Waged Work

A Reader

2/1

12/12

9 3

OR 4.10.93

Waged Work

A Reader

EDITED BY

Published by Virago Press Limited 1986
41 William IV Street, London WC2N 4DB

British Cataloguing in Publication Data

Waged work : a reader.
   1. Women—Employment—Great Britain
   I. Feminist Review
   331.4'0941   HD6135

   ISBN 0-86068-801-1

Photoset in North Wales by
Derek Doyle & Associates, Mold, Clwyd
Printed by Anchor Brendon Ltd, Tiptree, Essex

Contents

Introduction

Mandy Snell and Mary McIntosh

The general outlines of women's position in employment are probably depressingly familiar. In Britain, as in many other societies, women's waged work is 'women's work' – low paid, low grade and seen as largely unskilled. Women are concentrated in clerical work, in shop work and in catering, cleaning and other personal services. In manufacturing, women are concentrated in the semi- and unskilled jobs in industries like engineering, food, drink and tobacco, and clothing and textiles, which tend to be low paid (see Martin and Roberts, 1984).

Within women's work, Black women are concentrated in the lowest paid and lowest grade jobs, often involving heavy work (as in nursing and ancillary health service work, as well as jobs in factories and warehouses) or long and 'unusual' hours (such as shift work and cleaning). Black women are over-represented in declining areas of manufacturing, such as clothing, and are more likely than white women to work in poor or even dangerous conditions, in sweatshops or as homeworkers.

The articles collected here, all originally published in *Feminist Review*, cover the period from the mid-1970s to the mid-1980s and discuss many of the major debates on women and employment over that period. Because they have been published over several years, some of the articles are not up to date with current events, but we include them here because of their analysis and because they deal with important past situations. They focus on *waged* work and women's situation in the workforce. They highlight how much the economic situation has changed, and how little women's employment situation (in terms of what sort of work they are doing) has changed. They do not deal with *unwaged* work – women's domestic labour – though of course it lurks in the background as a major influence on women's position in general.

When the Equal Pay and Sex Discrimination Acts came into force in the mid-1970s, there was some initial optimism that they would open up opportunities for women at work. Looking back, there seems then to have been a relatively favourable economic situation. Unemployment was relatively low; companies were hiring and seeking labour; and unions were in a much stronger position to negotiate over changes of any kind. Yet, as Mandy Snell's article, written in the late 1970s, 'Equal Pay and Sex Discrimination', shows, the legislation had little effect on the detailed patterns of pay and jobs. Women's work continued to be undervalued and underpaid, and a range of attitudes and practices, combined with the weakness of the legislation itself, meant that there was little change in the long-established divisions between men's and women's work.

The continued problem of job segregation has been well demonstrated by Catherine Hakim (1979 and 1981) and by Jean Martin and Ceridwen Roberts (1984). It has been the focus both of theoretical debates, particularly among socialist-feminists, and of empirical investigations. Veronica Beechey, in her article 'Studies of Women's Employment', examines some of this recent research and assesses both the implications of the findings and interpretations and some of the more general theoretical frameworks developed. She looks at case studies of women's relationship to their work in three particular industries. All three studies emphasized the importance of women's position within the family for understanding their position at work. Veronica Beechey argues that this is too simple an analysis and that women's position in the occupational structure cannot simply be 'read off' from the sexual division of labour within the family. The processes of gender construction within the labour process itself must be analysed as part of any full explanation of job segregation.

Cynthia Cockburn, in her article 'The Material of Male Power' – and more fully in her book *Brothers* (1983) – shows how this process has taken place in the printing industry as changes in technology have been introduced in such a way as to make transformations in gender relations. A similar argument has been developed by Ann Game and Rosemary Pringle in their book *Gender at Work* (1984), in which they looked at six industries in Australia and show gender relations being 'constantly renegotiated and recreated' as technology changes and work is reorganized. Veronica Beechey's article is also critical of both labour process theory and dual and segmented labour market theories. She argues that while they have contributed towards our understanding of work in general and have affected the theoretical frameworks used to analyse women's employment, they cannot provide a general analysis of job segregation because they see gender relations at work as a by-product of the dynamics of capital accumulation and restructuring, rather than as a central concern. Nor have these theories recognized the crucial role of trade unions and of men in creating and maintaining divisions within the working class (Hartmann, 1976; Rubery, 1980; Beechey, 1983).

Anne Phillips and Barbara Taylor, in an earlier article 'Sex and Skill', address the same issues. They look at early socialist-feminist explanations for job segregation and the impact of radical feminist concepts on the thinking of Marxist feminists – in particular the recognition that the construction and maintenance of gender hierarchy must be analysed independently. They look at existing Marxist theories of the labour process and find that they do not deal adequately with the question of skill. They conclude that women's work is often 'deemed inferior simply because it is women who do it'. Skill is increasingly an ideological category, developed out of the struggle of men to retain their dominance in the sexual hierarchy at work, rather than a real distinction based on the nature of the jobs that men and women do. Phillips and Taylor argue that male workers, through this strategy, have tended to 'continually recreate for capital a group of "inferior" workers who can be used to undercut them'.

The issue of the role of men and trade unions is taken up in several of the other articles here. Cynthia Cockburn shares much of Phillips and Taylor's analysis of the construction of gender relations in the labour process, although she stresses the material basis of male power through men's access to the design and use of technical processes and productive machinery.

Many of the articles on work published in *Feminist Review* have concentrated on the sexual division of labour within the workplace. Yet, as Phillips and Taylor and Beechey point out, it is commonly believed that women's place in the labour force is in large part due to their place in the family. Because women still carry the major responsibility for childcare and the care of other dependants, and for housework, they are seen as less committed to the labour market and disadvantaged within it. Also, because of the expectation that men need a 'family wage' and women have a breadwinner to depend on, they are not thought to have a right to the better jobs (Land, 1980). As the prevalence of homeworking and part-time work amongst women in Britain illustrates, women do encounter very practical and material constraints on whether, when, where and how they do paid work. Nicola Charles, in 'Women and Trade Unions', argues from her study at the local level in a range of industries that the material conditions of women's lives affected the attitudes and practices of both the women and the trade unionists, reinforcing in turn women's secondary position in the workforce.

Suggestions that homeworking allows women to combine paid work and domestic responsibilities flexibly and comfortably are discussed in Sheila Allen and Carol Wolkowitz's article, 'Homeworking and the Control of Women's Work'. The authors argue that it is illusory to think that the homeworker is free to work when she wants and as long as she wants. Systems of control operate in homeworking just as they do in factories and offices. Their study in West Yorkshire shows how control is exercised by the suppliers through mechanisms such as piecework payment systems, the allocation and flow of work and conditions associated with the provision of machinery. These demands, combined with those of childcare and other unpaid domestic responsibilities, mean that many homeworkers are, in effect, working continuously.

In the 1980s we are experiencing a further worsening of the economic climate, with far-reaching implications for women's work. At this stage of the economic recession, Britain has unprecedentedly high levels of unemployment and is undergoing major industrial restructuring, including the restructuring of the labour force both within the country and internationally. So ours is a potentially stormy period, as the updraught of women's aspirations and expectations in the labour market collides with an economic cold front of stagnation, job losses and deskilling.

The picture is complicated, however, by the pattern of job segregation. Women and men are not spread equally in the different sectors of the economy, or in different types of work, or in different levels of work in terms of pay, power and 'skill'. Furthermore, these patterns are a complex product of management strategies, union practices, cultural stereotypes and of the choices that individual women and men tend to make. As such, the way in which patterns change as restructuring proceeds is not determinate, but is the object of ongoing struggles.

The outcome of some of these processes during the 1970s was explored in Irene Bruegel's article, 'The Reserve Army of Labour'. The expansion of women's employment in the post-war years has gone hand in hand with the growth of the labour-intensive service sector of the economy. Many of the lower paid jobs in this sector, and of comparable jobs in other sectors, have become identified as 'women's work'. The continued expansion of parts of the service sector has therefore mitigated the effects of the recession on women's employment opportunities. Women are not over-represented among the unemployed, but Bruegel maintains that they are, nevertheless, more disposable employees than men and that 'within any given industry or job women, particularly part-time women workers, have suffered from greater rates of job loss than men'. Since her article appeared in 1979, unemployment has grown and it now appears that these particular patterns of job loss may have been a once-and-for-all phenomenon and other processes are now in play. Her article has given rise to a heated debate and some writers have argued that in some situations women are less vulnerable to redundancy than men and more likely to find alternative employment, because of their willingness to work for lower pay and to work part-time (Perkins, 1983; Mayo, 1983; Beechey, 1983). Such an argument implies that during the recession some employers have restructured their labour process in such a way as to create these 'women's jobs'. To some extent this is clearly true; yet it is also true that the later stages of the recession have seen the disappearance of many low-paid and part-time jobs in certain labour-intensive and under-capitalized sectors such as clothing (Coyle, 1984).

Where jobs have not actually disappeared, they have come under increasing pressure from cost-cutting and rationalization. Angela Coyle's article, 'Going Private', looking at a phenomenon whose significance was not anticipated in the late 1970s, shows that the so-called 'privatization' of hospital cleaning services is reducing the cleaners' rates of pay and hours, intensifying their work and forcing them to accept new rotas. As well as selling off other major public enterprises, the current British Government is insisting that the National Health hospitals should put their cleaning, catering and laundry services out to private tender. In the short run, the private contractors achieve savings by cutting down on labour costs. In the long run, it is part of a government strategy to reduce wages and benefits and to deregulate the contract between employer and employee. Amina Mama's article, 'Black Women and the Economic Crisis', shows that Black women and especially women of Afro-Caribbean origin are often found in the lower reaches of the health services, and indeed of the other public services. These are jobs which, because of effective union organization and the absence of the profit motive, have been secure and with relatively good pay and conditions compared with many women's jobs in the private sector. Privatization and other moves to reverse the gains, however small, that have been made in public employment will hit women workers in the first place, and there will be many Black women among them.

Another form of restructuring of the labour force has been the geographical relocation of activities in order to tap a cheaper or more malleable supply of labour. Though service industries cannot easily relocate their operations, the clothing industry, a major employer of women in manufacturing, has a long history of sending routine work to women in rural areas who have few other job opportunities. Now the clothing and micro-electronic industries are 'putting out' on an international scale to women who work in Third World factories rather than at home, as Diane Elson and Ruth Pearson discuss in their article 'Third World Manufacturing'. The labour-intensive work draws upon skills in sewing and so forth that women are presumed to have already, and women, it seems, can be worked harder and paid less than men. Meanwhile, at home, employers are seeking new ways to use cheaper workers, to combat the competition from low-cost imports. The bigger clothing firms have shifted production to peripheral areas and small towns where there are many older, married women with few other chances of employment. Smaller firms continue to make use, as the clothing industry always has, of women working at home, fitting the paid work around their domestic obligations, as discussed in the article by Sheila Allen and Carol Wolkowitz. Others sometimes set up permanent or temporary 'factories' in suburban trading estates and invite women to come in for whatever hours suit them to do routine assembly work and packing, especially for the Christmas trade – at very low rates of pay. On a much larger scale, there is the decentralization of big government offices. While there are many reasons for this, among them must surely be the fact that 6,000 DHSS clerical workers in Longbenton in the North East of England and nearly 4,000 dealing with driving licenses in Swansea reduce the upward pressure on civil service salaries that comes from competition with private offices in the South East of England. Large private sector firms, too, are decentralizing the more routine elements of their clerical work and are often choosing areas of the country that were traditionally the homes of heavy industry – areas where there were few jobs for women, but ironically areas where there is now exceptionally high unemployment amongst men (Massey, 1983).

It is tempting to describe all of these changes in purely economic terms, as if they were the inevitable working out of the imperatives of the world capitalist economy producing a new gendered job market. But it is important to remember that these outcomes are also the product of struggles and negotiations between Third World governments and corporations, between unions and employers, between men and women within unions – over government policies on the regions, on wages and on terms of employment – and even between men and women within families. The literature on economic restructuring has tended to ignore these social processes, perhaps partly because, in the recent period, trade union resistance has not been very effective and workers often have been merely the victims of the logic of capital. Recent studies of labour market segmentation and of out-work by the Cambridge School, however, have begun to take account of some of these issues.

An area where there has been much more exploration of the social as well as the economic processes has been that of technological change and its impact on sex segregation. Here the debate has often been couched in terms of 'patriarchy v. capitalism' or 'feminism v. Marxism'. Cynthia Cockburn's article, 'The Material of Male Power', takes the question rather deeper, looking at the history of the compositors' craft in the printing industry and arguing that each new technique was introduced in such a way as to strengthen men's monopoly of the craft, even at the expense, sometimes, of efficiency from the employers' point of view. Cynthia Cockburn has developed her analysis further in her book *Brothers* (1983) where she also shows how the advent of electronic photo-setting has to some extent broken this pattern and women, often trained as typists, are beginning to find a place in composing. The male compositors, facing the destruction of their craft, often blame the women for undercutting their pay and privileges and strive to keep them excluded from the better areas of work.

On the whole, recent technological changes have tended to displace women workers who were previously doing routine clerical, typing and assembling work. Once again, however, Janine Morgall's article 'New Office Technology', written some years ago but confirmed by later developments, shows that the way new technology is introduced is not just an inevitable working out of capitalist logic but that there is room for women to mobilize to improve the division of labour and prevent the intensification of their work. Amina Mama makes the same general point, but with much gloomier implications. For Black women have been beginning to find a place in the lower rungs of office work just at the period when these more routine jobs are being displaced. Yet selection and training for any new jobs created by new technology often tend to be racist as well as sexist, so that Black women in particular are not getting a foot into these new areas.

However bleak the economic climate, struggles continue over the division of labour and the way the work is organized and there are political and social, as well as economic, factors affecting women's future. One area of such struggles much debated among feminists since the early 1970s is the trade union movement. A number of the articles in this collection are highly critical of the role that men in trade unions have played. Cynthia Cockburn sees compositors as perpetuating and creating a gender hierarchy in the face of technological change in the printing industry. Nicola Charles finds that local trade union activists (as well as most of the women workers that she interviewed) operate on the basis of a 'familial ideology' that defines women's labour market role as a secondary one, so that they marginalize women's interests and, she argues, weaken the unions themselves. Angela Coyle, while she recognizes the very real difficulties that unions face in privatization struggles, is nevertheless critical of the failure of the wider labour movement to give significant support, particularly when many other workers are likely themselves to be affected in future by privatization policies.

While Cockburn, Charles and Coyle all report essentially negative findings on trade unions, especially at the local level, there are more positive moves within unions which are not reflected in these articles. Women are beginning to hold more offices within union hierarchies and several unions now have a significant number of women on their national executives. Women delegates to the Women's Trade Union Congress bring considerable strength and vigour to a rich variety of motions and debates. Some unions have begun to take some women's issues more seriously, as shown, for example, by the number of unions making claims on the basis of 'equal pay for work of equal value' on behalf of their women members. Others have set up special training schemes for women activists and established equal opportunities committees or structures. As yet these have had little impact on women's position at the local level, let alone the overall pattern of women's work, but they have contributed to a growth in confidence and awareness amongst women members which is beginning to make itself felt in union structures and policies, despite economic and political conditions that are not at all favourable to women's employment prospects.

In addition, two other avenues have opened which potentially offer women some support and opportunities to put pressure on central government – European Economic Community (EEC) policy and legislation on women's rights in employment, and the initiatives in relation to women being taken in some local authorities. As Mandy Snell's article, among others, has indicated, legislation and policy on women's employment are unlikely to produce significant changes in the division of labour within the workplace. Without procedures and resources to implement the laws or policies, and without institutions to monitor and enforce them, little progress is likely. The EEC has adopted directives on areas such as equal pay, equal access to jobs, training and promotion, which have led to member countries passing or amending national legislation in order to comply with the directives. It is now pursuing the development of directives on granting rights to part-time and temporary workers and on the provision of parental leave to workers. It is also considering a directive to promote the setting up of positive action programmes for women. These directives, once adopted, open up channels which, however slow and cumbersome they may be, as Catherine Hoskyns argues in this volume, can be used by women in trade unions to put pressure on central government.

An example of this process working effectively is the question of equal pay for work of equal value. As a result of cases taken to the European Court of Justice under the equal pay directive, the Court ruled in 1982 that the UK was not complying with the Community directive on equal pay because the Equal Pay Act 1970 did not provide equal pay for work of equal value unless a woman was covered by a job evaluation scheme. The UK Government prepared minimal amendments to comply with the directive, but these were altered after considerable pressure from women's groups, trade unions, the Equal Opportunities Commission, the National Council for Civil Liberties (NCCL) and other groups. The resulting legislation, although still inadequate, has enabled a series of cases to be taken to industrial tribunal, and the first case (*Hayward* v. *Cammell Laird Shipbuilders Ltd*) was recently won. In this case a woman cook in a works canteen successfully compared her work to that of skilled shipyard craftsmen and won an increase of over £30 a week.

Clearly there are some complex issues with respect to the EEC. As Catherine Hoskyns points out, Community legislation is handed down 'from above' rather than arising from pressure from women in member states who are often cynical about the appropriateness of legislation as a solution to women's problems. Nonetheless, the Community and the European Court provide a means of 'going over the head' of an unfriendly or unwilling national government. However, the UK Government has shown itself capable both of resisting Community directives for long periods (for example, on the issue of equalizing retirement ages for men and women) and of implementing directives against their true spirit (for example, by implementing equal treatment with respect to certain benefits by equalizing downwards rather than upwards).

The other positive initiative has been the development since 1982 of more than thirty Women's Committees within local government. These have arisen partly as a result of the movement of feminists into the Labour Party (see *Feminist Review*, 1984) and perhaps also as a result of the entrance into local government of a generation of councillors and officers on the left who had grown up with an active women's movement and who had at least heard, if not fully understood, feminist debates on the Alternative Economic Strategy and so on.

Women's Committees are typically full policy-making committees of Councils with budgets to spend and some staff to develop and implement the Committee's policy. Most have taken as one of their main priorities improving the employment opportunities of women staff working for the local authority itself. Most Women's Committees have also looked at the services their Councils provide and how these can be made more responsive to the needs and demands of women. In some Councils this has meant appointing an officer in their economic development function to look at and pursue women's needs, in others it has meant putting pressure and demands on the relevant part of the Council to ensure that its economic development strategy and initiatives take into account women's employment needs.

Most Women's Committees are fairly small in terms of budget and support staff numbers, but the Greater London Council (GLC) with relatively well-resourced Women's as well as Industry and Employment Committees has been able to take a variety of positive initiatives on women's employment in London. These include: first, setting up an Equal Opportunities Unit which has introduced a series of positive measures to overcome the disadvantages faced by women working at the GLC itself; second, using its purchasing power to ensure that its contractors and suppliers comply with the Sex

Discrimination and Race Relations Acts ('contracts compliance'); third, giving priority, or at least particular consideration, to women in its industrial strategy and in the work of the Greater London Enterprise Board (GLEB) which gives grants and loans to firms and co-operatives; fourth, funding more than 250 women-only training places in non-traditional skills as well as prioritizing women on mixed courses; fifth, funding more than 4000 childcare places in London (approximately 1000 of them full-time); and sixth, supporting women's employment and industry-based projects and campaigns, as well as other campaigns such as those on homeworking and low pay which are particularly important for women.

The rapid growth of such large, well-resourced and well-staffed bureaucracies has led to discussions in the women's movement about 'femocrats' and the possible dangers of co-option. But with respect to employment, the main issue for women has been how to ensure that policies benefitting women are implemented by officers who may have different priorities once Councils start investing in the private sector (Bruegel, 1985).

Although all these initiatives are threatened because of rate-capping and the abolition of the metropolitan authorities, the initiatives taken by local authorities have shown that local political institutions can be used to bring women's employment issues to the fore and to resource and support local women's and trade union groups working on these issues.

These and related issues form an important part of *Feminist Review*'s ongoing work as a political journal. We welcome any new ideas, analyses and comments on these issues and invite prospective contributors to get in touch with the editorial collective at the address below:

Feminist Review
11 Carleton Gardens
Brecknock Road
London N19 5AQ

Equal Pay and
Sex Discrimination

Mandy Snell

The women's movement has always been ambivalent about the value of legislation in bringing about real change. On the one hand women have campaigned vigorously for legislation to improve women's domestic, economic and political position. On the other hand, women inevitably find that laws, once passed, are unsatisfactory and that the inequalities they were intended to remove still remain. Disappointed and increasingly cynical, many women have begun to question the effectiveness of legislation as a weapon in their continuing struggle for equality.

The Equal Pay and Sex Discrimination Acts came into force at the end of 1975. These Acts were intended to eliminate discrimination against women in pay and in employment. Both Acts rely heavily on enforcement through individual complaints to industrial tribunals, and much analysis and assessment of the effects and value of the legislation has concentrated on women's difficulties and lack of success in winning cases before these tribunals. Relatively little attention has been focused on the impact of the legislation in the workplace. What difference have the Acts made to women's pay and opportunities at shop floor and office level? Has discrimination been eliminated? What inequalities remain and why?

To answer these questions, this article describes the findings of the London School of Economics Equal Pay and Opportunity Project and discusses their implications for women in the workplace and for legislative and institutional action outside the workplace.

■ The Equal Pay Act

The Equal Pay Act contains two approaches to equal pay: one individual and one collective. The individual provisions require employers to give equal treatment for pay and terms and conditions of employment to men and women employed on like work (Section 1 (4)) or on work which, though different, has been given an equal value under a job evaluation scheme (Section 1 (5)). A woman is regarded as doing like work if her work is of the same or a broadly similar nature to a man's, and if the differences between the things that she does and the things he does are not of practical importance in relation to terms and conditions of employment. However, under Section 1 (3), unequal treatment of a man and a woman can be justified if the employer can prove that this is genuinely due to a material difference (other than the differences of sex) between the woman's case and the man's. The collective provisions apply to collective agreements, wages council orders and employers' pay structures. These cover a large number of employees, often in more than one organization. Under Sections 3, 4 and 5, an agreement containing a provision applying to men only or to women only can be referred to the Central Arbitration Committee for amendment to remove that discrimination. In addition, rates applying to women only should have been amended to not less than the lowest male rate in the agreement, wages order or pay structure. This means that all women covered by an agreement, order or pay structure should at least have had their rates brought up to the male minimum. Although most tribunal cases, and public interest, have focused on equal pay for like work,[1] this provision of the Act was little used in the organizations studied. They implemented almost exclusively through the use of the work of equivalent value provision (Section 1 (5)) and the provision relating to collective agreements (Section 3). As a result, the vast majority of women were entitled to and received, some benefit under the Equal Pay Act. Most women work in predominantly if not totally female occupations and therefore would not have been entitled to equal pay under the like work provisions. But the increased use of job evaluation and their coverage by collective agreements meant that most women who were not doing like work with men were still entitled to some increase in pay.

Nonetheless, groups of women were found in fifteen organizations who were not entitled to equal pay under any of the provisions of the Act because they were not doing like work and were not covered by job evaluation, an agreement or order or an employer's pay structure. The manual women were cleaners and canteen assistants who fell outside the collective agreements covering other manual workers in the same organization. The white collar women were clerical and secretarial workers in smaller organizations where no job evaluation, collective agreement or employer's pay structure existed.[2] With one exception, these groups of women were small, ranging from five to twenty-five women. The notable exception was an all-female pay structure covering more than 4,000 typists and secretaries. While the total number of women not entitled was relatively small, the incidence of such cases was high and suggests that large numbers of women, on a national scale, may fall completely outside the terms of the Act. If this is so, the question arises of how the Act could be amended to ensure the coverage of women who are now excluded. Various solutions have been put forward. One is to amend the Act to require equal pay for work of *equal value* rather than for *work rated as equivalent under a job evaluation scheme*. This approach however, may present practical difficulties. How is the work to be judged and by whom? Given the low status often attributed to women's jobs and skills, it is difficult to see how subjective assessment would be avoided in the absence of a systematic evaluation of the jobs involved. If disputes arose and a case was taken to tribunal, how would tribunal representatives assess the jobs if not by job evaluation? The idea of using a 'notional man' has also been suggested, but again it is difficult to see how women, employers, unions or tribunals would objectively assess what a man would be paid for work always undertaken by women.[3]

Some practical, non-legislative methods of overcoming women's lack of entitlement are suggested by the project findings:

1 wherever possible, women and unions should ensure that groups or individuals traditionally falling outside collective agreements are specifically included within them. In this way, women who are marginal workers in an organization can benefit from the higher pay and greater bargaining strength of the main body of workers. Women cleaners' rates in one organization doubled as a result of being brought up to the labourers' rate in the agreement covering engineering workers.

2 the extension of collective bargaining into white collar areas would increase women's coverage under the collective provisions of the Act.

3 women and unions could press for the integration of typist, clerical, secretarial and other female jobs into the pay and job structures covering men. This would ensure coverage by the collective provisions of the Act, and provide the basis for negotiating access to higher graded jobs from female job areas.

4 women in less well organized areas and industries could invoke Schedule 11 of the Employment Protection Act to obtain the general level of terms and conditions operative for comparable workers within the industry and district. Thus women in unstructured pay situations might benefit from the higher pay of some women in more formal pay systems.

5 women and unions should consider pressing for the introduction of participative job evaluation. Although job evaluation is a controversial issue for most unions, there is clear evidence from our project that job evaluation, properly carried out, has resulted in significant increases in pay for many women who would not otherwise have been entitled to them.

How has the Equal Pay Act affected women's pay?

The implementation of equal pay resulted in considerable and sometimes dramatic narrowing of differentials between the basic rates of main groups of manual and white collar women, and those of men. This narrowing represented real and significant increases in pay and there is no doubt that many women received substantial increases which they would not have otherwise received.

The extent of change in women's pay position can be shown by examining the position of manual women both before and after the Act (Table 1).

Before the Act, most women in manual jobs were on pay rates below those of any men in the organization (category A). This situation was not necessarily related to their jobs or their level of skill but was simply a result of their sex. Even where women were doing semi-skilled jobs such as machine operating and assembly work, they were on rates lower than the lowest and unskilled male labourers' rate. Most women were on a single 'women's rate' which was the same for all women regardless of job, or were in specially designated women's grades. Where women were on unisex, mixed pay grades, these had different and lower rates for women. After the Act the overall pay position of manual women had changed considerably. In most organizations women were paid on or above the lowest male rate, although

Table 1 Manual women's rates before and after equal pay, compared with manual men within the same organization. For nineteen organizations.*

All rates referred to are occupied rates

	No. of organizations	
	pre Equal Pay	*post* Equal Pay
Category A all women paid below the lowest male rate	16	3
Category B bulk of women paid below the lowest male rate	0	1
Category C bulk of women paid on or above lowest male rate, but below all other male rates	1	9
Category D substantial nos. of women paid as much as or more than substantial nos. of men	2	6
TOTAL	19	19

*Only nineteen organizations are included because for three out of the twenty-two where manual implementation was studied, full and reliable pay information was not obtainable.

many still were on rates which were below those of most men and which they did not share with any men in the organization.

These 'de facto' women's rates represent potentially dangerous situations. If there were a return to free collective bargaining, and given men's greater bargaining power, there would be little to prevent differentials between these groups of women and higher paid men from widening again and any benefits gained from the Equal Pay Act being wiped out.

The effects of the Act on pay for white collar women has been perhaps less spectacular, partly because many white collar women were in large commercial or public sector organizations where equal pay had been implemented before the Act was passed. Other white collar women were not entitled to equal pay and thus may not have received any pay increase as a result of the Act. Also, there was already a much greater overlap between men's and women's grades and rates prior to the Act than for manual women. Nonetheless, where white collar women were entitled to equal pay, many women received significant increases in pay. However, it should be noted that while women were in the same grade and on the same salary scale as men, they were often placed at a lower point on that scale. Furthermore, most women were still concentrated in lower grades, many of them on 'de facto' women's grades.

One factor which contributed to the narrowing of differentials was incomes policy. Flat rate increases, such as the £6 limit, represented larger increases for lower-paid workers.[4] As a result, some narrowing of differentials between women's and men's pay might have been expected anyway during the period of study. However, the degree of narrowing found was greater than could be attributed to the workings of incomes policy alone. Analysis of changes in pay for men and women over the period studied shows a much faster rate of increase in women's pay as against men's, even the lowest paid men's. This faster rate of increase was in part due to incomes policy but there is no doubt that it was also the result of special and larger payments given to women as part of equal pay implementation.[5]

The project also examined movements in earnings over the period studied. Many workers, particularly manual men, receive other payments in addition to basic rates which may increase their earnings considerably. Also, basic rates for many production workers are minimum or fallback rates while actual earnings consist largely of piecework or other incentive payments. To see if other components of earnings had been altered to recoup the cost of equal pay or to compensate men for women's increased earnings, earnings of main groups of manual and white collar women were compared with those of groups of men of a similar occupational or skill level.[6]

Overall, few such alterations to other components of pay were found. Actions taken which minimized the cost of equal pay or compensated men were confined largely to manipulation of basic rates and gradings. However, instances were found which suggest that more attention should be paid to ensuring that women who have equal basic rates have opportunities for equal earnings as well. For example, instances were found of deliberate alterations to incentive schemes as part of or as a result of equal pay implementation. In two cases women's piecework rates were 'tightened' to offset increases in their basic pay. This meant that the women involved would have to work much harder and produce more (in one case 40 per cent more) to earn the same amount of incentive pay as before equal pay. As a result, the women's average hourly earnings remained at 60 per cent of men's although their basic rate had been increased to 90 per cent. In another case, men found that their hourly earnings fell below those of some women when the women's rates were equalized with theirs. They went out on strike and settled when the company agreed to give them a guaranteed 103 per cent of the women's bonus earnings. Examples were also found where men's greater bargaining strength resulted in higher bonus earnings for men than for women on the same basic rate. Men had gained access to the jobs with higher potential bonus earnings and had negotiated more favourable incentive schemes or rates for their departments. In one organization for example, male departments negotiated new incentive schemes which enabled them to obtain high earnings for lower effort and output. As a result, women on the same basic rate but in different departments and on different schemes earned only 94 per cent of the men's earnings even when they achieved above average bonus performance.

Incentive schemes are complex and varied; rates and performance levels are a constant source of friction and negotiation in many organizations. Differences in earnings between departments or groups of workers are common and may reflect relative bargaining strength rather than differences in output or effort. In this situation it is important that women and unions monitor average hourly earnings of men and women in the same grade or on the same occupational or skill level to check that women are obtaining similar earnings for similar effort. If they are not, this indicates the need to examine incentive schemes, and access to them, for possible intentional or unintentional bias.

Amongst white collar women, differences in earnings were mainly related to placement on salary scales. Major factors involved were:

1 market pressures: managers often had discretion to pay above the bottom of the salary scale or to give extra increments to attract outsiders to join the organization or to induce employees to stay. Men benefit most often since they are more likely than women to be highly paid on entering and to be offered better paid jobs outside. This situation reflects past and present discrimination in both pay and opportunities and is unlikely to change unless women are

brought up to the average salary level for men in the organization with similar experience.[7]

2 merit pay: This is often highly discretionary and poorly defined. Assessment is often carried out by individual managers with little outside control. This provides scopes for conscious or unconscious prejudice towards women. In one case women managers were receiving considerably less merit pay than men although they had longer service as managers and better objective performance indicators than the men.

3 equal pay implementation: Sometimes women who were below the male minimum before equal pay were brought up to the minimum rather than to an appropriate place on the scale.

Again, these instances highlight the importance of monitoring actual earnings if real equal pay is to be achieved.

Are women getting equal pay?

In spite of considerable and sometimes dramatic increases in women's pay, overall women are still paid significantly less than men. This is obvious both from national figures on earnings (see Table 2) and from the distribution of men and women's pay rates in the organizations studied. As Table 2 shows, differentials in average hourly earnings have narrowed, but the gap is still large. If overtime pay was included, the gap would be larger still as men generally work longer hours than women.

Within the organizations studied, equal pay has improved women's pay position relative to men, but women are still concentrated in lower grades and on lower rates than men (see Table 1).

Table 2 Average gross hourly earnings (pence per hour) excluding the effect of overtime hours		
	1970	1977
Men	67.4	177.4
Women	42.5	133.9
Women's earnings as a percentage of men's	63.1	75.5
Equal Opportunities Commission, Second Annual Report 1977, Table 4.2.		

The major reason for women's continuing lower pay is lack of equal job opportunities. Most women work in less skilled and lower graded jobs, often in low paid industries, which will continue to be less well paid however fair the payment system. But there is also considerable evidence that while many women received substantial increases, they nonetheless received less than they might have done. This was primarily the outcome of actions taken by employers to minimize their obligations under the Act and of the strategies they adopted to implement the Act rather than the result of non-compliance with the legislation.

Non-compliance

The project team found only six clear-cut cases of non-compliance where sufficient evidence was available to enable the women to win a case before a tribunal or the Central Arbitration Committee. These cases affected altogether less than 100 women. With one exception, non-compliance involved the payment of women-only rates below the lowest male rate set in the relevant collective agreement or employer's pay structure. Under Section 3 of the Act, these women should have been brought up to the lowest male rate, if not to above it.

However, cases of possible non-compliance occurred in over half the organizations studied. These were cases where sufficient evidence was present to show less favourable treatment before a tribunal, but where management could have argued that differences of practical importance or genuine material differences existed which justified or explained the unequal treatment. Fourteen of these cases involved possible like work comparisons, often related to inspection or examination jobs in factories, packing and sorting jobs in warehouses or stores departments and general clerical jobs in white collar employment.

Most cases of non-compliance were not recognized by women within the organizations. As a result, they were not raised with management or the unions nor were any taken to tribunal. This lack of knowledge and consequently of action on women's part was the result of several factors: 1) the extent of job segregation between men and women meant that many women were not aware of the content of men's jobs. Most men worked in different departments. Sometimes they were in a different pay structure, e.g. monthly rather than weekly paid. Often their jobs had a different job title, although the work was similar. 2) a high degree of management discretion, confidentiality and secrecy regarding pay is still common, particularly in white collar jobs. Employees were often told not or chose not to reveal or discuss their earnings. As a consequence, low pay and inequalities in pay never came to light. 3) women's knowledge of pay levels was often restricted by their lack of knowledge of and involvement in pay determination and bargaining. This in turn was often the result of their lower level of involvement in union affairs and offices. In some cases, women were not aware that they were being paid below the minimum rate set in the agreement covering them or even that they were covered by an agreement at all. Even where women were aware of unequal pay, they were reluctant to take action. They feared unpleasantness or negative reactions from fellow workers or management and hostile attitudes on the part of male trade unionists. Some women could not face going to a tribunal. Given the relatively few cases of clear-cut non-compliance and the difficulties women face in identifying and proving cases of unequal pay, it seems unlikely that large numbers of women will gain significant improvements in pay through claims to industrial tribunals.[8] As the next two sections show, factors other than non-compliance were in any case found to be the major reasons for women's loss of potential benefit. But the high incidence of unrecognized cases suggests that some women would clearly benefit from a detailed examination of jobs and pay. In particular:

1 women should examine the content of their own jobs and those of men for possible like work comparisons. Women should learn more about their pay and how it is determined by asking to see any industry and/or company agreements or wages council orders covering them and any details of grades or rates or salary scales applying to them.

2 where pay is not discussed openly, women should initiate open discussion.

3 monitoring of hourly earnings and salary levels by grade and department should be introduced to help identify areas of unequal pay.

4 other terms and conditions, including non-monetary ones, should be examined. In several organizations women were treated less favourably with respect to uncertified absences from work and perks such as free meals and uniforms.

Minimization

A major reason for loss of potential benefit to women was actions taken by employers which had the effect of reducing their obligations under the law but which resulted in compliance with the law.[9] For example, where men and women were doing similar work before equal pay, employers in four organizations moved either all the men or all the women off the work to prevent like work comparisons. As a result, the employer was no longer obliged to raise the women's pay to that of the men. Other actions taken by employers to minimize their obligations included:

1 changing job content of men's and women's jobs to avoid like work comparisons.

2 the introduction or restructuring of grading systems, both at national and at company level such that women ended up on lower rates or grades regardless of their skill level. Often women were put into de facto women's grades, usually just above the lowest male rate (which only a few male labourers may have been on) and well below the bulk of men. In other cases women were brought up to the lowest and unskilled male rate, although they were clearly doing semi-skilled work and regardless of previous differentials between women workers.

3 altering job evaluation factors to favour men – in one case by giving undue weighting to heavy lifting and in another by changing the factors such that a former single operator's grade became two separate grades with the men in the higher one and women in the lower one.

4 depressing the lowest male rate relative to the skilled rate over the period of implementation to reduce the amount women's pay would have to be increased. In one case women were given five per cent less than they would have received had the differential between the lowest male rate and the skilled rate stayed the same.

5 bringing women up to the scale minimum on unisex salary scales and tightening piecework rates to offset increases in women's basic rates, both mentioned above.

In addition, actions were taken to compensate men or to restore their differentials with women whose rates had been equalized with theirs. Such actions included giving men additional duties and upgrading them, putting lower paid men on to bonus schemes to increase their earnings and 'red circling' men's higher pay. (Red circling is the process which prevents workers from suffering a drop in pay – for example when changes to the pay or grading system result in their rate or grade being lowered. The rates of such workers are preserved at the higher rate while new entrants go on to the lower rate.) In all these cases, the women received equal pay increases, but their pay position relative to the men concerned remained the same.

Employers' minimizing actions had a dramatic effect on women's pay. Examining the largest and most representative groups of women only, twelve cases were found, affecting more than 2,000 women, where women were underpaid between £2 and over £4 a week. Several examples illustrate how such actions reduced women's potential benefits:

case 1: bringing women to the scale minimum rather than to the appropriate place on the scale. As a result average salaries for women on the middle grade of the clerical structure in one organization were 93 per cent of the average salaries of men in the same grade.

case 2: separation of male and female jobs into different grades. Before implementation the main jobs women did and those men did were in the same grade, but women were paid 74 per cent of men's rates. During equal pay implementation the industry agreement was altered and a new grading scheme introduced which placed the women's jobs in the two lowest grades and the men's into the three highest. As a result, the gap between men's and women's rates narrowed to 83 per cent, but women received £2.75 a week less than they would have done under the previous grading scheme.

case 3: creation of grades to avoid equal pay comparisons. Prior to equal pay journeywomen were in the same category in the national agreement as journeymen, but paid at 75 per cent of their rates. To avoid paying women journeymen's rates, the category was split into several grades and the women put into the lower of them. Although the women's differentials narrowed to 90 per cent as a result of equal pay, the sixty women concerned would have been on a rate of £2.91 a week higher had the journeyman/woman category not been split. They would also have had their bonus rates equalized with those of journeymen which would have further increased their pay.

case 4: removal or 'red circling' of men doing the same jobs as women. In this case men and women did the same jobs, the women on days, the men on night shift. Women's basic rates were 78 per cent of men's. To avoid equal pay comparisons, the company moved men off the night shift. Where this was not possible, men's pay was 'red circled' as an anomaly. Had this not happened, more than 100 women would have been entitled to an increase of £4 a week to their basic rate.[10]

Strategies used for implementation

The other major factor in women's loss of potential benefit was the section of the Act used by employers to implement equal pay. The project examined main groups of women to see whether implementation under a different section of the Act than the one used would have benefitted them more. Overall, where job evaluation was used, women were more likely to be graded and paid at the appropriate skill level. In contrast, where employers used Section 3 (the collective provisions), women were often graded and paid below their skill level in relation to men in the same pay structure. For example, in seven out of twelve cases where Section 3 was used for implementation, large groups of women in semi-skilled jobs such as machine operator, assembler or inspector were underpaid in relation to their skill levels. In the project's judgement, these women would have been better off in pay terms had job evaluation, properly carried out, been the method of implementation.

This outcome was partly a result of the different requirements which different sections of the Act put on employers and unions and partly a result of the way the provisions of Section 3 were applied at establishment or company level. Implementation under Section 3 carried no obligation to pay women according to their skill level or the value of their work.[11] As a result, both at national and company level, women's rates in many cases were simply brought up to the lowest male rate or slotted into de facto women's rates without systematic consideration of women's skill levels. Sometimes this was deliberate minimization by employers. In other cases it was the consequence of the normal practice in some organizations of relying exclusively on industry agreements to determine pay. Where this was so, there was a tendency simply to slot women's jobs into the often sketchy structure of rates provided by the agreement.

Employers' actions were affected by a variety of factors:

1 fears of reactions from men. These were sometimes justified. During implementation, men in several organizations who objected to women being brought up to their rates put pressure on management for upgrading and additional bonus pay. In one case they went on

strike. In almost every case, management conceded to the men's demands in order to avoid possible disruption and conflict.

2 lack of pressure from unions, often due to lack of knowledge and active involvement in pay at local level. Shops stewards sometimes had not been involved in implementation because negotiations were carried out at industry or headquarters level. However, where unions intervened in implementation they played a crucial role, though not always a positive one. In several cases, unions actively colluded with management to minimize or allowed management to carry out such actions without protest. In three other cases, however, union intervention prevented minimizing actions by employers with consequent higher gradings and pay for the women involved.

3 the method and level of pay determination. Where job evaluation existed prior to equal pay or was introduced to implement it, employer action to reduce obligations was rare. Minimizing actions were difficult to carry out in well-constructed jointly agreed schemes without union knowledge and co-operation. Where, however, management and unions were determined to minimize, it was equally possible to do so under job evaluation as under any other method of determining pay. Where it was normal practice to apply the industry agreement with little or no change, few employers chose to alter or expand nationally agreed rates and grades at local level. Some organizations covered by agreements did introduce job evaluation at local level, partly to make equal pay implementation easier, but also to produce a more rational pay structure which would be acceptable to all the employees covered by it. But the absence of pressure from unions and complaints from women meant that change at local level was often kept to a minimum. Implementation of equal pay was a low priority for most employers and it is not surprising that many opted for the least costly and disruptive method of dealing with it.

The project findings indicate that the vast majority of women are receiving equal pay as defined by the Act, although many women are not receiving the pay that their skills and jobs merit. Because this situation is due to strategies and actions which in the main are not unlawful, little change can be expected through individual claims to tribunals. Possible amendments to the law and increased institutional action could be important and these are discussed in the concluding section of the article. But the most important implication of these findings for women in workplaces and in unions is the need for action in the workplace. Greater involvement by women in pay determination and bargaining is essential to identify and remove remaining inequalities in pay and to prevent actions in future to restore men's differentials. Most employers and many women believe that equal pay has been implemented and that no further action is needed. But our findings suggest that the issue should be re-opened in the workplace and women's jobs and pay reconsidered. Particular attention needs to be paid to the possibility of like work cases, to the likelihood of minimizing actions having taken place during implementation and also to the treatment of women's jobs in company and industry agreements and grading schemes. Analysis of movements in differentials between groups of men and women workers with the introduction of equal pay and examination of old and new grading schemes and agreements may indicate whether and how minimizing actions occurred. Consideration should also be given to the introduction of job evaluation, carried out jointly by management and unions and with the participation of women.

■ The Sex Discrimination Act

How has the Sex Discrimination Act affected women's opportunities at work?

The Sex Discrimination Act, unlike the Equal Pay Act, is essentially a negative and passive piece of legislation. Its aim is to eliminate discrimination on the grounds of sex in employment, education and in the provision of goods, facilities, services and premises. Although it permits positive discrimination in training in certain circumstances and gives the Equal Opportunities Commission (EOC) the duty of promoting equality of opportunity, it does not place an obligation on employers, unions or relevant government and other institutions to take positive steps to break down segregation in jobs and to create genuine equal opportunities in employment. It is therefore perhaps not surprising that the effects of the Act in the organizations studied have been very limited. Little has been done and little has changed.

With regard to personnel practices, changes have been few and on the whole superficial. Most employers assumed that their policies and practices met the requirements of the law without systematically examining them to ensure that they did so. The removal of overt discrimination from recruitment procedures was the most common area of change. Sex was removed from job advertisements and managers and personnel staff were instructed not to refuse women (or men) jobs out of hand on the basis of sex. Changes to training and promotion procedures were rare. Little use was made of the provisions in the Act which allow employers to discriminate lawfully. Few organizations took advantage of Section 7 which allows employers to specify one sex for a job where sex is a 'genuine occupational qualification' (GOQ). The three areas specified as GOQs were toilet cleaner, female searcher, and work involving night shifts. Less encouraging, there has been no use whatsoever of Section 48 which allows positive discrimination in training for jobs which have been largely the preserve of one sex. With few changes to practices, procedures, attitudes, and an economic situation where turnover and recruitment were in any case low, the effects of the Act on the employment of women in the organizations have been minimal. No large scale shifts of women into men's jobs took place and the occupational distribution of women was almost completely unchanged. However, a few small but potentially important changes occurred. A handful of women moved into traditionally male jobs: engineering apprentice, engineer, porter, supervisor. This latter case was particularly significant as a woman was promoted from the administrative side, which serviced the men, to supervisor over fifty men in the field. In two other cases considerable numbers of men moved into traditionally female jobs, in one case as a result of action to keep men out. Dexterity testing was introduced when the Act came in to screen out male applicants for all-female electronic assembly jobs. To the company's surprise, some men did well on the test and went on to successfully to complete the assembly training course. Within a year 30 per cent of assemblers were men.

Employers' limited response to the Sex Discrimination Act was strongly influenced by their attitudes to it. Many managers felt that the legislation was unnecessary and irrelevant because 'we already have equal opportunity here'. They believed that women were in the jobs they do best and which they wanted to do, as were men, and they could not see that any changes were necessary. Other managers recognized that discrimination existed within their organizations, but felt that changes were unnecessary as discriminatory practices and actions were unlikely to be identified and taken up by women and unions within the organization or by the EOC coming in from outside. As one personnel manager put it:

> Legislation doesn't mean a company will act differently. We won't change our personnel decisions, just how we go about

them ... Just as we keep a 'good' mix on race by finding reasons to reject most Asians, so we will find reasons to reject women for some jobs.

The Act seemed to them to require less specific action than other employment legislation and there were no perceived labour shortages to justify them. Another important factor was the absence of positive pressure from unions. There were few union initiatives beyond the demand for the inclusion of the TUC (Trades Union Congress) model equal opportunity clause in agreements.[12] Nor were unions generally involved in the limited actions taken by management. Several factors contributed to this absence of union pressure. Local union representatives often lacked detailed knowledge and understanding of the Act and its implications for practices in their workplace. The Act affected areas such as recruitment and promotion where, in some organizations, it was not union practice to intervene. Furthermore, many union representatives shared management's assumption that there was no need for action, either because they also believed women had equal opportunity or because they were hostile to the idea and consequences of equal opportunity.

These attitudes on the part of both management and unions have important implications for the likelihood of further changes in organizations. As will be discussed in the concluding section, these findings indicate a need for institutional and union action in terms of both education and enforcement if women are to obtain equality of opportunity at work.

Has the Act eliminated discrimination in employment?

In more than half the organizations studied, members of management admitted that they were continuing to discriminate against women (and in some cases men). In another seven organizations, managers indicated their intention to discriminate in future. Most cases involved direct discrimination in recruitment or promotion where suitable women (or men) had been or would be refused jobs because of their sex. Women were turned down for jobs as setters and as supervisors and men were refused jobs as sewing-machinists and as semi-skilled operatives. Other cases involved discriminatory practices. One company specified different and higher entry requirements for boys than for girls because it was assumed that boys would pursue a career in the industry while girls would do the bulk of the low-grade, repetitive clerical work.

The most common reasons given by the managers concerned for discriminating were that one sex was more suitable for certain jobs than the other, that women would leave or would have domestic problems and that men would object to women moving into male areas or becoming supervisors over them. No discrimination cases were taken to tribunal nor were cases brought up within the organizations by women or unions. The main reason was that most of the women were not aware that discrimination had occurred. In most cases, the women had applied from outside for jobs within the organization and were therefore unlikely to know the real reason for their rejection. Even in cases of promotion within the organization, the women involved often were unaware of discrimination. Although employers admitted their discrimination to us, they were careful to give legitimate reasons to the applicants.

In the few cases where women felt they had been discriminated against, they did not pursue the matter. The reasons given were, fears of unpleasantness and disruption at work, the difficulty of proving a case, the feeling that it was not worth the trouble involved and lack of support from the union. For example, union representatives in one organization dismissed women's complaints of discrimination with the statement that it was 'management's right to select whoever they want'. These findings highlight the difficulties women face in identifying and proving discrimination. As with equal pay, the implications are that individual claims to tribunals are unlikely to play a significant role in eliminating discrimination in the workplace. The project also found sixteen cases of possible indirect discrimination. These were cases where organizations applied conditions or requirements for hiring or promotion with which a considerably smaller proportion of women than men could comply and which the project team felt might not be justifiable in terms of the job itself. Examples included:

1 that employees be geographically mobile or willing to undertake lengthy residential training in order to be promoted. These requirements were difficult for married women with children to comply with and were not always justifiable as alternative methods of providing flexibility of labour and training were possible.[13]

2 maximum age restrictions for entry to jobs and seniority requirements for promotion. The former prevents women returning to work from entering certain occupations and the latter penalizes women who have left the labour force for child bearing and rearing.

In some cases these requirements were a means of restricting competition for jobs and promotion.

3 restriction of jobs to time-served workers. Few women have served the apprenticeships required. In most cases the flexibility and skills learnt during the apprenticeship were genuinely required, but this was not so in all cases.

Indirect discrimination is a complex concept and there was little awareness and even less understanding of its implications among women, unions and employers. This situation is not confined to workplaces; unions at national level, the media and many women activists have failed to recognize the potential importance of this provision of the Act. Unlike direct discrimination cases, individual cases of indirect discrimination can be used to eliminate practices or requirements which discriminate against large numbers of women. This is illustrated by the *Price* v *Civil Service Commission* case. Linda Price successfully claimed that restricting entry to the executive class of the Civil Service to people under twenty-eight was indirectly discriminatory because many women are unable to take up or establish a career in their twenties because they are out of the labour force raising their children. As a result, the Civil Service must modify its entry and career structure to eliminate this discrimination.

Barriers women face in the workplace

In spite of the sex discrimination legislation, a variety of factors within the workplace continue to limit women's opportunities. These factors can be grouped into five categories:

1 *Job and promotion criteria which act as barriers to women*
Many job and promotion criteria which act as barriers to women are legitimate and related to actual demands of the job, but some are a matter of convenience or tradition, or reflect male career patterns. Even where such criteria are justifiable, the barriers they create could be removed or overcome by structuring jobs somewhat differently or by giving women special training. Examples included:
Lifting. Lifting requirements prevented women in many organizations from moving into better paid jobs or into jobs which traditionally led to higher graded jobs. Management and unions tended to assume that all the jobs concerned were too heavy for women without actually examining the content of the jobs. In fact, women could do many of these jobs and some said that they would like to. Other jobs could

have been altered and machinery introduced to make them easier for both men and women to do.

Hours of work. Women's reported inability and unwillingness to do shift or overtime work was often given as the reason why women did not move into better paid career jobs. While often true, there was considerable evidence that some women wanted or needed to work longer and different hours. In one case, the introduction of new machinery and shift work in one organization led to female redundancies and men replacing women. Had the employers consulted the women, they might have found that some women would have preferred shift work to no work at all.[14] Another barrier was the lack of part-time work, especially in jobs involving responsibility. Few organizations had examined their work flow to see whether it would be possible or even advantageous to employ people part-time rather than full-time.

Traditional promotion paths and criteria. In many organizations women do not have access to traditional promotion paths. For example, it is common in engineering to select supervisors from setting and from time-served jobs, which women have not done in the past, often because of discrimination. Similarly, promotion to supervision and management is often from technical and shop floor jobs rather than from the clerical and administrative side. But some managers and supervisors admitted that their jobs could be done just as well by people from the administrative side if they were given some technical support and training.

2 *Attitudes to women and work*

Attitudes in and of themselves need not be important; much depends on the organization's procedures and practices (or lack of them) and the scope they provide for managers' attitudes to affect women's opportunities. In many organizations, individual managers and supervisors make decisions to hire, train and promote individuals. We found considerable evidence that they may be doing so on the basis of assumptions about men and women which may not always be true. Several attitudes were prevalent to some extent in all the organizations. There was widespread acceptance of job segregation in manual jobs and strong views on the suitability of certain jobs for men (those involving lifting or mechanical tasks) and for women (those involving dexterity or repetitive work). Many men felt that women should not be asked to do dirty, heavy or potentially dangerous work. Women were thought to be capable of many jobs, especially in the white collar sector, but it was believed that they did not want or were not able to do them because of family responsibilities. It was often said that women did not want responsibility or a career.

Although many managers assumed a lack of interest on women's part, there were some women in nearly every organization who wanted more responsibility or the chance to move into traditionally male jobs. A further sign of women's interest was the increase in applications from women for higher-graded or men's jobs after the Sex Discrimination Act came in.

3 Personnel policies and practices

Many organizations have personnel policies and practices which are not unlawful but which can operate to women's disadvantage. For example, in most organizations the managers or supervisors have the final say in selection procedures. Given their attitudes and assumptions about women, it is not surprising that many have continued to discriminate against women.

Perhaps more important for women is the lack of certain personnel procedures, particularly with respect to training and promotion. Many organizations lack formal appraisal procedures where employees can discuss their career aspirations and problems systematically with their supervisors. In other cases there is no system of internal advertising for jobs. People are simply appointed. Both these practices can militate against women. Unless women have the extra confidence to push themselves forward, many managers will assume they are not interested in a career and will pass them over for promotion. Women's opportunities are also limited by the lack of pre-promotion training and training for adults. Training before, rather than after, promotion might particularly benefit and encourage women by increasing their confidence, credibility and skills. Without opportunities for day release and other formal training for adults, older women cannot obtain the training they need to overcome the effects of past discrimination or to catch up when they re-enter employment.

4 Effects of other employment policies

Other changes made in organizations affected women's opportunities. Most such actions are taken for good business reasons and indeed may be a move towards 'good practice'. But their impact on women had not been considered. For example, several organizations are attempting to professionalize supervision and management by recruiting graduates to replace managers and supervisors who traditionally had been trained up from within. As a result, women who have worked their way up through the grades and who could now expect to move into management and supervisory positions find that their paths are blocked by young male and (a few) female graduates. In another case, manual men made jobless by restructuring were taken on as supervisors in related clerical areas. As a result, posts which women were poised to move into were closed to them.

5 Structural and organizational factors

A number of organizational and structural factors were found which in effect severely limit women's opportunities. As mentioned earlier, some industries have age and career structures which make careers for women difficult. Another organizational factor is decentralized operating units. In many large organizations it is not normal practice for Head Office to interfere in local operations. Policy is set out generally at Head Office level but interpreted locally. This explains the failure of some company equal opportunity policies to have any effect. While the interest in and knowledge of the legislation was concentrated at Head Office level, the interpretation of policy and selection and promotion decisions took place at local level where interest and knowledge were low.

These barriers, while not unlawful, indirectly restrict women's opportunities in the workplace. They illustrate the subtle way in which established structures, practices and attitudes interact to limit women's opportunities, often without an intention to discriminate on anyone's part.

The continued existence of discrimination and the presence of subtle barriers in spite of sex discrimination legislation highlights the need for action by women and unions in the workplace. The first step is an audit of the distribution of men and women by grade, job and department; this should throw up areas where discrimination or barriers seem likely. Next, personnel practices and procedures should be investigated to see that they provide genuine equal opportunity for men and women. Job and promotion criteria should be examined to ensure that they are relevant to job performance and that no direct or indirect discrimination is taking place. Promotion paths should be identified and reviewed to see if they favour men and if so, whether they could be replaced by other equally effective routes. Particular attention should be paid to identifying where discrimination in the past or women's different career patterns prevent women from getting on. Finally, the initial investigation should include an analysis of applications for jobs, training and promotion to see how many women apply in the first place. Once areas of discrimination and barriers have been located, action will be needed to remove them. The action taken will depend to a large extent on the support for equal opportunity in the organization and the union's bargaining strength and its willingness to use it. Also some changes may require major alterations to organizations' structures and practices and thus are unlikely to be won easily. However, there are several areas which any programme for action should include:

1 increased and special training for women is crucial if they are to overcome the effects of past discrimination and other barriers and move into male areas. Such training is also important for increasing women's confidence as well as skills. Under Section 48 of the Sex Discrimination Act, positive discrimination in training is allowed in certain circumstances.

2 women, union representatives and line and personnel managers need more training on the law itself, its implications in the workplace and on what discrimination and equal opportunities involve. Positive programmes are unlikely to be effective in an atmosphere of ignorance, misunderstanding or hostile attitudes.

3 regular monitoring of women's position in the organization and of practices will be necessary to assess progress and to isolate problems areas.

■ Conclusions and implications

At workplace level, the legislation has had little impact. Although most women received some increase in pay as a result of the Equal Pay Act, many are still underpaid in relation to the men they work with and in relation to their level of skill and effort. Furthermore, the Sex Discrimination Act has not eliminated discrimination in employment nor has it led to any significant degree of desegregation of jobs. Most women are still concentrated in low-grade, low-paid women's jobs with little prospect of better paid jobs or promotion. This is largely because so little use has been made of the rights and powers conferred by the Acts, rather than because of the content and wording of the Acts themselves. While public attention has focussed on tribunal cases and consequently on the limitations of the law, it is clear that the absence of action and negative action by employers, unions, women and the Equal Opportunities Commission has been the major factor responsible for the limited effectiveness of both Acts at workplace level. Difficult economic circumstances and other employment legislation enacted during the same period created problems to which employers gave a higher priority. In the absence of pressures to do otherwise from women and unions within the organization or from the EOC or other institutions outside the organization, it is not surprising that many employers chose to minimize costs, effort and disruption wherever possible.

These findings suggest that the main need is for action to make the legislation as it stands more effective rather than for amendments to the Acts. In the long term there will almost certainly be a need to amend and strengthen the legislation to make it more punitive, as has been found necessary in the United States. In the short term there are clearly areas where amendments would help to clarify and strengthen the law. In particular, large numbers of women would benefit from the extension of the formal powers of the Central Arbitration Committee to allow it to investigate and make amendments to collective agreements where, in spite of modifications made to remove overt discrimination, discrimination in practice remains. Amendments are also needed to extend the scope of the Acts and to shift the burden of proof in discrimination cases on to the employer to make it easier for women to win individual cases. But amendments alone are unlikely to bring about significant changes to pay and practices in the organizations studied. Above all, what is needed is action by the EOC and trade unions. Both are in a position to take action and both have the power and indeed the obligation to women to do so.

Under the Sex Discrimination Act, the EOC was given the duties of working towards the elimination of discrimination and of promoting equality of opportunity. To these ends, it has been given a variety of rights and powers which could considerably increase the effectiveness of both Acts if used firmly and effectively. In particular, the EOC has the power under Section 57 to conduct formal investigations into organizations. This could be used to investigate organizations and industries where discrimination in pay and employment practices are thought to be particularly widespread. Such investigations are essential in view of the project findings: that no further action on equal pay or sex discrimination is likely in most organizations and that little change can be expected through individual tribunal cases given the difficulties women face in identifying and proving discrimination.

On equal pay, action on collective agreements and job evaluation could be particularly useful. First, the EOC could undertake an independent investigation into industry and company agreements in the light of the extent of minimization and de facto women's grades found. Agreements made both before and after equal pay could be examined for evidence of changes introduced in order to minimize. Where discriminatory agreements are found, they could be referred to the CAC by the Secretary of State under his existing powers if the parties to the agreement were not prepared to act. Secondly, the EOC could issue detailed guidelines on job evaluation. While job evaluation led to more equitable pay results for women in most cases, there can be weaknesses in the way job evaluation schemes are set up and applied and these are difficult for women and, in some cases, tribunals to recognize. As a result minimization and lack of compliance may not be noticed. Such guidelines should cover methods of job evaluation (both analytical and non-analytical) including factors and weightings, composition of panels and their training, appeals and maintenance systems, application of pay to results and arrangements for red circling. Emphasis should be placed on how discriminatory schemes can be recognized and on what type of information would be required to show less favourable treatment.

Trade unions are in a key position to identify inequalities in pay and practices and to take action to change them. Our findings show that where unions put pressure on employers, either negatively or positively, their action always had a significant impact. However, union action has often been lacking at local level.[15] Indeed, the existence of equal pay and sex discrimination legislation is to some extent an indictment of union apathy on these issues.

Unions can be most effective through the normal processes of collective bargaining and use of their industrial strength in the workplace. The issues of equal pay and opportunity need to be taken up and fought for in the workplace rather than before tribunals. There is a danger that some unions may opt for the narrow definitions and limited channels of redress established in the Acts. While unions should of course take full advantage of the resources and support that the legislation provides, it is crucial that they go beyond the definitions set by the Acts to fight for genuine equality of pay and opportunity.

Earlier sections have indicated some of the actions unions might take at workplace level. In addition, there is a particular need for action at national level on three issues:

1 The initial responsibility for some cases of minimization and de facto women's grades clearly lay with industry level negotiators.

Where unions have been party to industry agreements they should examine them for such inequalities, and if necessary, renegotiate them.

2 Unions should provide more detailed information and guidance on the legislation and its implications for shop stewards and other lay officers. The project found that information sent to local representatives by union head offices often concentrated on what the legislation said ('your rights') while local representatives needed guidance and specific examples of what this meant in practice and how they might identify and change discriminatory practices in their organizations ('what you can do'). Training and exercises on equal pay and opportunity should also be incorporated into the basic training for shop stewards. Such training should cover potential problem areas such as positive discrimination, indirect discrimination and hostile attitudes on the part of male members.

3 Unions should consider how women's participation in union offices and negotiations could be increased. The project findings make it clear that women's greater involvement in unions and pay determination is essential if women are to safeguard their interests at work.

Finally, what are the implications of these findings for women's campaigns for equality of opportunity at work? First, although the Acts have had only a limited effect on women's pay and opportunities, this effect should not be underestimated. As a result of the Equal Pay Act many women received considerable increases in pay which they would not otherwise have received. The Sex Discrimination Act has opened some job opportunities to women which formerly were closed to them. Perhaps most importantly, both Acts have raised women's level of awareness and expectations. While the Acts in and of themselves will not bring equality of opportunity, they clearly have provided the basis and impetus for further campaigning action.

Secondly, the findings highlight the need for campaigns directed at pay and practices in the workplace. Many women's campaigns are directed at winning social facilities such as abortion and nurseries which are needed to enable women to take advantage of equality of opportunities at work. While these campaigns are essential, social provisions alone will not make women's opportunities equal when at work. If women are to win real equality at work, action on both fronts is needed.

■ Notes

The article is based on the research of the London School of Economics project which monitored the implementation and the effects of the Equal Pay and Sex Discrimination Acts in twenty-six organizations over the period 1974-1977. The project was funded by the Department of Employment and the Nuffield Foundation. The findings described are the product of the whole team's efforts, but the views expressed are those of the author and may not always be shared by the other members of the team.

1   The Equal Pay Act was amended in 1984, the Sex Discrimination Act is due to be amended during 1986, and further case law since this article was written have affected the interpretation of the Acts. Detailed reports and analysis of equal pay and sex discrimination tribunal cases can be found in *Industrial Relations Review and Report, Industrial Relations Law Report* and Incomes Data Services' *Brief.* Details of the legislation and how to use it can be obtained from the National Council for Civil Liberties (NCCL). In some cases the NCCL and the Equal Opportunities Commission (EOC) will provide legal advice and support.

2   Many women are covered by an employer's pay structure – that is a formal pay or grading structure which has been set up by the employer. Such pay structures are common in larger white collar organizations. If such a structure is known or 'open to be known' to employees, it can be referred to the Central Arbitration Committee (CAC) to be amended on the same basis as collective agreements. The project findings suggest that many women are not aware that they are in such a structure and therefore perhaps entitled to an increase in pay under the collective provisions of the Act.

3   See the NCCL report, *Amending the Equal Pay and Sex Discrimination Acts*, for a fuller discussion of these and other possible amendments.

4   Not all low-paid workers received the full £6. For example, under the 1975 industry agreement for the retail multiple grocery and provisions trade (Great Britain), the two lowest and predominantly female grades received increases of £5.20 while the top three predominantly male grades got the full £6.

5   Equal pay settlements were exempt from incomes policy.

6   All terms and conditions of employment are covered by the Equal Pay Act, including other components of pay such as free uniforms. Only pensions and provisions relating to maternity, death and retirement and protective legislation are not covered.

7   A Court of Appeals decision, *Fletcher* v *Clay Cross*, has ruled that an employer cannot claim market pressures as a reason for paying a woman less. The Court of Appeals observed that 'if any such excuses were permitted, the Act would be a dead letter'.

8   Of 2,493 equal pay cases taken to tribunal in 1976 and 1977, 1,421 were withdrawn, 768 lost and only 304 won. Of 472 sex discrimination cases, 276 were withdrawn, 155 lost and 41 won.

9   Actions involving job segregation and the alteration of job content for one sex would probably have been unlawful had they taken place after the Sex Discrimination Act came in.

10 This case is similar to that at Trico where women were working alongside higher paid men whose pay had been protected by red circling. Although the employer took the case to a tribunal which ruled in his favour, the women stayed out on strike until the company was forced to give them equal pay.

11 For example, prior to equal pay some agreements had one women's rate, a skilled male rate and an unskilled male rate. As there was no semi-skilled male rate, Section 3 only required that semi-skilled women be brought up to the unskilled rate. However, had there been a semi-skilled male rate, Section 3 would have required that semi-skilled women be brought up to it.

12 The model clause includes provisions for both sides to review the operation of the equal opportunities policy periodically and for complaints of unequal treatment to be dealt with through agreed grievance procedures. However, there has been no use of these potentially important provisions by the unions concerned.

13 Some banks and insurance companies require geographical mobility of those wishing to make a career. Frequent moves at the convenience of the organization are said to be necessary to provide employees with varied experience and to prevent stagnation. Some employees, and in one case the union, feel that this requirement is not justified once initial training has been completed. They argue that if all posts were advertised internally, employees could apply to move if and when it suited their family circumstances.

14 The Factories Act 1961 limits the hours that women in manual jobs can work. Employers can, however, apply for an exemption order if it is in the public interest to maintain or increase efficiency of the industry. If the right to apply for such an order were extended to unions and women, this would provide flexibility in cases where women need or want to work shifts or nights without removing the overall protection which the law provides.

15 In recent years most unions at national level have begun to take equal pay and opportunity seriously. TASS (the Technical Administrative and Supervisory Section of the Amalgamated Union of Engineering Workers) and APEX (the Association of Professional, Executive, Clerical and Computer Staff) have been particularly active on these issues. But nationally agreed policies often have had little effect at local negotiating level.

The Reserve Army of Labour 1974-1979

Irene Bruegel

The idea that women workers are particularly useful to capital as a reserve army of labour – to be brought in and thrown out of wage labour as the interests of capital dictate – has a wide currency amongst Marxists and feminists (Bland *et al*, 1978; Beechey, 1978; Counter Information Services, 1976; Adamson *et al*, 1976). Such a theory clearly has important implications: it places the specificity of female labour within a general Marxist model of capital accumulation and so provides some material basis for the differentiation of male and female wage labour, and it also shows up the similarities between the situation of women as wage labourers and that of other groups of workers such as immigrants.

The theory has, however, been challenged. While no one disputes that women have provided a reservoir of labour to be tapped in times of boom and labour shortage, some Marxist-feminists have questioned the assumption that female labour is particularly 'disposable' in times of economic crisis. This note examines the argument in the light of the experiences of women workers in Britain in the years 1974-78. It concludes that, taken as a whole, women's employment opportunities have been protected from the worst effects of the crisis by the continued expansion of service work in the period. Nevertheless, individually, women have been more susceptible to redundancy when compared to men in similar circumstances. Thus the reserve army of labour model holds, but the simple version needs qualification.

■ Marx and the industrial reserve army

Marx (1867) saw the expansion of a reserve army of labour as an inevitable outcome of the process of capital accumulation (*Capital*, Vol. I). As capital accumulated, it threw certain workers out of employment into a reserve army; conversely, in order to accumulate, capital needed a reserve army of labour. Without such a reserve, capital accumulation would cause wages to rise, and the process of accumulation would itself be threatened as surplus value was squeezed. While Marx did note that certain workers – the pauperized lumpen-proletariat – might bear the brunt of unemployment, he was concerned to show how the expansion of capitalism inevitably drew more and more people into a labour reserve of potential, marginal and transitory employment, rather than to identify any group of workers as particularly vulnerable. Marx did not consider women as a group in his reserve army of labour model. Nevertheless, the extension of women's involvement in wage labour in all western economies clearly fits the picture of the continued expansion of the reserve army drawn by Marx. Braverman (1974) and Kolko (1978) both argue this in relation to the United States. In Britain the net expansion of 2.5 million workers achieved between 1951 and 1971 was made up almost entirely (2.2 million) of women coming into wage labour. This expansion meant, as Marx argued it would, that wages, particularly in those industries where women predominate, have been kept down. The process becomes self-fuelling. Increasingly, the maintenance of family living standards has come to depend on two or more wage packets,[1] and all adult female labour has become potential wage labour – as many as a quarter of mothers of pre-school children are now employed (Office of Population Census and Surveys, 1978).

In the sense of providing a labour *reserve*, women's labour power has clearly become an important part of what Marx saw as the industrial reserve army.

■ The hypothesis of greater 'disposability'

This isn't really at issue. What is in dispute is whether women bear, to a disproportionate extent, the burden of unemployment in times of crisis, whether they are *more* 'disposable'. This is what the notion of women as a reserve army of labour has come to mean, notwithstanding Marx's use of the term.

There are a number of grounds on which one would indeed expect that women's labour power would be more readily dispensed with in times of redundancy (Barron and Norris, 1976). MacKay *et al* (1971) concluded in their study of the engineering industry that 'there was a greater propensity to dismiss females in preference to males in a redundancy situation'.[2] They point to the fact that redundancy procedures often stipulated that, after people over the age of retirement, part-time and married women workers should be picked out for the sack. The seniority principle of last in, first out would also tend to discriminate against women, even if there was no explicit discrimination (Jenness *et al*, 1975).[3] Daniel and Stilgoe (1978) found that half of the firms in their survey of 300 companies operated the seniority principle in making redundancies. A Department of Employment Survey of redundancies in 1975-76 (Department of Employment, 1978) does confirm the vulnerability of shorter service workers, despite the bias in the Redundancy Payments Act which tends to increase the vulnerability of older (and hence more long-serving) workers. Significantly, the survey doesn't distinguish between male and female workers.

The fact that women tend to work in smaller, less unionized workplaces may also make them more vulnerable to redundancy. However, the poor record of many unions in fighting redundancies, particularly amongst part-time women workers (Counter Information Services, 1976), suggests that lower levels of unionization may not be a particularly important handicap as such.

MacKay *et al* (1971) also saw the higher rates of redundancy amongst women as a reflection of their lower levels of skill; employers are likely to keep on skilled men or put them on short time when work is slack because their skills are not easily replaced and, on dismissal, they may move elsewhere.[4] Women, on the other hand, can be more easily replaced or re-engaged when trade picks up, so there is much less of a deterrent to giving them the sack. The dependency of working wives, which forces them to live where their husbands work, contributes to this pattern. Twilight shifts in particular are closed down and started up again on the basis of a captive, relatively immobile workforce of married women. In the United States, where there is in any case more job mobility, the lesser mobility of married women is seen to contribute to higher levels of unemployment amongst women (Ferber and Lowry, 1976; Niemi, 1976).

The current pattern of limiting redundancies by freezing appointments (Daniel and Stilgoe, 1978) may also increase the relative vulnerability of women workers. This is because family responsibilities often force women to leave work for a period; as a result, at any given point in time, women workers are more likely to be looking for work than men.[5]

Moreover, ideology in the form of the notion that a woman's place is in the home may well contribute to a greater vulnerability of women to unemployment. The onslaught on married women working – blaming them, in effect, for the level of unemployment amongst men – is perhaps not as strong as it was in the 1930s,[6] nevertheless, it is still evident,[7] with youth unemployment in particular being 'explained' by the tendency of married women to work. Unemployment amongst women is never considered the personal and social problem which male unemployment is.[8] As a result, women's confidence in their right to work is weaker than men's, and may well contribute to a higher 'voluntary' redundancy rate as well as fuelling discriminatory practices by managements and unions.

These arguments, taken together, suggest that, other things being equal, one could expect women to be more vulnerable to unemployment than men. However, Gardiner (1976) and Milkman (1976) suggest different ways in which everything is not equal, in which female labour is quite distinct from male labour. Gardiner argues that the cheapness of female labour would lead capital to substitute women for men, rather than sack women in preference to men. This is indeed Marx's argument, and such a fear certainly underlay attempts by organized workers to exclude women from large areas of employment. Such a fear indeed led the Trades Union Congress into endorsing the provisions which forced unemployed women into domestic service before the war (Lewenhak, 1977). In this way women could be prevented from competing for men's jobs. However, it is not at all clear that such substitution (of women for men) would be especially common in periods of slump; the returns on, and the possibilities of, substituting women for men are greater when the economy is expanding.[9]

Gardiner's argument also conflicts with the point Milkman makes; namely that the sexual division of wage labour is so rigid as to preclude both the substitution of male by female labour (as in Gardiner's account) and the effective substitution of female by male labour (as in the 'women as a dispensable labour force' account). What Milkman is arguing is that the segregation of women into women's work is of such ideological importance that it cannot be breached, even where it would yield capital cheaper labour.[10] Hence for Milkman the pattern of women's employment and unemployment over the cycle of booms and slumps simply reflects the fortunes of 'women's' industries and occupations. While the degree of segregation is great (Hakim, 1978), Milkman's argument cannot be sustained. As is shown below, the effect of a slump in any given industry is different for women than for men. Secondly, the pattern of segregation of women's work and men's work is not naturally determined, nor easily explained by 'ideology'. It reflects, in part, economic factors, and follows, in some degree, the dual labour market division (Barron and Norris, 1976). This means that women tend to be recruited to less stable areas of employment (Baudouin et al, 1978); a job is 'women's work' partly *because* it doesn't offer stable and continuous employment.[11] Catering work in schools and colleges is a prime example of the use of female labour for 'unstable and seasonal work'.

■ Unemployment amongst women

If one looks at figures for women's unemployment over recent years, both in Britain and elsewhere, there seems to be little basis for either Gardiner's or Milkman's objections to the reserve army model. Between 1974 and 1978 in Britain the official rate of unemployment amongst women increased more than three times as fast as that of men. In Holland, Italy, Spain and Belgium (OECD, 1976; Wernecke, 1978) the rate of increase in unemployment was also greater amongst women than men. In other countries the level of unemployment amongst women is higher, although the rate of increase is on a par.[12] However, there are always severe problems in using the official statistics of unemployment as a measure of the effects of crisis on women's employment. In Britain, only women registered at the labour exchange are counted as unemployed.[13] Given this narrow definition, something like half the women who say they are looking for work are not counted as unemployed (General Household Survey, 1976; Dex, 1978). This complicates the assessments of changes over time (quite apart from hiding the real extent of unemployment amongst women), because it is likely that the proportion of unemployed women who do register does vary over time (General Household Survey, 1974, 1976). Given a shift in unemployment towards younger people and hence towards single women, the proportion of women registering has probably risen (Moore, Rhodes et al, 1978). To some extent then, the fast rise in official unemployment amongst women overestimates the real rise.

Nevertheless, from what evidence there is, it would seem that 'real' unemployment amongst women has risen faster than amongst men, the rise being particularly fast amongst single women.[14] Moore, Rhodes et al's estimates of the real unemployment level suggest that women have been disproportionately affected; while women are only 41 per cent of the labour force, they accounted for 53 per cent of the net rise in real unemployment. Thus the unemployment figures, even allowing for changes in registration, do not substantiate Gardiner's argument. Neither, however, can they be said to prove the disposability model, because it is single women who appear to have been particularly badly affected, while the hypotheses outlined above tend to emphasize the particular vulnerability of married women workers (Beechey, 1978), rather than women workers as a whole. However, even figures derived from surveys pose problems for measuring unemployment amongst 'housewives', and the survey figures could well underestimate the impact of a crisis on married women's employment. This is because unemployed housewives who would otherwise work may not consider themselves to be looking for work in a climate of restricted employment, childcare facilities, transport provisions and so on, and so wouldn't therefore be counted as unemployed by a survey such as that undertaken by the General Household Survey. Because of the difficulties with any of the measures of unemployment, in this article employment figures rather than unemployment figures will be used to analyse the impact of the crisis on women's employment opportunities.

■ Trends of women's employment

In attempting to evaluate a 'disposability' model, it is important to clarify exactly what the model proposes. On the one hand, the idea that women might cushion men from the full impact of recession could be taken to imply that women's employment opportunities, taken as a whole, deteriorate relative to men's in times of recession. On the other hand, it can be taken to mean that any individual women is more susceptible to redundancy and unemployment than a man in an equivalent situation would be. This distinction is important.

At first glance the first form of the model appears to have little validity. In the years 1974-78 female employment *rose* by 145,000 jobs, while the number of men at work fell by 361,000, a pattern repeated in a number of countries. However, this pattern is simply a reflection of the long-term trend towards an increasingly female labour force. In 1951 only 32 per cent of the labour force were women; by 1977 over 40 per cent were. Had there been no recession and past trends had continued, then the rise in women's employment between 1974 and 1978 would have been greater than the 145,000 jobs created. This point is illustrated in Figure 1, which shows how in each recession since the war the rate of growth of female employment slowed down relative to periods of expansion. If one takes into account the increasing need and desire for women to seek paid work, then it is far from clear that the rise in female employment over the last few years really signals a lesser deterioration in women's employment prospects relative to men's. The number of women seeking work between 1974 and 1977 increased faster, at 4 per cent, than the number of jobs created (1.5 per cent). Moore, Rhodes *et al* (1978) calculated the shortfall in male jobs relative to male workers between 1973 and 1977 to be 615,000; for the smaller female labour force the shortfall was some 680,000.

Turning to the second form of the 'disposability' model, Figure 2 makes it clear that in every industry[15] employing a substantial number of women and where employment declined between 1974 and 1977, the rate of employment decline was greater for women than for men. Of the major industries, only construction, public and miscellaneous services and the public administration sector, where reclassification has distorted the picture,[16] do not conform to this trend. In manufacturing as a whole, women lost nearly 9 per cent of their jobs, in a period when male manufacturing jobs fell by less than 5 per cent. The losses were particularly great in the new growth sectors such as electronics. Similar trends are found throughout western manufacturing (OECD, 1976; Baudouin *et al*, 1978). What kept women's employment buoyant as a whole was the continued expansion of parts of the service sector (Figure 3); for example, professional and scientific and miscellaneous services. The growth of these matched the falls in employment elsewhere, despite public sector cuts.[17] To a degree, then, Ruth Milkman is right; the particular pattern of women's employment, the concentration in a limited range of the expanding service sector, has limited the impact of the recession on women's opportunities as a whole. If women had not been concentrated in 'women's work' – catering, nursing, teaching, cleaning – but had been distributed amongst industries in the same way as men, then the impact of the 1974-77 crisis would have been far greater – a decline of jobs of almost half a million, compared to an actual increase in the period of 140,000.[18] Thus, as in the United States (OECD, 1976), the

Annual changes in female employment, 1950-1978 (June-June), Great Britain.

Figure 1

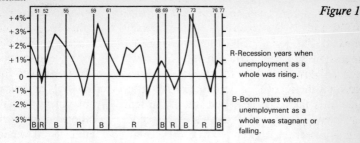

R-Recession years when unemployment as a whole was rising.

B-Boom years when unemployment as a whole was stagnant or falling.

Changes in employment by industry, 1974-1977 (percentage change for each group), Great Britain.

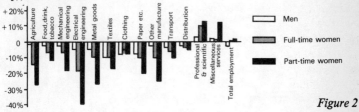

Figure 2

Components of change in women's employment, 1974-77, Great Britain. Change by industry.

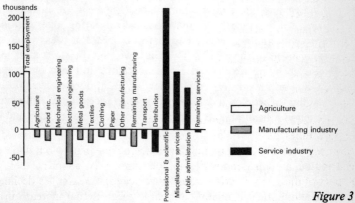

Figure 3

Source: Department of Employment

Annual change in manufacturing employment, male and female, 1950-1978, Great Britain.

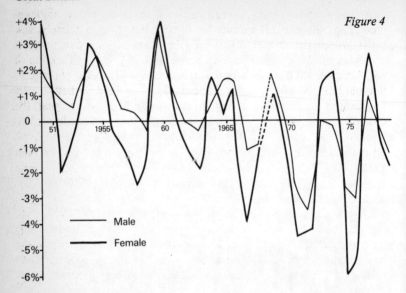

Figure 4

Source: Department of Employment

'favourable' industrial distribution of women has cushioned women's employment, *taken as a whole*, against the worst effects of the crisis.

In manufacturing the impact of the crisis has fallen disproportionately on women. As in all previous post-war recessions, women's employment has fallen faster than men's (Figure 4), in a way which conforms to the reserve army model. Comparing one period of recession with another, women appear to be becoming less vulnerable than they were in the 1950s. This may well be due to a shift away from the declining textile and clothing sectors and into more stable clerical and administrative employment. What it does show is that the vulnerability of women industrial workers to recession is not a recent phenomenon attributable to legislative changes such as the Equal Pay Act.

■ Part-time work

It is part-time women workers who have been made to bear the brunt of the decline in employment. The pattern in electrical engineering shows this up particularly well. Between 1974 and 1977 38,000 unskilled and semi-skilled jobs were lost; 18,000 of these were part-time women workers, compared to a 5 per cent job loss amongst men. The 'selection' of women for redundancy does not imply any breakdown in the sex stereotyping of jobs – men taking women's work – as Milkman's argument implies. Rather, it highlights the function of part-time employment in a capitalist economy. Wherever short-term fluctuations in demand for labour are expected, whether the fluctuations are from day to day, month to month, or year to year, the cost of dealing with such fluctuations for the capitalist is less when women, particularly part-time women, have been employed (Hurstfield, 1978). This phenomenon is well illustrated by the mini boom of 1973-74; part-time employment of women in manufacturing increased by 15 per cent in that year, to fall subsequently by 10 per cent in 1974-75 and 8 per cent in 1975-76. In every industry where employment declined between 1974 and 1977, the rate of decline for part-time women exceeded that of men and full-time women (Figure 2). It is part-time women workers, who form an increasing proportion of women workers (40 per cent are now part-time), who conform most closely to the model of women as a disposable reserve army. Nevertheless, in certain areas of work, their numbers are still increasing rapidly.

■ Conclusion

Over the last few years there have been two conflicting processes at work affecting women's employment. On the one hand, within any given industry or job, women, particularly part-time women workers, have suffered from greater rates of job loss than men. This has come about partly, no doubt, through explicit or barely veiled discriminatory policies, but more important, probably, has been the exploitation of the weaknesses of married women's labour market position, weaknesses which derive in one way or another from primary definition of women as housewives and mothers. On the other hand, the continued expansion of parts of the service sector on the basis of the availability of cheap female labour has mitigated the effects of the crisis on women's employment opportunities. It is important to recognize that the 'protection' that women's jobs have had through the expansion of the service sector is a protection based on the cheapness of female labour. The low pay offered to women in the expanding service sectors virtually precludes any wholesale takeover by men, even when unemployment is high. Given certain technological constraints which have until now made the service sectors highly labour intensive (Braverman, 1974; Harris and Taylor, 1978), the service sector did require a 'reserve army' of cheap labour to draw on to expand its output. As a result, in virtually all capitalist countries the expansion of service industry went hand in hand with the expansion of women's paid employment in the post-war years. Since services were less vulnerable to recession than other sectors of employment, they have afforded women a certain protection from unemployment in times of recession. However, with the development of microprocessors this 'protection' is likely to wear thin, since the advantages women offer to capital – cheap and relatively docile labour – becomes less and less relevant (Counter Information Services, 1979; Downing and Barker, 1979). Moreover, the type of work women do – low level, repetitive and boring – is probably more susceptible to rationalization, whether it is manufacturing or service work, than ever before. In Germany, where rationalization of office work has gone further than in Britain (Cooley, 1979), service work no longer protects women's employment as a whole from the impact of crisis (Däubler-Gmelin, 1977); the degree of protection in the United States is also significantly less than in Britain (OECD, 1976). Thus the analysis in this note must be seen in its historical perspective.

While it is probably true for all periods that the marginal position of married women in the labour force has made them, individual for individual, more vulnerable to redundancy than male workers, the particular form of capitalist expansion and restructuring over the last thirty years – the expansion of labour intensive public and private services and administrative occupations – greatly extended the employment opportunities of women. The result was that women's employment continued to expand even when men's jobs were being cut back fast.

The long-term shift towards women in the workforce cushioned women's employment against the shorter term (cyclical) recessions. The signs are that this particular phase of capital restructing may be over; that one of the bases of the long-term expansion of female employment – the cheapness of female employment – may be declining in relative significance, given new technological developments. Hence many groups of women who have traditionally regarded their jobs as secure will find themselves threatened with rationalization on a scale comparable to the wholesale elimination of jobs in the traditional male strongholds – mining, railways, docks. The implications of this analysis are not that the solution lies in attempting to equalize the incidence of increasing unemployment between men and women. Rather, it is that the fight for jobs will increasingly be a fight for women's jobs. Thus if the labour movement is to be able effectively to resist unemployment, now more than ever before it urgently needs to devise more effective strategies of defending women's jobs and the right of women to work.

■ Notes

This article appeared in *Feminist Review* No. 3, 1979.

1 This point comes out very clearly in the Royal Commission on the Distribution of Income and Wealth (Research Report 6, 1978). When wives do not go out to work, the chances of a family in Britain today being in poverty are almost one in three; where wives work, the chances are nearer one in fourteen.

2 MacKay *et al*, p.375, give the following figures for redundancies in Birmingham and Glasgow over the 1959-66 period:

	Average quarterly redundancy rate	
	Birmingham	Glasgow
skilled men	.1	.6
all men	.2	.5
all women	.9	.6

3 The degree to which 'last in, first out' (LIFO) loads redundancy on to women depends on how the procedure is applied. If it was adopted company or plant wide, then women would indeed be particularly vulnerable. It seems in practice that unless the whole plant is closed, redundancies tend to be brought in shop by shop. Given the high level of job segregation within a workplace, this means that the LIFO procedure would tend to be applied separately to groups of men and women and would not necessarily lead to a higher rate of redundancy amongst women. As Jennes *et al* (1975) point out, where women have broken through into male dominated jobs, as in the United States steelworks, the LIFO procedure will work against them.

4 British statistics on short time working do not distinguish between men and women. Däubler-Gmelin's research in Germany shows that men are far more likely to be put on short time than women but far less likely to be made redundant.

5 This is reflected in turnover figures. These show that over industry as a whole, for every 100 women in work, nearly forty are taken on in a year, compared to thirty men; at the same time, nearly forty leave, compared to thirty men (*Department of Employment Gazette*, November 1978).

6 Rowbotham 1973, Milkman 1976, Humphries 1976 all present evidence

of hostility to married women workers in Britain and the United States in the 1930s. In both countries various bars were put on married women working; nevertheless, the long-term expansion in women's wage labour was not halted.

7   Occasional calls are made even today to sack married women. In 1977 the *Daily Mail* ran a campaign, 'Weed out the Working Wives', but no major party has explicitly questioned the right of married women to work.

8   Government figures for unemployment amongst women are seriously inadequate and, even more disturbing, the various job creation schemes show a distinct bias towards male workers; in 1976 84 per cent of the young people on the Job Creation Scheme were boys, despite the fact that unemployment levels for girls are equally bad. One of the ill-fated Manpower Services Commission's posters did feature a girl, but the problem of youth unemployment is seen as a problem of boys out on the streets, of potential disruption to the social order.

9   The process of substitution is rarely one where a woman takes on a job that was previously held by a man. More often substitution takes place in the context of capital restructuring, of bringing in new machinery which transforms a skilled job into a semi-skilled or unskilled one, or of moving jobs around the country. In either case the substitution of female for male labour, while bringing in long term savings in wage costs, requires capital investment. Such investments are unlikely to be made where output is stagnant and wage rises are restricted.

10 Milkman maintains that it is 'ideologically' important to retain the image of women as dependent and passive, despite the drive to exploit their labour power. Milkman sees this contradiction only being resolved by segregating women into 'women's work'.

11 This is not to say that all areas of unstable employment are filled by women. Immigrant men fulfil a similar role in the economy; the construction industry, with very large fluctuations in demand for labour, is almost wholly dependent on male immigrant labour (Baudouin, 1978). Nor are all areas of women's work highly unstable, but in general women's work is characterized by a greater degree of instability in employment.

12 The OECD gives the following figures of relative unemployment rates (1975):

	Australia	France	Germany	Italy	Belgium	United States
male	3.2	3.5	4.5	2.9	4.4	8.0
female	5.0	7.9	5.2	4.9	9.9	9.2

13 This is justified on the grounds that: 'Many married women who state they are seeking work may be expressing a future intention rather than a current activity. In practice they are more inclined to attach conditions to the work they are prepared to take – working hours, ease of travel,

availability of nursery schools and so on – and they can only be described as unemployed in a restricted sense.' (Cmnd 5157 Unemployment Statistics: Report of the Interdepartmental Working Party, 1972.)

14 Calculating from the General Household Survey data 1974 and 1976:

	1974-76
change in total male unemployment (registered and unregistered)	+10%
change in total female unemployment (registered and unregistered)	+28%
change in single female unemployment (registered and unregistered)	+42%

15 The data used are the Department of Employment annual census (June) of employment by industry, analysed at the 27-industry Standard Industrial Classification level. Unfortunately, data on occupational groups are not available on an annual basis. Such information would have been helpful for the analysis because the jobs (occupations) women do within an industry tend to be very different from those of men. In theory, the higher rate of job loss for women within each industry could be due to the particular vulnerability of the *jobs* that women do, rather than the vulnerability of women in any particular area of work. This point has been checked as far as possible with the published statistics for the electrical engineering industry. When the broadly defined industry is disaggregated into its nine constituent industries, the pattern of higher job loss for women in each of the declining industries remains; similarly, when each occupation within electrical engineering is analysed from the annual returns, there is still a tendency for women to suffer a higher rate of job loss in each of the declining occupations.

16 Some 60,000 to 70,000 workers in public administration were reclassified into other services in the period under review.

17 Despite the public sector cuts, net employment in the public services has continued to grow, albeit at a much slower rate than previously. In the year 1977-78 the growth in female employment has been so slow that it has barely matched the declines elsewhere. See Hughes (1978) for a further discussion.

18 This is calculated using a 'shift and share' analysis. Expected growth in total employment on the basis of the male distribution is $\sum_i (\frac{M_i}{M} F).R_{fi}$

where M = total male employment 1974

M_i = male employment in industry 1974

F = total female employment 1974

R_{fi} = rate of change of female employment in industry in 1974-77.

Sex and Skill

Anne Phillips and Barbara Taylor

It is time the working females of England began to demand their long suppressed rights ... In manufacturing towns, look at the value that is set on woman's labour, whether it be skilful (sic), whether it be laborious, so that women can do it. The contemptible expression is, is it made by woman, and therefore cheap? Why, I ask, should woman's labour be thus undervalued? ... Sisters, let us submit to it no longer ... but unite and assert our just rights! ('A Bondswoman' (Frances Morrison) writing to a radical working class newspaper, *The Pioneer*, 12 April 1834.)

Waged work in Britain, as in every other advanced capitalist country, is sharply differentiated along sexual lines. There may be few occupations left which are entirely the preserve of either men or women, but most men workers are employed in jobs where the workforce is at least 90 per cent male, while most women workers work in jobs which are at least 70 per cent female (Hakim, 1978). Even when men and women do work in the same industry, sexual demarcations are still rigidly maintained: women sew what men design and cut out; women serve what men cook; women run machines which men service; and so on and on ... Everywhere we turn, we see a clear distinction between 'men's work' and 'women's work', with women's work almost invariably characterized by lower pay, lack of craft traditions, weak union organization, and – above all – unskilled status.[1] Wherever women workers are, whatever jobs they do, they nearly always find themselves occupying the lowest rung on the skill ladder, earning wages which are commensurate, it is claimed, with the low level of training, ability or concentration required for the job.

In this paper we want to suggest that the classification of women's jobs as unskilled and men's jobs as skilled or semi-skilled frequently bears little relation to the actual amount of training or ability required for them. Skill definitions are saturated with sexual bias. The work of women is often deemed inferior simply because it is women who do it. Women workers carry into the workplace their status as subordinate individuals, and this status comes to define the value of the work they do. Far from being an objective economic fact, skill is often an ideological category imposed on certain types of work by virtue of the sex and power of the workers who perform it.

This hypothesis needs some qualification. Obviously it is true that there are jobs which require training, and it is also true that women workers (as well as some men workers, especially Blacks or Asians) have generally been refused access to this training, thereby ensuring their exclusion from areas of work requiring more knowledge and initiative. Moreover domestic responsibilities – particularly childcare – curtail women's ability to enter training programmes even when these are open to them, as well as making it generally more difficult for women to climb up the job ladder. Part-time work and outwork, which are nearly always classified as unskilled, are often the only options open to women with small children. We are not denying this. But to suggest that the remarkable coincidence between women's labour and unskilled labour in our economy is solely the result of discriminatory training programmes, or even of home responsibilities, is surely naive, since it implies that with educational upgrading and the provision of more day-nurseries women would take their place alongside skilled men workers, and gender-ghettoes in waged work would disappear. We think the problem goes much deeper than this. In order to see how much deeper it goes, however, we must begin to rethink the meaning of skill itself and the economic categories through which skill has been defined.

How can we make sense of the rigid sexual segregation of waged work? At first glance, there seems to be nothing in the nature of capitalism itself which requires this division of labour on a sexual basis. In principle, capitalism is the first mode of production which treats all members of society as equals. It does not divide up the species into those that are born free and those that are born slaves; it does not divide us into the complex hierarchy of ranks which characterized feudalism. For Marx and Engels it was this that gave capitalism its revolutionary nature. Here, they argued, was a form of social organization which would destroy these divisions and gradations, sweep away national, religious, sexual distinctions, reduce everything to the naked 'cash-nexus'. Capital is interested only in labour-power – of whatever sex, race or rank in society – and selects its labour-power on the purely quantitative basis of how much it can contribute to profits. How then do ghettoes of 'women's work' arise?

When Marxist-feminists first began to ask this question, they usually answered it in terms of the needs of capitalism itself. Employers benefit, it was argued, from the existence of a pool of cheap, unskilled labour which can be used to undercut men workers and fuel expansionist sectors. Women workers are particularly useful as this 'reserve army of labour' because their family responsibilities and (usually) partial dependence on a man's wage ensure that they are viewed (and often view themselves) as secondary workers, who can be pushed back into their primary sphere – the home – whenever they are not needed on the labour market. Women's family role makes them particularly vulnerable as workers, and their vulnerability is capital's strength. They are the super-exploitables.

In recent years, however, many Marxist feminists have become uneasy about the assumptions embodied in this style of argument. After all, 'if women's subordination within society predates capitalism, then surely one cannot hope to explain it in terms of the inherent logic of the capitalist system?' (Mackintosh, 1981). More specifically, since work – whether waged or unwaged – has always been divided along sexual lines, surely we cannot hope to explain the sex segregation of capitalist waged work solely in terms of the profit imperatives of capitalism itself? Under the impact of radical feminism – which insists that women are oppressed by men, not just by systems of productive relations – some socialist women began searching for explanations which lay in the realm of family life, sexual relations, and the cultural formation of gender differences. The concept of 'patriarchy' began to be employed – not as a fully worked out theory of gender dominance, but as a way of indicating that such a theory was necessary; that it was no longer adequate to treat sexual oppression as a by-product of economic class relations. The construction and maintenance of gender hierarchy was argued to have its own 'laws of motion', and it is these which theorists of patriarchy have been attempting to explore.

These developments represent a major advance for feminist thinking. For until we shake ourselves loose of theoretical inhibitions and begin to explore freely the uncharted terrain of gender relations, we shall never make sense of the specificity of our experience as women. But there is a sense in which these developments have not been radical enough. For in attempting to push past the categories of Marxist economic analysis, we have left these categories untouched and unchallenged. In arguing against 'economism' – the reduction of sex oppression to capitalist economic imperatives – we have, in effect, left Marxism to the male Marxists, many of whom would very much like to believe that capitalist production relations have nothing to do with sexual relations and that the struggle between capital and labour is unconnected to – hence unchallenged by – the sex struggle. This is surely not our aim. We do not want to find ourselves simply tacking the Woman Question onto a finished theory of the 'economy'. We want to take the issue of gender hierarchy into the heart of Marxist economic analysis itself.

An article by Heidi Hartmann (1979) highlights this need to rethink economic categories in the light of feminism. According to Heidi Hartmann, the Marxist analysis of capitalism provides us only with a theory of the different 'places' required by capitalist production. It explains why a hierarchy of labour is necessary within the waged workforce, but tells us nothing about why *women* end up at the bottom of this hierarchy:

> Marx's theory of the development of capitalism is a theory of the development of 'empty places' ... Just as capital creates these places indifferent to the individuals who fill them, the categories of Marxist analysis, 'class', 'reserve army of labour', 'wage-labourer', do not explain why particular people fill particular places. They give us no clue about why *women* are subordinate to *men* inside and outside the family and why it is not the other way around. *Marxist categories, like capital itself, are sex-blind.* The categories of Marx cannot tell us who will fill the empty places. (Hartmann, 1979: 7-8)

Hence the need for an additional theory of the patriarchal relations which assign women to subordinate places in the social hierarchy. Left to its own devices, capitalism might well have fulfilled the prophecies of Engels and others, and effectively destroyed sexual divisions within the family by drawing women indiscriminately into wage labour. But patriarchy intervened, and ensured through the development of the family wage system that women's subordinate position within the family be reproduced within waged labour.

Two assumptions lie behind this argument. The first is that sexual oppression can and must be theorized independently of the specific economic forms – capitalist or otherwise – in which it appears. Patriarchy has its own history, its own effects. As a working assumption, a starting-point for feminist investigation, that is a crucial presupposition. The second assumption, however, is more dubious. This is the idea that the capitalist economic system operates like an impersonal machine, geared to the extraction of surplus value, and indifferent to the sorts of people absorbed into its workings. As wage labourers, we are all just cogs in this machine: a 'variable capital' which is incorporated – regardless of sex, colour or nationality – into the remorseless cycle of capital accumulation. Heidi Hartmann points out that 'pure capitalism' in this form has never existed; that capitalism in its historical development encounters individuals who are already sex-stratified, and that this pre-existing structure of sexual stratification – patriarchy – then becomes harnessed to capital's need for different types of labour. But an understanding of this 'actual capitalism', she argues, will be based on our examination of the interaction of the two separate dynamics – that of patriarchy, for which we have as yet no developed analysis, and that of the capitalist economic machine, for which we can simply turn to the existing body of Marxist theory.

The particular interpretation of Marxism on which this argument is based is not, we should add, one which is unique to Heidi Hartmann. 'Economism', that is, the idea that capitalism develops through the mechanical operation of certain objective laws of material development, has been the dominant rendering of Marx since the late nineteenth century. It is an interpretation which has not only expelled gender as a determinate social factor, but – at its extreme limits – has managed to expel *all* social factors from its analysis, leaving instead only the relentless grinding-through of an inner logic of capitalist development, in which the imperatives of profitability push capitalist society along a pre-destined route. On this account capitalism is not only 'sex-blind', but blind to the entire fabric of social existence in which it is historically located. It is, to mix our metaphors yet further, an economic train carrying us all in one direction, regardless of who we are or the historical baggage we carry.[2]

There have always been critics of this economistic interpretation of Marxism, and in recent years they have launched their attacks from a number of different directions. But in particular, there has been a spate of literature exploring the changing structure of capitalist work processes which has attempted to replace the Economic Machine view of Marxism with a dynamic, historical account of capitalist development, an account that undermines the dichotomy between 'objective laws' and 'subjective' consciousness which has been so prevalent in socialist thinking. These writings on the labour process have not been notable for their feminist content, but they do offer some basis for a re-assessment of the relationship between sex and skill.

The 'labour process' discussions were generated partly by the publication of Harry Braverman's *Labour and Monopoly Capital* in 1974, which was quickly followed by a series of articles and books amplifying and extending his thesis; in Britain, most of this work has been carried out under the auspices of the Conference of Socialist Economists (Conference of Socialist Economists, 1976; Brighton Labour Process Group, 1977; Gorz, 1978). The innovative core of all these writings has been the insistence that capitalist production relations develop not as a mechanical logic of surplus extraction, but through a process of struggle, embedded in history. Changes in the organization of work cannot be treated simply as technological innovation demanded by capital's search for higher profits; they are the outcome of continuous tension between capitalists and workers – and, we would argue in extension of this thesis, of tensions between workers themselves, particularly between men and women workers. According to Harry Braverman and others, capitalism's capacity to make profits depends on the degree of command it can assert over its workers. Unless capital can directly control the organization of work – the labour process – it cannot dictate how much surplus value is produced. When knowledge and training are required to make a product, the worker who has that knowledge – who understands how things are made, and just what kind of operations must be performed to make things a certain way – also has power over the speed and quality of the work. If however, that craft knowledge can be transferred from the worker to the technical experts or managers, and the worker reduced to the performance of routine operations within a process s/he no longer fully comprehends, capitalist control over production is greatly increased. The worker becomes 'de-skilled', as the knowledge which was once part of the job becomes part of the power of capital itself. Changes in the production process are introduced, therefore, not as a way of achieving some abstract goal of economic 'efficiency', but as a way of breaking the control of powerful groups of workers who are able to obstruct the demands of profitability. However much capital might like to deal with workers as an abstract 'variable capital' which just produces surplus value on demand, it has been forced to deal with real people, with men and women who have had varying degrees of control over their work. And the continuing transformation of jobs under capitalism – the creation and re-creation of what Heidi Hartmann calls 'empty places' – arises out of the struggle for control between capital and these real workers, in which the power of the workers themselves becomes a key factor shaping and defining the jobs they do.

Interpreting capitalist development in this way leads directly into a re-definition of skill categories. In its attempts to assert its control over the labour process, Harry Braverman argues, capital has continually reduced the skill component in all forms of labour, making all work increasingly alike and increasingly dull, dreary and degraded. This homogenization, he argues, has been masked by the multitude of distinctions foisted on us by government statisticians and academic sociology – blue-collar/white-collar, old working class/new working class, skilled, semi-skilled, unskilled – but the underlying reality is one of growing convergence. Office work and factory work, for example, have been subjected to the same dreary processes of routinization, to the point where any attempt to distinguish the former as mental labour from the latter as manual becomes almost entirely specious. The conventional view of the 'upgrading' of work in the twentieth century is thus an illusion, based partly on this assumption that the expanded sector of office work is more skilled than manual labour, and partly on the practice of classifying all machine operatives as semi-skilled, even when the content of their work may involve less judgement or require shorter training than jobs previously defined as unskilled general labour. Braverman is not denying that some skilled work remains, but is arguing that existing skill labels fool us into believing there is a great deal more of it around than is the case.

This scepticism with regard to skill classifications helps us as feminists to turn a more critical eye on divisions which have previously been taken for granted, and is something which anyone with an eye to the operations of the Equal Pay Act, with its recurrent downgrading of typically 'feminine' skills such as dexterity against typically 'masculine' qualities like strength, might already have concluded. Braverman himself is mainly concerned to dismiss skill categories as mystifying, but we would regard them as highly illuminating – not perhaps of the content of the work performed, but of the sexual hierarchy which permeates capitalism. If skill distinctions are not necessarily about real work differences, what are they about? Three examples help to illustrate the answer.

In a recent study (Rubery and Wilkinson, 1979) it is suggested that the skill distinctions between the work of producing paper boxes and that of producing cartons can only be understood as historical associations between typically 'male' work and skill. Paper boxes are produced by women working on hand-fed machines; the work is considered – and paid – as unskilled labour. Cartons are produced under a more automated process, and the work hence requires less individual concentration but it is treated as semi-skilled work. It is hard to escape the conclusion that it is because of the similarities between the work of men and women in the carton industry that women in carton production are considered more skilled than box workers. Men and women work in a similar process; men are recognized as semi-skilled rather than unskilled workers; therefore carton production must be semi-skilled. The women producing paper boxes are simply women producing paper boxes, and however much the work itself might seem to qualify for upgrading, it remains unskilled because it is done by typically unskilled workers – women (Craig, Rubery, Tarling and Wilkinson, 1980).

In this example, the association between skill and sex is quite complex. Since both kinds of work are done by women, it seems to be the comparability between men's and women's jobs in the carton industry that forces a recognition of women in carton production as semi-skilled. Much more common than this is our second example, clerical work, where a new kind of labour is created which is defined as 'female' from its beginnings, and which is allowed no comparability with previous or existing men's jobs. The transformation of the male 'black-coated worker' of the nineteenth century into today's temp typist and file clerk occurred through the enormous expansion of all forms of office work in the period following the First World War. The new class of clerical workers had little in common with the clerks of the previous century, and the skill component of their work was immediately downgraded into typically 'female' abilities – including as usual dexterity, ability to carry out repetitive tasks, and so on. In this case it was not that men's jobs were deskilled, and women drawn into them, but that a new category of work was created which was classified as 'inferior' not simply by virtue of the skills required for it but by virtue of the 'inferior' status of the women who came to perform it. It is interesting to speculate whether the downgrading of the newly created skills would have occurred with so little struggle if the thousands of young women who came to fill the offices in this century had instead been young men. We can at least state with some certainty that the entire personal service aspect of clerical labour (as in virtually all the service work performed by women) would not in this case have developed in the same way.

The third example, based on Ben Birnbaum's analysis of the English clothing industry (Birnbaum, n.d.), goes further in indicating how this identification of men with skilled and women with semi-skilled or unskilled status has been generated through the struggles of men workers to retain their dominance within the sexual hierarchy. Throughout this century, machining in the clothing trade has been done by both men and women. But where it was done by men it was classified as skilled; where it was done by women it was classified as semi-skilled. As in the previous examples, it was a supposed non-comparability between men's and women's work which made this distinction possible: the women worked in larger workshops, in a more sub-divided labour process, machining men's garments, while the men worked in smaller shops machining women's garments. And in successive re-definitions of the basis for skill classification, differences were always employed in such a way as to ensure skilled status for the men and semi-skilled for the women. Initially the two sectors operated with different definitions of skill; predictably machining in the sector controlled by men turned out to be skilled, and machining in the sector controlled by women, semi-skilled. When in 1926 the wages council enforced a single basis for skill classification for the two sectors, it was drawn up in such a way as, once again, to confirm the men machinists as skilled and the women as semi-skilled. Ben Birnbaum argues that the distinctions cannot be rationalized in terms of the content of the work – it arose out of the struggle of men workers from the Russian, Jewish and Polish communities to retain their social status within the family, even when excluded by their position as immigrants from the 'skilled' jobs they might otherwise have done. Forced as they were to take on machining work usually done by women as semi-skilled, they fought to preserve their masculinity by re-defining (their) machining as skilled labour. Within the clothing trade he concludes 'the only way to become skilled was to change one's sex'.

What all of these examples indicate is the extent to which skill has become saturated with sex. It is not that skill categories have been totally subjectified: in all cases *some* basis was found in the content of the work to justify the distinctions between men's and women's work.

But the equations – men/skilled, women/unskilled – are so powerful that the identification of a particular job with women ensured that the skill content of the work would be downgraded. It is the sex of those who do the work, rather than its content, which leads to its identification as skilled or unskilled.

Ben Birnbaum's analysis is also important because he suggests that the imperative operating to enforce skill distinctions in garment production was the need of men workers to retain domestic authority. The men were denied access to the skilled jobs they considered theirs by right. Faced with this they struggled to acquire skilled status and skilled rates of pay for jobs usually deemed semi-skilled. For them, craft status was identified with manhood, and the struggle to maintain their position in the upper level of the labour hierarchy was fuelled by a determination to maintain the traditional balance of power in families where men had always acted as primary breadwinners.

This pattern of development – the sexualization of skill labels following the actual de-skilling of work processes – is one which has been repeated throughout the course of the nineteenth and twentieth centuries. It has been closely interwoven with the continuous battle between organized craftsmen and employers over the control of production. The outcome of this battle has been uneven (though not for Harry Braverman, who tends to regard capital as all-powerful). But to the extent that capital has succeeded in demolishing the actual craft knowledge and abilities of men workers, it has eroded the material basis for skill distinctions, thereby creating a workforce with a thin layer of skilled men at the top and a mass of unskilled workers at the bottom. Men workers have fought long and hard against this process, fought to retain their craft position, and failing all else, at least their craft labels. And in these struggles, craft has been increasingly identified with masculinity, with the claims of the breadwinner, with the degree of union strength. Skill has been increasingly defined *against* women – skilled work is work that women don't do.

Historically, this outcome is hardly surprising. The main protagonists were after all capital and the organized male working class; it was the power of the craftsmen that capital was most concerned to break with its weapon of de-skilling, and it was these workers who were in the best position to defy the process. In this history capital has been far from sex-blind. Since it is concerned not just with a logic of surplus extraction, but with an assertion of command, it is necessarily sensitive to those social relations which make some workers already more subordinated than others. The women who machine fashion garments in their own home are not subjected to the employer's control over their every movement: they can stop the machine at any moment; they can work at any time of day or night; they can get up to make a cup of tea when they decide to. But they are less powerful than the most de-skilled of men machine operatives, because they are chained to the home by their young children, denied access to any other form of employment, made totally dependent on their employer's decisions about how much to pay them. For them it is what they are as women, rather than the way their work is organized, that brings them under capital's control. Or as one early textile manufacturer explained to a questioner during the struggle over factory hours in the early nineteenth century, he liked to employ married women who had 'families at home dependent on them for support' because they were 'attentive, docile' and 'compelled to use their utmost exertions to procure the necessaries of life' (Marx, 1976: 526n). Since 'docility' could be induced in women by their economic and social subordination, it was primarily the more powerful and stroppier men workers who had to be countered with technical and organizational innovations aimed at de-skilling their jobs. This is not to say that women's jobs have been protected from the processes of de-skilling, but merely to emphasize that the confrontations over de-skilling have taken place on an already sexually defined terrain – between capital and skilled men workers.

In these struggles, the preservation of *masculine* skills became the issue which provided much of the force to workers' resistance. Where capital tried to undercut men's power by introducing women workers onto jobs previously defined as 'male' – as in textiles in the early nineteenth century, or engineering during the First World War – hostility was open and fierce. It is an irony of great concern to feminists that one of the most celebrated episodes in the history of British class struggle – the Shop Stewards' Movement of the First World War – drew its strength from the resistance of men workers to a dilution of their jobs by women. Here the battle against deskilling was reinforced and fuelled by the rejection of women's entry into men's jobs. The perpetuation of sexual hierarchy has been inextricably interwoven with the struggles against the real subordination to capital, as claims to skilled status have come to rely more and more on the sex of the workers and less and less on the nature of the job.

The result is deeply contradictory for men workers, who thereby continually recreate for capital a group of 'inferior' workers who can be used to undercut them. But as well as this, the identification of 'women's work' with unskilled work has masked the process through which capitalist work in general has become more routinized, more deadening, more a denial of the humanity of those who perform it. The segregation of women's work from men's conceals from many men workers the ways in which we are all becoming 'women workers' now; all subject to (in Harry Braverman's phrase) a 'degradation of labour' which gives to all jobs the classic features of women's employment.

As feminists we face two tasks. The first is to re-think economic categories in the light of feminism; 'economics' cannot be left unchallenged by the feminist critique. Capitalist production relations develop in and through confrontations between capital and workers, and the form which these confrontations take is often dictated by the deep divisions within the working class between men and women. Gender hierarchy enters directly into the development of capitalist relations, and a Marxism which fails to recognize this will not be sufficient for us. The second task is to re-organize economic struggles themselves – a task which has long been understood by feminists who find themselves in an uneasy alliance with a trade union tradition whose concern with differentials, with the maintenance of existing skill hierarchies, seems to leave little space for feminist politics. We might suggest that it is only when the socialist movement has been freed from its ideology of masculine skills that it will be able to confront the nature of capitalist work itself, and make the transformation of that work the focus of a future strategy. Perhaps then – in a struggle to claim for both men and women the lives now given over, day-by-day, year-by-year, to the crippling dictates of capitalist production – a new basis for sexual unity might begin to be forged.

■ Notes

This article appeared in *Feminist Review* No. 6, 1980.

The article was originally written for presentation at the Nuffield Conference on De-skilling and the Labour Process, in November 1979, and later discussed by the Conference of Socialist Economists Sex and Class Group. We should like to thank Sue Himmelweit for her comments on the first drafts and for her encouragement to rewrite it for *Feminist Review*. In revising it we have gradually come to realize that it opens up many more questions than it resolves. We put it forward, therefore, not as a finished 'position' but as a way of sharing our questions with other feminists, in the hope that a wider dialogue may ensue.

1   This process of identification of women with lack of skill seems if anything to be increasing. To give just one example; in 1911 women performed 24 per cent of all skilled jobs and 15.5 per cent of all unskilled; by 1971 they performed only 13.5 per cent of skilled manual work and just over 37 per cent of the unskilled (Bain and Price, 1972; cited in Hakim, 1978).

2   Clearly at one level the argument that the capital-labour relation is not a gender relation is correct; inasmuch as the capital-labour relation is a *value relation* it is not a relation between people at all, but between abstract quantities of dead and living labour. The circuit of capital as a value-circuit is not the story of real men and women entering into concrete social relations with one another, but an account – *abstracted from these relations* – of changing value forms. The mechanism whereby this abstraction occurs is not, of course, a theoretician's brain, but the market – through which all qualitative relations become expressed in quantitative terms. But: 'the capitalist labour process is the unity of the processes of valorization and the real labour process on the adequate basis of a specific form of social organization of labour' (Brighton Labour Process Group, 1977: 6). As a process which occurs in time, over time, a capitalist labour process is embedded in history, in inherited social relations. As a *concrete historical* process, the capitalist labour process must situate itself within existing patterns of social dominance and subordination. As a use-value – that is, in its historic existence – labour is concrete labour, characterized as much by its femaleness as any other of its attributes – and in our society 'femaleness' is a condition of relative powerlessness. As a concrete material process, capitalist production employs labours which are 'male' and 'female', and hence in a relation of power to one another. There is no pure 'economics' free of gender hierarchy, no Marxist science which can direct its gaze where women are not.

Third World
Manufacturing

Diane Elson and Ruth Pearson

Since the late 1960s a new type of wage employment has become available to women in many Third World countries: work in 'world market factories' producing manufactures exclusively for export to the rich countries. In these factories the vast majority of employees are usually young women between the age of fourteen and twenty-four or -five. While these women are only a small proportion of all Third World women, theirs is an important case to study, because the provision of jobs for women is often seen as an important way of 'integrating women into the development process', a demand which emerged from the United Nations Conference of International Women's Year which took place in 1975 under the tutelage of various international development agencies.

The idea that women's subordinate position stems from a lack of job opportunities, and can be ended by the provision of sufficient job opportunities, is deeply rooted and held by a wide spectrum of opinion, from international development agencies, government bureaux and mainstream Marxists to many women's organizations. Our work in the Workshop on the Subordination of Women in the process of development at the Institute of Development Studies, Sussex University, has led us to reject this perspective as a starting point. We do not accept that the problem is one of women being left out of the development process. Rather, it is precisely the relations through which women are 'integrated' into the development process that need to be problematized and investigated. For such relations may well be part of the *problem*, rather than part of the *solution*. Our starting point, therefore, is the need to evaluate world market factories from the point of view of the new possibilities *and* the new problems which they raise for Third World women who work in them.

■ Why have world market factories emerged in the Third World?

World market factories represent a relocation of production of certain kinds of manufactured product from the developed countries, where they continue to be consumed, to the Third World. These products are often classified into two groups, those using old established (or 'traditional') technologies, such as garments, textiles, sporting equipment, toys, soft goods, furniture, etc; and those using modern technologies, such as electrical goods and components for the electronics industry.

The stress on the modernity (or otherwise) of the technological base can, however, be misleading. For the sophisticated, highly knowledge-intensive processes which produce the technological base for something like the electronics industry remain located in a few developed countries, in particular Japan and the USA. The parts of such an industry which are relocated to the Third World share many characteristics with world market factories based on old-established technologies: *their production processes are standardized, repetitious, call for very little modern knowledge, and are highly labour-intensive.* In many cases the reason for the high labour intensity is that the production processes are assembly-type operations which have proved difficult and/or costly to mechanize further.

Subcontracting from large corporations

World market factories typically produce on sub-contract to the order of a particular overseas customer, and the customer arranges the marketing of the product. The world market factory may be owned by indigenous capitalists, or may be a wholly owned subsidiary of its overseas customer, or may be a joint venture of some kind between Third World businessmen and the overseas customer. World market factories producing components for the electronics industry are typically wholly or partially owned subsidiaries of Japanese, North American or European multinationals. Large multinational trading and retailing firms based in developed countries have been very important in the development of trade in final consumer goods from world market factories. Large US and European retailing firms, like Sears Roebuck, Marks and Spencers and C & A Modes, now place very large contracts with world market factories. In South East Asia the huge Japanese trading firms (such as Mitsubishi, Mitsui, Sumitomo, and so on) are very important customers of world market factories. For instance, it has been estimated that about 40 per cent of South Korea's foreign trade is in the hands of the four major Japanese trading firms, and in the case of Thailand the percentage is said to be even higher.

Some world market factories producing final consumer goods do no more than assemble together parts supplied by their customers. Typical cases are the sewing together of products like garments, gloves and leather luggage, the design and cutting of the parts having been carried out in the developed country by the customer. For instance, trousers are cut out in Germany, then flown in air-containers to Tunisia, where they are sewn together, packed and flown back for sale in Germany. In such cases, the world market factory is fully integrated into the production process of the customer firm, even though in formal terms it may be independent.

Through the provision of material inputs, or design capacity, or working capital, the customer may control the production process to the extent that, though the supplier has formal autonomy, in practice the customer is operating a new and more sophisticated version of the 'putting-out' system. The transfer of the goods across national boundaries, though ostensibly organized through market sales and purchases, may in substance be a transfer between two departments of an integrated production process. A good test is the ease with which, if the specific contracts under which it is operating were broken, the world market factory would be able to find alternative buyers for its product, or alternative sources of supply of the same inputs.

In some cases there is some scope for local initiative, a certain relative autonomy. Hong Kong is a good example of the form that such relative autonomy might take: faced with import controls, Hong Kong businessmen in the garment industry have successfully switched to new product lines which cater for the higher quality rather than the cheaper end of the market. And while the vast bulk of Hong Kong's garment industry output is contracted for by large western buying groups, and is made to their specifications, the number of manufacturers developing and marketing their own products has begun to increase.

But in general the degree of autonomy enjoyed by world market factories is very limited because they lack the means to develop new technologies. For example, the locally owned and developed consumer electronics industry in Hong Kong (producing radios, watches, TV games etc.) has been in difficulties with quality control in some items because of the lack of local technical know-how. All the evidence suggests that world market factories *cannot* create a new technical basis for capital accumulation: the lack of technology transfer is one of the main criticisms made of world market factories by Third World governments.

Why is production relocated to the Third World?

The fundamental reason is to try to overcome the limits to profitability posed by labour in developed countries. While the exploitation of labour is a necessary condition for the profitability of capital, it also confronts capital with potential opposition.[1] The relation between capital and labour can never be completely determined by what would suit capital. Individual capitals may try to get round this problem by manipulating the market for their product, but the existence of other capitals limits their ability to do this. In the case we are considering, the competition between capitals producing labour-intensive manufactures in the USA and Western Europe on the one hand, and Japan on the other, was particularly important. In the 1960s the problem posed by labour in Japan was much smaller than the problem posed in the USA and western Europe. Japanese wage rates were lower and productivity higher, so that Japanese firms could undercut the prices which American and European firms had to charge if they were to cover their costs. To some extent the effects of this on American and European firms could be offset by state intervention, such as import controls. But this kind of intervention tends to be limited by the competition that goes on between capitals in different industries in a national economy. Though import controls tend to increase the profitability of firms in protected branches of industry, by enabling them to charge higher prices, they tend to decrease the profitability of firms in other branches, by for instance, raising wage costs because of a rise in the cost of wage goods, such as textiles and garments.

The limitations that competition places on strategies in the market means that eventually some action has to be taken in the process of production. This may take the form of investment at *existing* locations in new technology that will reduce the need for labour and/or reduce labour costs by permitting greater control over the labour force in the factory or the substitution of cheaper labour, and so on. (For the classic recent discussion of this possibility, see Braverman, 1974.) Or it may take the form of investment at *new* locations, with or without new technology, to take advantage of a labour force which is cheaper and easier to control.

In the case of labour-intensive manufacturing in the late 1960s, capital was faced with a technological barrier in that automation was either too difficult or too costly for many of the assembly processes. At the same time, advances in the technology of transport and communication reduced the costs of locating production at a distance from the market it served; and governments in an increasing number of Third World countries were actively supplying the infrastructure necessary for labour-intensive manufacturing. Governments in the USA and western Europe also took action to facilitate relocation of production, modifying their tariff provisions to provide for duty-free re-entry of goods assembled abroad from parts and components exported from the developed country. Governments of Third World countries set up Free Trade Zones, and provided a wide range of incentives for firms to locate in them.[2]

All this has provided a powerful incentive to relocate production to areas of the Third World where a suitable labour force is available. It must be a labour force which offers a ratio of output to money costs of employment superior to that which prevails at existing centres of capital accumulation in the developed countries. And this superior ratio must be achieved *without* superior technology. It is by now well documented that this has been achieved in world market factories by a combination of much lower costs of employment, and matching or even higher productivity than that achieved in developed countries. Wages in world market factories are often ten times lower than in comparable factories in developed countries, while working hours per year are up to 50 per cent higher. Additional costs, such as social security payments, fringe benefits and work clothing are also much lower. The US Tariff Commission found that productivity of workers in foreign establishments assembling or processing products of US origin generally approximates that of workers with the same job classification in the US. Several other studies have reported instances of productivity substantially higher than in the US. This is not being achieved through superior technology; it is the result of greater intensity of work, of greater continuity of production: in short greater control over the performance of the labour force.

The greater degree of control is facilitated by the measures which have been taken by Third World governments to suspend workers' rights in world market factories. Many Third World countries which in the past had enacted progressive labour legislation, often as a result of the contribution of trade union struggles to the fight against imperialism, have by now incorporated the official trade union organization into the state apparatus, and either suspended, or failed to enforce, major provisions of that legislation. Workers in world market factories have been left exposed by the abrogation of their rights on such matters as minimum wage payments, contributions to insurance funds, limitations on the length of the working day and week, security of employment, redundancy conditions and payments, and the right to strike. Free Trade Zones have particularly stringent controls on the activity of workers' organizations, but in some countries, particularly in South East Asia, the whole country is covered by such controls; and the power of the state is vigorously used to enforce them. It is ironic that in the name of improving the lives of the poorest groups in the Third World by creating more employment opportunities for them, many governments have actively reduced the ability of the poor to protect themselves against the most blatant forms of exploitation.

The situation of workers in world market factories cannot, however, be analysed simply in terms of class struggle and national struggle. It has also to be analysed in terms of gender struggle.

■ The employment of women in world market factories

Why is it young women who overwhelmingly constitute the labour force of world market factories? This question is conspicuous by its absence from most of the studies done by economists (Lim, 1978, is a notable exception). One reason may be that the type of jobs done by women in world market factories in the Third World are also done by women in the First World. It might seem to follow that the labour force of world market factories is predominantly female because the jobs to be done are regarded as 'women's work'. But to note that jobs are sex-stereotyped is not to explain why this is so. After all, capitalist firms are compelled by competitive forces to select their labour force and constitute their division of labour on the basis of profitability, not ideology. If it were more profitable to employ men in world market factories to do jobs done by women in the developed world, then this is what capitalist firms would do, particularly as they do not face the situation of more or less full employment of the male labour force which prevailed in the fifties and sixties in the developed world. We might expect the pressures of unemployment and poverty to induce men to accept jobs that in developed countries have been stereotyped as 'women's work'. In fact, this is what we find in a large number of 'white collar' jobs, such as typing and clerical work. (Boserup, 1970). But this does not seem to have happened in world market factories.

The reproduction in world market factories of the sexual division of labour typical in labour-intensive assembly operations in developed countries must therefore rest upon some differentiation of the labour force which makes it more profitable to employ female labour than male labour in these jobs. *Female labour must either be cheaper to employ than comparable male labour, or have higher productivity, or some combination of both; the net result being that unit costs of production are lower with female labour.* In general the money costs of employing female labour in world market factories do seem to be lower than the money costs of employing men would be. Kreye found that women's wages in world market factories are in general 20 per cent to 50 per cent lower than wages paid for men in comparable jobs (Frobel *et al*, 1979). Direct productivity comparisons between male and female workers are hard to make, since so few men are employed in comparable labour-intensive assembly operations. In the few documented cases where men have been employed (in Malaysian electronics factories and Malawi textile factories), their productivity was in fact lower than that of women employed in the same plants. Firms running world market factories seem firmly convinced that this would generally be the case.

What produces this differentiation? The answers that companies give when asked why they employ women, as well as the statements made by governments trying to attract world market factories, show that there is a widespread belief that it is a 'natural' differentiation, produced by innate capacities and personality traits of women and men, and by an objective differentiation of their income needs in that men need an income to support a family, while women do not. A good example is the following passage in a Malaysian investment brochure, designed to attract foreign firms:

> The manual dexterity of the oriental female is famous the world over. Her hands are small and she works fast with extreme care. Who, therefore, could be better qualified *by nature and inheritance* to contribute to the efficiency of a bench-assembly production line than the oriental girl (emphasis added).

Women are considered not only to have naturally nimble fingers, but also to be naturally more docile and willing to accept tough work discipline, and naturally less inclined to join trade unions, than men; and to be naturally more suited to tedious, repetitious, monotonous work. Their lower wages are attributed to their secondary status in the labour market which is seen as a natural consequence of their capacity to bear children. The fact that only young women work in world market factories is also rationalized as an effect of their capacity to bear children – this naturally means they will be either unwilling or unable to continue in employment much beyond their early twenties. Indeed the phenomenon of women leaving employment in the factory when they get married or pregnant is known as 'natural wastage', and can be highly advantageous to firms which periodically need to vary the size of their labour force so as to adjust to fluctuating demand for their output in the world market.

While we agree that there is a real differentiation between the characteristics of women and men as potential workers in world market factories, in our view it is far from being natural.

Where do women get their skills?

The famous 'nimble fingers' of young women are not an inheritance from their mothers in the same way that they may inherit the colour of her skin or eyes. They are the result of the *training* they have received from their mothers and other female kin since early infancy in the tasks socially appropriate to woman's role. For instance, since industrial sewing of clothing closely resembles sewing with a domestic sewing machine, girls who have learnt such sewing at home already have the manual dexterity and capacity for spatial assessment required. Training in needlework and sewing also produces skills transferable to other assembly operations:

> ... manual dexterity of a high order may be required in typical subcontracted operations, but nevertheless the operation is usually one that can be learned quickly on the basis of traditional skills. Thus in Morocco, in six weeks, girls (who may not be literate) are taught the assembly under magnification of memory planes for computers – this is virtually darning with copper wire, and sewing is a traditional Moroccan skill. In the electrical field the equivalent of sewing is putting together wiring harnesses; and in metal-working, one finds parallels in some forms of soldering and welding (Sharpston, 1976: 334).

It is partly because this training, like so many other female activities which come under the heading of domestic labour, is socially invisible and privatized, that the skills it produces are attributable to nature, and the jobs that make use of it are classified as 'unskilled' or 'semi-skilled'. Given that 'manual dexterity of a high order' is an admitted requirement for many of the assembly jobs done by women in world market factories, and that women working in the electronics industry have to pass aptitude tests with high scores, it is clear that the categorization of these jobs as 'unskilled' does not derive from the purely *technical* characteristics of the job. The fact that the training period required within the factory is short, and that workers do not take long to become highly proficient once this period is over, does not detract from this conclusion. Little training and 'on the job' learning is required because the women are already trained:

> It takes six weeks to teach industrial garment making *to girls who already know how to sew* (Sharpston, 1975: 105, emphasis added).

In objective terms, it is more accurate to speak of the jobs making a demand for easily trained labour, than for unskilled labour. But of course skill categories are not determined in a purely objective way (Braverman, 1974). In particular, jobs which are identified as 'women's work' tend to be classified as 'unskilled' or 'semi-skilled', whereas technically similar jobs identified as 'men's work' tend to be classified as 'skilled' (Phillips and Taylor, this volume). To a large extent, women do not do 'unskilled' jobs because they are the bearers of inferior labour; rather the jobs they do are 'unskilled' because women enter them already determined as inferior bearers of labour.

Women's subordination as a gender

The social invisibility of the training that produces these skills of manual dexterity and the lack of social recognition for these skills is not accidental. It is intrinsic to the process of gender construction in the world today. For this is not simply a process of gender differentiation, producing two 'separate but equal' gender roles of women and men, any more than apartheid produces two 'separate but equal' roles for Blacks and whites in South Africa. Rather it is a process of *subordination* of women as a gender (Whitehead, 1979). This is not only an ideological process, taking place in the realm of attitudes and values. It is not just a matter of people ascribing lesser value to women's gender roles; of simply failing to see the contribution that women make; or of believing that it is only right and proper for women to accept a second place to men. Although ideology plays a role, we would argue that the subordination of women as a gender cannot be understood simply as a matter of 'patriarchal attitudes'.

Rather it is a material process which goes on not just in our heads, but in our practices. In claiming that it is a material process we do not intend to reduce it to an economic process, to be analyzed only in terms of labour; but rather to emphasize that it cannot be changed simply through propaganda for more 'enlightened' views, and that it requires practical changes in daily living. We would suggest that this process of subordination of women as a gender can be understood in terms of the exclusion of women as a gender from certain activities, and their confinement to others; where the activities from which women as a gender are excluded are some of those which are constituted as public, overtly social activities, and the activities to which women as a gender are confined are some of those which are constituted as private, seemingly purely individual activities.

The constitution of activities as public or private, social or individual, of course differs over time, and between different kinds of society, and is itself a matter of struggle, not a pre-determined 'given'. The importance of activities in which the social aspect is dominant, which are overtly represented as social, is that these confer social power. This is not to say that *no* power is conferred by activities in which the private aspect is dominant: but in our view it is a mistake to see private power as co-equal with social power. Social power is collective power, reproducible through social processes, relatively autonomous from the characteristics of particular individuals. But private power is purely individual power, contingent on the specific characteristics of particular individuals, reproducible only by chance.

A distinction can usefully be made between relations which are *gender ascriptive*, that is, relations which are constructed intrinsically in terms of the gender of the persons concerned; and relations which are not gender ascriptive, but which can nevertheless be *bearers of gender* (Whitehead, 1979: 11). An example of the first is the conjugal relation: marriage is a relation necessarily involving the union of persons of definite and opposite genders. A union between persons of the same gender is not marriage. An example of the second is the sexual division of labour in the capitalist labour process. Though the capital-labour relation is not gender ascriptive, it is nevertheless a bearer of gender (Phillips and Taylor, this volume). Gender ascriptive relations are clearly the fundamental sites of the subordination of women as a gender, and in them women's subordination may take a literally patriarchal form, with women directly subject to the authority of the father, their own or their children's. But male hegemony in gender ascriptive relations does not always assume a patriarchal form.

Rather it is a matter of the extent to which women's social being can only be satisfactorily established through the mediation of a gender ascriptive relation, whereas the same is not true for men. This kind of gender subordination is not something which an individual woman can escape by virtue of choosing to avoid certain kinds of personal relation with men. For instance, it means that the *absence* of a husband is as significant as his presence for the establishment of a woman's identity. As Elizabeth Phillips of the Jamaica Women's Bureau has pointed out:

> The apparent independence of women from men can be misleading: while women may not be directly subordinate to a particular member of their male kin, they are nonetheless subject to an overall culture of male dominance.

For women, unlike men, the question of gender is never absent.

Behind the mirage of docility

It is in the context of the subordination of women as a gender that we must analyse the supposed docility, subservience and consequent suitability for tedious, monotonous work of young women in the Third World. In the conditions of their subordination as a gender, this is the appearance that women often present to men, particularly men in some definite relation of authority to them, such as father, husband, boss. A similar appearance, presented by colonized peoples to their colonizers, was brilliantly dissected by Franz Fanon, who showed how the public passivity and fatalism which the colonized peoples displayed towards the colonizers for long periods concealed an inner, private rebellion and subversion. But this passivity is not a natural and original state: to achieve it requires enormous efforts of self-repression. The 'native' is in a state of permanent tension, so that when he does resist, it tends to be with a spontaneity and intensity all the stronger for having been so long pent-up and hidden: action not negotiation is the characteristic response (Fanon, 1969: 48).

That self-repression is required for women to achieve an adequate level of docility and subservience can be demonstrated on an everyday level by differences in their behaviour when authority figures are present and absent. An example is the behaviour observed by Noeleen Heyzer (1978) in a world market factory producing textiles in Singapore. Here the women workers were always on guard when the supervisors were around, and displayed a characteristic subservience; but in the absence of supervisors behaviour changed. Far from displaying respectful subservience, workers mocked the supervisors and ridiculed them. Another indication that the 'private' behaviour of women workers in their peer group differs from their behaviour when outsiders are present comes from the fact that some electronics factories on the Mexican border have introduced a few men on to production lines formerly the exclusive province of women in the belief that this will improve the discipline and productivity of the women. The stress that such self-repression can impose and the 'non-rational' forms its relief may take is exemplified in the well-documented occurrence of outbreaks of mass hysteria among young women factory workers in South East Asia.

It is interesting that governments and companies are unwilling to trust completely the personal docility of women workers and feel a need to reinforce it with that suspension of a wide variety of workers' rights which is such a selling point of Free Trade Zones. Nevertheless, in spite of being faced with extensive use of state power to control labour unions and prevent strikes, women workers in world market factories have at times publicly thrown off their docility and subservience and taken direct action, though their level of participation in trade unions is reported to be very low. There are indications that these struggles tend to erupt outside the official trade union framework, taking for instance the form of 'wild cat' sitdowns or walk-outs, rather than being organized around official negotiations.

Secondary status in the labour market

A major aspect of the gender differentiation of the labour force available for employment in world market factories is what is generally referred to in the literature as women's 'secondary status' in the labour market (Lim, 1978: 11). The main characteristics of this secondary status are that women's rates of pay tend to be lower than those of men doing similar or comparable jobs: and that women tend to form a 'reserve army' of labour, easily fired when firms want to cut back on their labour force, and easily re-hired when firms want to expand again. This tends to be explained in terms of 'women's role in the family' or 'women's reproductive role'. In a sense this explanation may be true, but it is ambiguous in that for many people 'women's role in the family', 'women's reproductive role', is an ahistorical fact, given by biology. What has to be stressed is that women's role in the family is socially constructed as a subordinated role – even if she is a 'female head of household'. For it is the female role to nurture children and men, work which appears to be purely private and personal; while it is the male role to represent women and children in the wider society. And it is the representative role which confers social power.

This kind of gender subordination means that when a labour market develops, women, unlike men, are unable to take on fully the classic attributes of free wage labour. A man can become a free wage labourer

> ... in the double sense that as a free individual he can dispose his labour-power as his own commodity and that, on the other hand, he has no other commodity for sale ... he is free of all the objects needed for the realization of his labour-power (Marx, 1976: 237).

A woman is never 'free' in this way: she has obligations of domestic labour, difficulties in establishing control over her own body, an inability to be fully a member of society in her own right; but also the possibility of obtaining her subsistence from men in exchange for personal services of a sexual or nurturing kind, of realizing her labour power outside the capitalist labour process. It is this gender difference which gives women a 'secondary status' in the labour market. Our purpose is not to deny the social reality of this secondary status. But it is to take up a critical stance towards it, rather than view it as 'natural': nature does not compel the tasks of bringing up children to be the privatized responsibility of their mother while depriving her of the social power to secure, in her own right, access to the resources required for this, thus forcing her into a dependent position.

This secondary status arising from women's subordination as a gender means that women workers are peculiarly vulnerable to super-exploitation, in the sense that their wages will not need to cover the full money costs of the reproduction of their labour power, either on a daily or a generational basis. It also means that women tend to get lower wages than men, even when those wages contribute to the support of several other people, as do the wages of many of the young women who work in world market factories (or indeed of many women workers in developed countries). Sending a daughter to work in such a factory is in some cases the only remaining strategy for acquiring an income for the rest of the family.

■ The interplay of capital and gender: the limits to liberation through factory work

Ever since large numbers of women were drawn into factory work in the industrial revolution in nineteenth-century England there has been a strong belief that wage work can liberate women from gender subordination. The classical Marxists tended to see the entry of women into wage work as a substitution of one form of domination, 'the rule of the husband over the wife', by another, the domination of capitalists over workers (Engels, 1976: 171-8), so that the struggle of working women became part of the general class struggle. Liberals have always tended to see jobs for women as leading to female emancipation by providing women with financial independence; and have viewed the lack of equal pay, equal working conditions and equal opportunities for women in the capitalist economy as the result of out-moded prejudice and discrimination. Such attitudes are expected to be gradually undermined as women demonstrate their capacities in the very visible sphere of wage work – which is overtly social, unlike domestic production. The fact that the social relations of factory work are not intrinsically gender ascriptive, but are rooted in an impersonal cash nexus, gives some plausibility to such views.

For instance, it seems plausible that competition between women and men for jobs would tend to undermine any material basis for gender differentiation of the labour force in world market factories. If intially capitalists prefer to employ women because they can be paid low wages, can be trained quickly and appear to accept easily the discipline of factory life, then surely high male unemployment will tend to undermine this preference as men are induced to accept the same wages and working conditions and to acquire the same attributes that make women employable, in order to get a job. The end result of such a process would be a labour force undifferentiated by gender, with women and men doing the same jobs, in the same conditions, for the same wages, modified only by personal preferences or prejudices for this or that kind of employment or employer. There would be no objective basis for gender differentiation.

But this argument fails to consider *how it is* that women have acquired the characteristics that make them initially the preferred labour force. If men are to compete successfully, they also need to acquire the 'nimble fingers' and 'docile dispositions' for which women workers are prized. But for this, they would require to undergo the same social experience as women. In order to compete successfully, men would need to experience gender subordination. But since men and women cannot *both* simultaneously experience gender subordination, this could only happen if women were to be freed from gender subordination; that is, a reversal, rather than an elimination of gender differentiation. Competition between women and men in the labour market can tend to produce, in certain circumstances, signs of such a reversal (Engels, 1976: 173-4), signs which provoke the traditionalist critique of women's participation in wage work as an overturning of the natural order of things. But these signs of the reversal of gender roles are themselves a demonstration of the fundamental interdependence of the labour force characteristics of women and men. Although, as competitors in the labour market, women and men may at first appear as atomized individuals, they are never completely separated. *They are always linked through gender ascriptive relations, and their labour market relations become bearers of gender.*

The important point about the development of capitalism is that it does offer a form of interdependence – the cash nexus – which is not gender ascriptive. But although capitalist production is dominated by the cash nexus, in the sense that it must be organized to make a profit, it cannot be organized solely through cash relations (through wages and prices) but requires a specific hierarchical managerial organization: the capitalist labour process. It has to be organized through the giving of orders, as well as the making of payments. It it because of this that capitalist production may be a bearer of gender, though it is not intrinsically gender ascriptive (Phillips and Taylor, this volume; Whitehead, 1979). Typically, the giving of orders in the capitalist labour process is defined as a male prerogative; while the role of women is defined as the carrying out of orders.

Another intrinsic limit is that the socialization of the reproduction of labour power cannot be accomplished completely through the cash nexus. A great deal of the labour required to provide the goods and services needed for the reproduction of labour power quite clearly can be socialized through the cash nexus: the monetization of labour processes formerly carried out domestically, and socialized though the gender ascriptive relations of marriage, is one of the hallmarks of capital accumulation (Braverman, 1974, ch. 13). But the establishment of the social identity of children, their social integration, cannot be accomplished solely through the cash nexus. One implication of this is that the 'de facto' position of women workers as major contributors to the family income does not automatically mean that they will become socially recognized as 'breadwinners', and that their secondary status in the labour market will be ended. For the position of breadwinner is not constituted purely at the economic level: it is also constituted in the process of establishing the connexion of the family with the wider society. The breadwinner must be also the public representative of the family. Ann Whitehead (1978) suggests that the wage itself, though clearly not a gender ascriptive form, tends to become a bearer of gender, in the sense that wages of male and female family members are not treated as interchangeable, but are earmarked for different things.

The recognition of this limitation does not mean that we must therefore deny capitalism *any* liberating potential: the alternative, cash-based forms of socialization it entails do tend to undermine and disrupt others forms of socialization, including the gender ascriptive relations which are fundamental to the subordination of women as a gender. In this way they provide a material basis for struggle against the subordination of women as a gender. But there is no way that capitalist exploitation of women as wage workers can simply *replace* gender subordination of women. Indeed, the capitalist exploitation of women as wage workers is parasitic upon their subordination as a gender.

The dialectic of capital and gender

We would like to distinguish three tendencies in the relation between the emergence of factory work and the subordination of women as a gender: a tendency to *intensify* the existing forms of gender subordination; a tendency to *decompose* existing forms of gender subordination; and a tendency to *recompose* new forms of gender subordination. We are not suggesting that these are mutually exclusive tendencies – any specific situation might well show signs of all three. They are, moreover, not categories which can be aggregated to produce a uni-dimensional conclusion that the position of women is getting worse or better. Rather, they are suggested as ways of analysing particular conjunctions of forces shaping women's lives, in the hope that this will help clarify the strategic possibilities facing women in those situations.

There is evidence of all three tendencies at work in the case of women employed in world market factories. One example of the way existing forms of gender subordination may be intensified is the case of a multinational corporation operating in Malaysia which believes in deliberately trying to preserve and utilize traditional forms of patriarchal power. Instead of undermining the father's authority over the daughter by encouraging 'modern', 'western' behaviour, it pursues a policy of reinforcement:

> The company has installed prayer rooms in the factory itself, does not have modern uniforms but lets the girls wear their traditional attire, and enforces a strict and rigid discipline in the work place (Lim, 1978: 37).

The enhanced economic value of daughters certainly provides a motive for fathers to exert more control, including sending them to work in the factories whether they wish to or not. On the other hand, the ability to earn a wage may be an important factor in undermining certain forms of control of fathers and brothers over young women, an advantage which has been mentioned frequently by Malaysian women working in world market factories. However, this does not mean that there is a reversal of the authority structure of the family. There is considerable empirical evidence that their wages do not confer greater status or decision-making power on the women, even though they may be the chief source of family income.

As an example of the way existing forms of gender subordination may be *decomposed*, we can cite Myrna Blake's observation (1979) of the importance of factory work as a way of escaping an early arranged marriage in some Asian countries. But the ability to resist arranged marriage and opt for 'free-choice' marriage is two-edged. In the conditions of a society dominated by the capitalist mode of production, 'free-choice' marriage tends to take on the characteristics of the dominant form of choice in such societies, a *market* choice from among competing commodities. And it is women themselves who take on many of the attributes of the competing commodities, while it is men who exercise the choice. This tendency towards the recomposition of a specifically capitalist, 'commoditized' form of making marriages is actively encouraged by the management styles of some of the large American multinational electronics companies which provide lessons in fashion and 'beauty care' and organize beauty contests and western-style dances and social functions for their employees. This is rationalized as the provision of fringe benefits which naturally appeal to the 'feminine interests' of the young women workers. Such interests are indeed 'feminine' in a situation where many young women are competing in a marriage market hoping to attract a husband. But they stem not from the eternal structure of the feminine psyche, but from concrete material conditions in which a young woman's face may be quite literally her fortune.

Although one form of gender subordination, the subordination of daughters to their fathers, may visibly crumble, another form of gender subordination, that of women employees to male factory bosses, is just as visibly built up. Work in world market factories is organized through a formal hierarchy with ordinary operators at the bottom controlled by varying levels of supervisors and managers. In study after study the same pattern is revealed: the young female employees are almost exclusively at the bottom of this hierarchy; the upper levels of the hierarchy are almost invariably male. Only among the lowest level of supervisors is it at all common to find women. The relationship of female employees to male bosses is qualitatively different from the relationship of male employees to male bosses. One important feature is that the sexual element in the relation between female employee and male boss is not contained and shaped by kin relations. This is one of the reasons why factory girls are often regarded as not quite 'respectable'. In some cases sexual exploitation is quite widespread – in the Masan Free Export Zone in South Korea, for example, numerous instances have occurred of sexual abuse of women employees by Japanese supervisors.

This *recomposition* of a new form of gender subordination in which young women are subject to the authority of men who are not in any family relation to them can also have the effect of intensifying more traditional forms of gender subordination of wives to husbands. The fact that a wife works in a factory means that she will be subject to the authority of other men and this may be a powerful reason for a husband wishing to confine his wife to the home. Husbands' dislike of their wives working in factories is mentioned by Linda Lim (1978) as one of the reasons why so few married women are employed in world market factories in Malaysia.

Instability of employment

But the problem is not simply that young women may, through factory work, escape the domination of fathers and brothers only to become subordinate to male managers and supervisors – and escape the domination of managers and supervisors only to become subordinate to husbands or lovers. There is also the problem that the domination of managers and supervisors may be withdrawn – the women may be sacked from her job – while the woman is without the 'protection' of subordination to father, brother, husband.[3] She may be left dependent on the cash nexus for survival, but unable to realize her labour power in cash terms through working in the factory.

This problem is particularly acute for women who work in world market factories. Some change in some distant, unknown part of the world may at any moment undercut their position, leaving their product and their labour power without a market. The recession in world demand in 1974 provoked massive cutbacks in employment in many world market factories: for instance about one-third of all electronics workers in Singapore lost their jobs (Grossman, 1979: 10).

Moreover, there is still a possibility of a resurgence of competition from firms located in developed countries. The very success of world market factories has made them vulnerable to retaliation. So far this has mainly taken the form of the growth of restrictions on imports of manufactures, particularly of consumer goods like textiles, garments and shoes. More recently there have been signs of fresh attempts to revolutionize the production process in developed countries, to eliminate the advantage which cheap labour gives to world market factories in the production of labour-intensive goods (Pearson, 1986). At the request of the European Clothing Manufacturers' Federation, the Commission of the EEC is funding a research programme on ways of automating garment making. The fact that the mass of capital continues to be accumulated in developed countries means that market demand, technical know-how and finance continue to be concentrated there, so that world market factories, representing relatively small dispersions of capital accumulation, are inherently vulnerable to changes in the conditions of accumulation in developed countries.

The hiring and firing practices of particular firms do, however, add to the inherent precariousness and instability of employment in world market factories. The preference of firms for young workers means that workers in their early twenties who have not yet left voluntarily are the first to be dismissed if it is necessary to retrench the labour force. Pregnancy is often grounds for dismissal. Or women are dismissed on the grounds that they can no longer meet productivity or time-keeping norms. A deterioriation in performance is, in fact, often the result of some disability caused by the work itself. Women employed in the garment industry on the Mexican border tend to suffer from kidney complaints and varicose veins. Women using microscopes every day in the electronics industry suffer eye strain and their eyesight deteriorates. Shift work, which is common in electronics and textile factories, can produce continual fatigue, headaches and a general deterioration of health. The net result is that it is often those workers who have already acquired new consumption patterns, responsibilities, and in many cases, debts, who lose their jobs, rather than those who have just entered factory life.

If a woman loses her job in a world market factory after she has re-shaped her life on the basis of a wage income, the only way she may have of surviving is by selling her body. There are reports from South Korea, for instance, that many former electronics workers have no alternative but to become prostitutes (Grossman, 1979: 16). A growing market for such services is provided by the way in which the tourist industry has been developed, especially in South East Asia.

■ Conclusions

Our conclusions may be summarized as follows: there are inherent limits to the extent to which the provision of wage work for women through capitalist accumulation can dissolve the subordination of women as a gender. Rather than ending such subordination, entry into wage work tends to transform it. While there is a tendency for the decomposition of some existing forms of gender subordination, such as the control of fathers and brothers over the lifestyles of young women, there is also a tendency to the recomposition of new forms of gender subordination, both through the recomposition of gender ascriptive relations in new forms, and through relations which are not intrinsically gendered becoming bearers of gender. Indeed, the decomposition tendency itself helps to strengthen the recomposition tendency. For the former, while bringing independence of a sort, also brings vulnerability. This is particularly true when, as is the case with world market factory employees, this tendency affects only a small proportion of the relevant age cohort, and an even smaller proportion of the total female population of the society concerned. As an insurance against this vulnerability, individual women may often have little choice but to actively accept, indeed seek, the 'protection' of new forms of gender subordination.

What can women do?

Official reports about the problems of women in the Third World usually end with a list of policy recommendations which various official bodies, acting 'in the interests of women', should implement. But we orient our discussion of action around the concept of 'struggle' rather than around the concept of 'policy'. It is not that we see no role for official state agencies, whether national or international, in the process of action, but rather that our orientation towards them is to ask, not what *solutions* should they offer women, but how can women use them for purposes women have determined. For we take the most fundamental objective of action to be the development of women's capacity for self-determination.

In our view the development of world market factories does, in itself, provide a material basis for a process of struggle for self-determination. The most fundamental way in which it does this is by bringing together large numbers of women and confronting them with a common, cash-based authority: the authority of capital. This is not the effect of most alternative forms of work for young Third World women, such as unremunerated labour in the family, or work in the 'informal sector' in petty services or 'out-work', or work as domestic servants (Blake, 1979: 11). In these other cases women tend to be more physically isolated from one another; or they are confronted with a different, more personalized form of authority, or they relate to one another not as members of the same gender or class, but as members of particular households, kin groups etc.

Struggle as workers

The most obvious possibility for struggle which this suggests is struggle as *workers* around such issues as wages and conditions of work. It is therefore, at first sight, disappointing to find a low level of formal participation in trade union activities by women employed in world market factories; and evidence that in many cases they do not identify themselves as workers, or develop 'trade union consciousness' (Cardosa-Khoo and Khoo Kay Jin, 1978). But we need to bear in mind the *limitations*, as well as the possibilities, of factory-based struggle about work-related issues; and the *shortcomings* of official trade union organizations in many parts of the world.

The basic limitation in the ability of workers, no matter how well organized, to secure improvements in pay and conditions of work is set by the fact that control over the means of production lies ultimately with management, and not with the workforce. The limits within which workers in world market factories are confined are particularly narrow because of the ease with which the operations carried out in them might be relocated, and because the management so often enjoys the backing of particularly coercive forms of state power. The ability to secure improvements tends to be very much conditioned by particular rates of accumulation at particular localities. It is noticeable that it is in countries like Hong Kong and Singapore where the rate of investment has been high that wage rates in world market factories have tended to rise. A higher proportion of married, and older, women tends to be found in world market factories in these countries, symptomatic of a tighter labour market.

Besides the rate of accumulation, another important consideration is the extent to which other social groups will support workers in particular factories in campaigns for better pay and conditions of work. In the case of women working in world market factories, such support within their own countries is likely to come mainly from either professional and technical elite groups, or from religious organizations. There is a material basis for the support of the first group in the fact that the pay and conditions of employment in world market factories so often offend the sense of justice and fairness encouraged by other aspects of the development of capitalism, rooted in the equalizing and liberalizing aspect of the market economy. Unfortunately such support tends to be limited: while many members of professional and technical elite groups are willing to support the workers' right to a fair day's pay for a fair day's work, they are not so willing to face all the implications of genuine self-determination for workers, including the workers' right to control the means of production. The support offered by religious groups can often be in many ways more radical, because it tends to draw on a different set of values, rooted in a more organic vision of society. Such groups, in some countries, have become very involved in the struggle of workers in world market factories. However, from the point of view of women, such support may be particularly double-edged, because religious values tend so often to encourage the subordination of women as a gender.

However, no matter how effective and far-reaching the support given by religious or other groups to the workforce, the struggle for better pay and conditions of work remains contradictory. To a considerable extent, the success of the workforce in this struggle is predicated upon the success of management in making profits.

Management's ability to displace labour with machinery means that the existence of a trade-off between the number of jobs available, and the pay and conditions of work associated with them, is not simply an ideological invention of orthodox economics. But the story does not end there. The actions which individual capitalists take (and must take, owing to competitive pressures) to relocate and re-shape production on an international scale have repercussions which tend to undermine the viability of their continued control over the means of production. To put it schematically, the international relocating and reshaping of production has repercussions which tend to undermine the national and international systems of money and property rights which underpin, and are necessary for, capitalist control over the means of production. Current manifestations of this are the world-wide problems of inflation, the lack of a stable international currency, and the massive increase in international indebtedness of precisely those Third World countries which have been most 'successful' in export-oriented industrialization.

The main lesson we would draw from this is that struggle at the level of the factory cannot be judged solely in terms of its effects on pay and conditions of work. It has to be judged not simply as an instrument for making economic gains, but as a way of developing the capacities of those involved in it, particularly the capacity for self-organization. In this context, participation in collective action in the factory itself, even of a sporadic and spontaneous character, is more important than purely formal membership of a trade union: it also helps factory workers to understand the world-wide structure of the forces which shape their lives, and helps prepare them for struggle, not just in the factory where they work, but against the economic system of which it is a part.

Struggles as women

Struggles arising from the development of world market factories will, however, remain seriously deficient from the point of view of *women* workers if they deal only with economic questions of pay and working conditions, and fail to take up other problems which stem from the recomposition of new forms of the subordination of women as a gender. Many of these problems present themselves as a series of 'personal' 'individual' difficulties: how to attract a husband or lover; how to deal with the contradictions of female sexuality – to express one's sexuality without becoming a sex object; how to cope with pregnancy and childcare (Blake, 1979: 12). The concern of women workers with these problems is not a sign that they are 'backward' in consciousness as compared with male workers, but that for women, it is gender subordination which is primary, while capitalist exploitation is secondary and derivative. This is not to say that women spontaneously recognize that their 'personal' problems are reflections of their subordination as a gender. If social relations were so transparent there would be little need to write essays like this – or consciously to analyse women's position and to plan and organize struggle.

The forms that workers' organizations have traditionally taken have been inadequate from women's point of view because they have failed to recognize and build into their structure the specificity of gender. Trade unions, for instance, have been organized to represent 'the worker', political parties to represent 'the working class'. The failure to take account of gender means that in practice they have tended to represent *male* workers. Working women have tended to be represented only through their dependence on male workers. In addition, the specific problems that concern women as a subordinated gender are often problems which it is not easy for conventional forms of trade union or working class political activity to tackle. New forms of organization are required that will specifically take up these problems, offering both practical, immediate action on them, and also revealing the social roots of what at first sight appear to be a series of individual, personal problems whose only common denominator lies in the supposed 'natural' propensities and capacities of women as a sex.

The employment of women in world market factories does provide a material basis for 'politicizing the personal' because of the way it masses together women not simply as workers but as a gender. Women are brought together in the factory, not by virtue of being the daughter of this man, the mother of that; the sister of this, the wife of that; but simply by virtue of being women, of having the characteristics of a subordinated gender. In factory employment, women are abstracted out of particularized gender ascriptive relations.

So, a practical reality is given to the concept of women as a gender, in the same way that a practical reality is given to the concept of labour in general (Marx, 1973: 103-5). This creates a basis for the struggle of women factory workers as members of a *gender*, as well as members of a *class*. This is not to say that such struggle will automatically take place – it will happen only if new forms of organization are consciously built. To some extent this is already happening. Women workers in various parts of the Third World have formed sector-based organizations which link women in different factories operating in the same industry; and 'off-site' organizations to tackle issues like housing, education and sanitation, which remain the responsibility of women.

Of course, limitations and contradictions similar to those discussed in the case of activity to improve pay and working conditions in the factory beset the struggle to ameliorate other aspects of women workers' lives, especially those in the so-called 'personal' domain. *Just as a limit is set to the former by capitalists' class monopoly of the means of production, so a limit is set to the latter by men's gender monopoly of the means of establishing social being, social presence.* Accordingly women's struggle as a gender should not be judged in purely instrumental terms, as achieving this or that improvement in the position of women; but should be judged in terms of the way that the struggle itself develops capacities for self-determination. The development of conscious co-operation and solidarity between women on the basis of recognition of their common experience of gender subordination is even more important a goal than any particular improvement in the provision of jobs or welfare services to women, more important than any particular reform of legal status, and than any particular weakening of 'machismo' or 'patriarchal attitudes'. Improvements which come about through capital accumulation or state policy or changing male attitudes can be reversed. Lasting gains depend upon the relationships built up between women themselves.

This is the point that needs impressing upon all those policy advisers, policy makers and policy implementers at national and international levels who wish to 'include women in development', 'enhance the status of women' and so on. The single most important requirement, the single most important way of helping, is to make resources and information available to organizations and activities which are based on an explicit recognition of gender subordination, and are trying to develop new forms of association through which women can begin to establish elements of a social identity in their own right, and not through the mediation of men. Such organizations do not require policy advisers to tell them what to do, supervise them and monitor them; they require access to resources, and protection from the almost inevitable onslaughts of those who have a vested interest in maintaining both the exploitation of women as workers, and the subordination of women as a gender. The most important task of sympathetic personnel in national and international state agencies is to work out how they can facilitate access to such resources and afford such protection – not how they can deliver a package of ready-made 'improvements' wrapped up as a 'women's programme'.

■ Notes

This article appeared in *Feminist Review* No. 7, 1981.

This paper has developed out of discussions in various feminist forums with women from both the Third World and the First World. We should like to thank the other members of the Subordination of Women Workshop, Institute of Development Studies, University of Sussex; and the participants in the international conference on the Continuing Subordination of Women in the Development Process, held at IDS, September 1978; and the participants in the IDS Study Seminar on Women and Social Production in the Caribbean, held in Puerto Rico, June-July 1980. Special thanks to Josephina Aranda, Jane Cardosa-Khoo, Sonia Cuales, Noeleen Heyzer, Ros Malt, and Moema Viezzer.

1   Exploitation of labour: in this essay used in a technical sense, derived from Marx, to mean the process of compelling workers to work longer than the time necessary to produce the goods they themselves consume.

2   Free Trade Zones: special areas which are exempt from normal import and export regulations, and also from many other kinds of regulation, such as protective labour legislation, and taxation law.

3   It may seem paradoxical to talk of the protection afforded by subordination, but the paradox lies in the social relations themselves. When the social identity of women has to be established through their relations with men, the absence of father, brother or husband, is often disadvantageous.

The Material
of Male Power

Cynthia Cockburn

A skilled craftsman may be no more than a worker in relation to capital, but seen from within the working class he has been a king among men and lord of his household. As a high earner he preferred to see himself as the sole breadwinner, supporter of wife and children. As artisan he defined the unskilled workman as someone of inferior status, and would 'scarcely count him a brother and certainly not an equal' (Berg, 1979: 121). For any socialist movement concerned with unity in the working class, the skilled craftsman is therefore a problem. For anyone concerned with the relationship of class and gender, and with the foundations of male power, skilled men provide a fertile field for study.

Compositors in the printing trade are an artisan group that have long defeated the attempts of capital to weaken the tight grip on the labour process from which their strength derives. Now their occupation is undergoing a dramatic technological change initiated by employers. Introduction of the new computerized technology of photocomposition represents an attack on what remains of their control over their occupation and wipes out many of the aspects of the work which have served as criteria by which 'hot metal' composition for printing has been defined as a manual skill and a man's craft.[1]

In this paper I look in some detail at the compositors' crisis, what has given rise to it and what it may lead to in future. Trying to understand it has led me to ask questions in the context of socialist-feminist theory. These I discuss first, as preface to an account of key moments in the compositors' craft history. I then isolate the themes of *skill* and *technology* for further analysis, and conclude with the suggestion that there may be more to male power than 'patriarchal' relations.

■ Producing class and gender

The first difficulty I have encountered in socialist-feminist theory is one that is widely recognized: the problem of bringing into a single focus our experience of both class and gender. Our attempts to ally the Marxist theory of capitalism with the feminist theory of 'patriarchy' have till now been unsatisfactory to us (Hartmann, 1979a).

One of the impediments I believe lies in our tendency to try to mesh together two static structures, two hierarchical systems. In studying compositors I found I was paying attention instead to *processes*, the detail of historical events and changes, and in this way it was easier to detect the connexions between the power systems of class and gender. What we are seeing is *struggle that contributes to the formation of people within both their class and gender simultaneously*.

One class can only exist in relation to another. E.P. Thompson wrote 'we cannot have two distinct classes each with an independent being and then bring them into relationship with each other. We cannot have love without lovers, nor deference without squires and labourers.' Likewise, it is clear we cannot have masculinity without feminity: genders presuppose each other, they are relative. Again, classes are made in historical processes. 'The working class did not rise like the sun at an appointed time. It was present at its own making ... Class is defined by men [sic] as they live their own history' (Thompson, 1963). The mutual production of gender should be seen as a historical process too.

So in this paper I set out to explore aspects of the process of mutual definition in which men and women are locked, and those (equally processes of mutual creation) in which the working class and the capitalist class are historically engaged. Capital and labour, through a struggle over the design and manipulation of technology that the one owns and the other sets in motion, contribute to forming each other in their class characters. Powerfully-organized workers forge their class identity vis-à-vis both capital and the less organized and less skilled in part through the same process. And men and women too are to some extent mutually defined as genders through their relation to the same technology and labour process. In neither case is it a balanced process. By owning the means of production the capitalist class has the initiative. By securing privileged access to capability and technology the man has the initiative. Each gains the power to define 'another' as inferior.[2] I will try to draw these occurrences out of the story of the compositors as I tell it.

■ Components of power

The second theoretical need which an examination of skilled workers has led me to feel is the need for a fuller conception of the material basis of male power, one which does not lose sight of its physical and socio-political ramifications in concentrating upon the economic.

As feminism developed its account of women's subordination one problem that we met was that of shifting out of a predominantly ideological mode and narrating also the concrete practices through which women are disadvantaged. Early literature relied on 'sexist attitudes' and 'male chauvinism' to account for women's position. Socialist feminists, seeking a more material explanation for women's disadvantage, used the implement of Marxist theory, unfortunately not purpose-designed for the job but the best that was to hand. The result was an account of the economic advantages to capital of women as a distinct category of labour and their uses as an industrial reserve army. The processes of capitalism seemed to be producing an economic advantage to men which could be seen uniting with their control over women's domestic labour to form the basis of their power.[3]

Many feminists, however, were dissatisfied with what seemed a narrow 'economism' arising from Marx (or through misinterpretation of Marx according to the point of view). The ideological vein has been more recently worked with far more sophistication than before, in different ways, by Juliet Mitchell on the one hand and Rosalind Coward on the other (Mitchell, 1975; Coward, 1978). But, as Michèle Barrett has pointed out, while 'ideology is an extremely important site for the construction and reproduction of women's oppression ... this ideological level cannot be dissociated from economic relations' (Barrett, 1980).

There is thus a kind of to-ing and fro-ing between 'the ideological' and 'the economic', neither of which gives an adequate account of male supremacy or female subordination. The difficulty lies, I believe, in a confusion of terms. The proper complement of *ideology* is not the *economic*, it is the *material*.[4] And there is more to the material than the economic. It comprises also the *socio-political* and the *physical*, and these are often neglected in Marxist-feminist work.

An instance of the problems that arise through this oversight is Christine Delphy's work, where a search for a 'materialist' account of women's subordination leads her to see marriage in purely economic terms and domestic life as a mode of production, an interpretation which cannot deal with a large area of women's circumstances (Delphy, 1977).

It is only by thinking with the additional concepts of the socio-political and the physical that we can begin to look for material instances of male domination beyond men's greater earning power and property advantage. The socio-political opens up questions about male organization and solidarity, the part played by institutions such as church, societies, unions and clubs for instance.[5] And the physical opens up questions of bodily physique and its extension in technology, of buildings and clothes, space and movement. It allows things that are part of our practice ('reclaiming the night', teaching each other manual skills) a fuller place in our theory.

In this account I want to allow 'the economic' to retire into the background, not to deny its significance but in order to spotlight these other material instances of male power. The socio-political will emerge in the shape of the printing trade unions and their interests and strategies. The physical will also receive special attention because it is that which I have found most difficult to understand in the existing framework of Marxist-feminist thought. It finds expression in the compositor's capability, his dexterity and strength and in his tools and technology.

■ Physical effectivity is acquired

One further prefatory note is needed. In 1970, when Kate Millett and Shulamith Firestone, in their different ways, pinned down and analysed the system of male domination, they spoke to the anger that many women felt (Millett, 1971; Firestone, 1971). But many feminists were uneasy with the essentialism inherent in their view, and especially the biological determinism of Firestone and its disastrous practical implications.

Marxist-feminist theory has consequently tended to set on one side the concept of the superior physical effectivity of men, to adopt a kind of agnosticism to the idea, on account of a very reasonable fear of that biologism and essentialism which would nullify our struggle. I suggest however that we cannot do without a politics of physical power and that it need not immobilize us. In this article I use the term physical power to mean both corporal effectivity (relative bodily strength and capability) and technical effectivity (relative familiarity with and control over machinery and tools).

To say that most men can undertake feats of physical strength that most women cannot is to tell only the truth. Likewise it is true to say that the majority of men are more in their element with machinery than the majority of women. These statements are neither biologistic nor essentialist. Physical efficiency and technical capability do not belong to men primarily by birth, though DNA may offer the first step on the ladder. In the main they are appropriated by males through childhood, youth and maturity. Men's socio-political and economic power enables them to do this. In turn, their physical presence reinforces their authority and their physical skills enhance their earning power.

Ann Oakley, among others, has made the fruitful distinction between biologically-given sex (and that not always unambiguous) and culturally constituted gender, which need have little correlation with sex but in our society takes the form of a dramatic and hierarchical separation (Oakley, 1972).

The part of education and that of childrearing in constituting us as masculine and feminine *in ideology* is the subject of an extensive lieterature (e.g. Wolpe, 1978; Belotti, 1975). But there is evidence to show that *bodily difference* also is largely a social product. With time and work women athletes can acquire a physique which eclipses the innate differences between males and females (Ferris, 1978). Height and weight are correlated with class, produced by different standards of living, as well as with gender.[6] Boys are conditioned from childhood in numberless ways to be more physically effective than girls. They are trained in activities that develop muscle, they are taught to place their weight firmly on both feet, to move freely, to use their bodies with authority. With regard to females they are socialized to seize or shelter them and led to expect them in turn to yield or submit.

While so much of the imbalance of bodily effectiveness between males and females is produced through social practices it is misguided to prioretize that component of the difference that may prove in the last resort to be inborn.[7] More important is to study the way in which a small physical *difference* in size, strength and reproductive function is developed into an increasing relative physical *advantage* to men and vastly multiplied by differential access to technology. The process, as I will show, involves several converging practices: accumulation of bodily capabilities, the definition of tasks to match them and the selective design of tools and machines. The male physical advantage of course interacts with male economic and socio-political advantage in mutual enhancement.

The appropriation of muscle, capability, tools and machinery by men is an important source of women's subordination, indeed it is part of the process by which females are constituted as women. It is a process that is in some ways an analogue of the appropriation of the means of production by a capitalist class, which thereby constituted its complementary working class. In certain situations and instances, as in the history of printers, the process of physical appropriation (along with its ideological practices) has a part in constituting people within their class and gender simultaneously.

■ The hand compositor: appropriation of technique

Letterpress printing comprises two distinct technological processes, composing and printing. Before the mechanization of typesetting in the last decade of the nineteenth century compositors set the type by hand, organizing metal pieces in a 'stick', and proceeded to assemble it into a unified printing surface, the 'forme', ready for the printer to position on the press, coat with ink and impress upon paper.

The hand compositor, then, had to be literate, to be able to read type upside down and back to front, with a sharp eye for detail. He had to possess manual dexterity and have an easy familiarity with the position of letters in the 'case'. He had to calculate with the printers' 'point' system of measurement. Furthermore he had to have a sense of design and spacing to enable him to create a graphic whole of the printed page, which he secured through the manipulation of the assembled type, illustrative blocks and lead spacing pieces. The whole he then locked up in a forme weighing 50lbs or more. This he would lift and move to the proofing press or bring back to the stone for the distribution of used type. He thus required a degree of strength and stamina, a strong wrist, and, for standing long hours at the case, a sturdy spine and good legs.

The compositor used his craft to secure for himself a well-paid living, with sometimes greater and sometimes less success depending on conditions of trade. Through their trade societies (later unions) compositors energetically sought to limit the right of access to the composing process and its equipment to members of the society in a given town or region, blacking 'unfair houses' that employed non-society men.

Comps deployed all the material and ideological tactics they could muster in resistance to the initiatives of capital in a context of the gradual, though late, industrialization of printing. Capitalists continually aimed for lower labour costs, more productive labour processes, the 'real subordination' of labour. Their two weapons were the mobilization of cheap labour and the introduction of machinery. They repeatedly assaulted the defences of the comps' trade societies. The organized, skilled men saw their best protection against capital to lie in sharply differentiating themselves from the all-but-limitless population of potential rivals for their jobs, the remainder of the working class.

They sought to control the numbers entering the trade and so to elevate their wage-bargaining position by a system of formal apprenticeship. They tried to limit the number of apprentices through an agreed ratio of boys to journeymen and to keep the period of apprenticeship as long as possible. The introduction of unapprenticed lads, 'the many-headed monster', the 'demon of cheap boy labour' was always a source of fear to compositors. Comps' jobs were kept within the class fraction by the custom of limiting openings wherever possible to members of existing printer families.

Thus the struggles over physical and mental capability and the right of access to composing equipment was one of the processes in which fractions of classes were formed in relation to each other.

How did women enter this story? The answer is, with difficulty. Women and children were drawn into industrial production in many industries in the first half of the nineteenth century, but in printing their entry was almost entirely limited to the bookbinding and other low-paid finishing operations held to require no skill. Girls were not considered suitable for apprenticeship. Physical and moral factors (girls were not strong enough, lead was harmful to pregnancy, the social environment might be corrupting) were deployed ideologically in such a way that few girls would see themselves as suitable candidates for apprenticeship. A second line of defence against an influx of women was of course the same socio-political controls used to keep large numbers of boys of the unskilled working class from flooding the trade.

Women who, in spite of these barriers, obtained work as non-society compositors were bitterly resisted and their product 'blacked' by the society men; i.e. work typeset by women could not be printed. Their number remained few therefore (Child, 1967). After 1859 a few small print shops were organized by philanthropic feminists to provide openings for women. It is worth noting that these enterprises did prove that women were in fact physically capable, given training and practice, of typesetting and imposition, though they did not work night shifts and male assistants were engaged to do the heavy lifting and carrying. These projects were dismissed by the men as 'wild schemes of social reformers and cranks'.[8]

The process of appropriation of the physical and mental properties and technical hardware required for composing by a group of men, therefore, was not only a capitalist process of class formation, as noted above, but also a significant influence in the process of gender construction in which men took the initiative in constituting themselves and women in a relation of complementarity and hierarchy.

■ The mechanization of typesetting: appropriation of the machine

The compositors' employers had for years sought to invent a machine that could bypass the labour-intensive process of hand typesetting. They hoped in so doing not only to speed up the process but to evade the trade societies' grip on the craft, introduce women and boys and thus bring down the adult male wage. The design of such a machine proved an intractable problem. Though various prototypes and one or two production models were essayed in the years following 1840, none were commercially successful. It was only when highspeed rotary press technology developed in the 1880s that typesetting became an intolerable bottleneck to printing and more serious technological experiment was undertaken. Among the various typesetting machines that then developed, the overwhelmingly successful model was the Linotype. It continued in use almost unchanged for sixty or seventy years.

The Linotype was not allowed to replace the hand typesetter without a struggle.[9] The men believed the Iron Comp would mean mass unemployment of society members. They did not (as an organized group) reject the machine out of hand, however. Their demand was the absolute, exclusive right of hand comps to the machine and to improved earnings. Their weapons were disruption, blacking and deliberate restriction of keyboard speeds. The outcome of the struggle was seen finally by both print employers and compositors as a moderate victory for both sides. There was unemployment of hand compositors for a few years in the mid-nineties, but with the upturn of business at the end of the Great Depression, the demand for print grew fast and the demand for typesetters with it. Indeed, the first agreement between the London Society of Compositors (LSC) and the employers on the adaptation of the London Scale of Prices to Linotype production was a disastrous error for the capitalists, who had underestimated the productive capacity of their new force of production and overestimated the strength of the organized comps. The bosses only began to share fully in the profits from their invention when the agreement was revised in 1896. A lasting cost to the comps was an increasing division of labour between the two halves of their occupation: typesetting and the subsequent composing process. They did succeed however in continuing to encompass both jobs within the unitary craft and its apprenticeship as defined by their societies.

Those who really lost in the battle scarcely even engaged in it. They were the mass of labour, men and women who had no indentured occupation and who, if organized at all, were grouped in the new general unions of the unskilled. Jonathan Zeitlin firmly ascribes the success of the compositors (in contrast to engineers) in routing the employers' attempt to break their control of their craft in the technological thrust of the late nineteenth century to the former's success in ensuring that during the preceding decades no unskilled or semi-skilled categories of worker had been allowed to enter the composing room to fill subordinate roles (Zeitlin, 1981). And the incipient threat from women had been largely averted by the time the Linotype was invented. An exception was a pocket of female compositors in Edinburgh who had entered the trade at the time of a strike by the men in 1872 and had proved impossible to uproot.

A more sustained attempt was made by employers ten years later to introduce women to work on another typesetting process that was widely applied in the book trade: the Monotype. The Monotype Corporation, designers of the machine, in contrast to the Linotype Company Ltd., opened the way to a possible outflanking of the skilled men by splitting the tasks of keyboarding and casting into two different machines. Men retained unshaken control of the caster, but an attempt was made by employers to introduce women onto the keyboards, which had the normal typewriter lay.

In 1909-10 the compositors' societies organized a campaign, focusing on Edinburgh, to eliminate women from the trade once and for all. They succeeded in achieving a ban on female apprentices and an agreement for natural wastage of women comps and operators. This male victory was partly due to an alliance between the craft compositors and the newly organized unions of the unskilled men in the printing industry (Zeitlin, 1981).

That there were large numbers of women, literate, in need of work and eminently capable of machine typesetting at this time is evidenced by the rapid feminization of clerical work that accompanied the introduction of the office typewriter, in a situation where the male incumbent to the office was less well organized to defend himself than was the compositor (Davies, 1979). Men's socio-political power, however, enabled them to extend their physical capabilities in manual typesetting to control of the machine that replaced it. (The gender bias of typesetting technology is discussed further below.) The effect has been that women's participation in composing work, the prestigious and better-paid aspects of printing, was kept to a minimum until the present day, not excluding the period of the two world wars. The composing room was, and in most cases still is, an all-male preserve with a sense of camaraderie, pin-ups on the wall and a pleasure taken in the manly licence to use 'bad' (i.e. woman-objectifying) language.

■ Electronic composition: the disruption of class and gender patterns

In the half-century between 1910 and 1960 the printing industry saw relatively little technical change. Then in the 1960s two big new possibilities opened up for capital in the printing industry as, emerging from post-war restrictions, it looked optimistically to expanding print markets. The first was web offset printing, with its potential flexibility and quality combined with high running speeds. The logical corollary was to abandon the machine-setting of metal type and to take up the second component of 'the new technology': letter assembly on film or photographic paper by the techniques of computer-aided photocomposition. The new process began to make inroads in to the British printing industry in the late sixties and swept through the provincial press and general printing in the seventies. The last serious redoubt of hot metal typesetting and letterpress printing is now the national press in Fleet Street.

Photocomposition itself has gone through several phases of development. At first, the operation comprised a keyboarding process whereby the operator tapped a typewriter-style keyboard producing a punched paper tape. The operator worked 'blind', that is to say he saw no hard copy of his work as he produced it. The 'idiot tape' was fed into a computer which read it, made the subtle line-end decisions formerly the responsibility of the operator and output clean tape. This second tape drove a photosetter, each impulse producing a timed flash of light through a photographic image on a master disc or drum. The result was a succession of characters laid down on film or bromide paper. The columns of text were taken by the compositor, cut up, sorted and pasted in position on a prepared card, later to be photographed as a whole and reproduced on a printing plate.

In the latest electronic composing technology there is no such photomatrix of characters. The computer itself holds instructions that enable it to generate characters, in an almost limitless range of type faces and sizes and at enormously rapid speeds, on the face of a cathode ray tube. The inputting operation is performed with a keyboard associated with a video display unit on which the operator can assist computer decisions and 'massage' the copy into a desired order before committing it to the computer memory. The matter is transmitted direct from computer to photosetter and may now be produced in complete sections as large as a full newspaper page, making paste-up unnecessary.

The process is clearly seen by capital as a means of smashing the costly craft control of the compositor. The system is greatly more productive and requires less manpower. It would require less still if operated in the manner for which it is designed, i.e. avoiding two keyboarding processes by having typists, journalists, editors and authors key matter direct onto the computer disc for editing on screen and thence to direct output.

The work is much lighter, more sedentary. The abilities called upon are less esoteric, more generally available in the working population outside print. Inputting requires little more than good typing ability on the QWERTY board, something possessed by many more women than men. The implications for compositors of this twist in their craft history are dramatic. Combined with a recession it is causing unemployment in the trade, something unknown since the thirties. The individual tasks in the overall process have become trivialized and the men feel the danger of increased sub-division, routinization and substitution of unskilled workers.

The union response has not been to reject the new technology. Instead it has fought an energetic battle to retain the right to the new equipment as it did to the old. It resists 'direct input' by outsiders, asserts exclusive right to the photosetting keystroke (if necessary to a redundant second typing), to paste-up and the control of the photosetters, and where possible, to the computers. It is demanding increased pay and reduced hours in exchange for agreement to operate the new technology. And it is insisting (in principle at least) that all composing personnel get the chance to retrain for all aspects of the *whole* photocomposing job ... an uphill struggle for re-integration of the now transformed craft.

■ Skill and its uses

An extensive literature has demonstrated the effect of craft organization on the structure of the working class. 'The artisan creed with regard to the labourers is that the latter are an inferior class and that they should be made to know and kept in their place' (Hobsbawm, 1964). The loss of demands on manual skill brought about by electronic photocomposition does not necessarily mean the job has become more 'mental'. On the contrary, present-day compositors feel their new work could be done by relatively unskilled workers. Many members feel they have lost status and some resent the strategic necessity to seek amalgamation of the National Graphical Association (NGA) with the unions representing the less skilled.

Our account shows however, that the purposeful differentiation between skilled and unskilled workers was also a step in the construction of *gender*. This is a more recent conception. Heidi Hartmann has suggested that 'the roots of women's present social status' lie in job segregation by sex and demonstrates the role of men and their unions in maintaining women's inferiority in the labour market by deployment of skill (Hartmann, 1979B). The fact that females in the closed-shop NGA (which embodies a large proportion of the better paid workers in the printing industry) until recently amounted to no more than 2 per cent of its membership is directly connected with the fact that women's average earnings have always been lower relative to men's in printing then in manufacturing occupations as a whole. Through the mechanisms of craft definition women have been constructed as relatively lacking in competence, and relatively low in earning power. Women's work came to be seen as inferior. Now that the new composing process resembles the stereotype of 'women's work', it is felt as emasculating. The skill crisis is a crisis of both gender and class for comps.

Anne Phillips and Barbara Taylor propose that skill is a direct correlate of sexual power. 'Skill has increasingly been defined against women ... far from being an objective economic fact, skill is often an ideological category imposed on certain types of work by virtue of the sex and power of the workers who perform it' (Phillips and Taylor, this volume).

It is important to recognize this ideological factor. It has become increasingly important in printing with the advance of technology. The compositor sitting at a keyboard setting type is represented as doing skilled work. A girl typist at a desk typing a letter is not – though the practical difference today is slight. Nonetheless, the formulation here again, posing the ideological as foil to the economic, leads to an under-emphasis on the material realities (albeit socially acquired) of physical power and with them the tangible factors in skill which it is my purpose to reassert.

Phillips and Taylor cite several instances of job definition where the distinction between male and female jobs as skilled and unskilled is clearly no more than ideological. But in printing, and perhaps in many other occupations too, unless we recognize what measure of reality lies behind the male customary over-estimate of his skill we have no way of evaluating the impact of electronic photocomposition, the leeching out of the tangible factors of skill from some tasks and their relocation in others, out of the compositor's reach.

What was the hot metal compositor's skill? He would say: I can read and calculate in a specialized manner; I can understand the process and make decisions about the job; I have aesthetic sense; I know what the tools are for and how to use them; I know the sequence of tasks in the labour process; how to operate, clean and maintain the machinery; I am dexterous and can work fast and accurately under pressure, can lift heavy weights and stand for hours without tiring. No one but an apprenticed compositor can do *all* these things.

There are thus what we might call tangible factors in skill – things that cannot be acquired overnight. They are both intellectual and physical and among the physical are knack, strength and intimacy with a technology. They are all in large measure learned or acquired through practice, though some apprentices will never make good craftsmen. The relative importance of the factors shifts over time with changing technology. Skill is a changing constellation of practical abilities of which no single one is either necessary or sufficient. Cut away the need for one or two of them and the skill may still be capable of adaptation to remain intact, marketable and capable of defence by socio-political organization.

The tangible factors in skill may be over-stated for purposes of self defence and are variably deployed in socio-political struggle. Thus, against the unskilled male, defined as corporally superior to the skilled, hot metal comps have defended their craft in terms of (a) its intellectual and (b) its dexterity requirements. Against women, with their supposed superior dexterity, the skilled men on the contrary used to invoke (a) the heavy bodily demands of the work and (b) the intellectual standards it was supposed to require.[10] (Among comps today it is sometimes done to keep a list of the 'howlers' they detect in the typescripts coming to them from the 'illiterate' typists upstairs.)

The bodily strength component of the compositor's craft may be isolated to illustrate the politics involved. Men, having been reared to a bodily advantage, are able to make political and economic use of it by defining into their occupation certain tasks that require the muscle they alone possess, thereby barricading it against women who might be used against them as low-cost alternative workers (and whom for other reasons they may prefer to remain in the home). In composing, the lifting and carrying of the forme is a case in point. Nonetheless, many compositors found this aspect of the work heavy and it was felt to be beyond the strength of older men. They were always torn between wishing for unskilled muscular assistants and fearing that these, once ensconced in part of the job might lay claim to the whole.

The size and weight of the forme is arbitrary. Printing presses and the printed sheet too could have been smaller. And heavy as it is, the mechanization exists which could ease the task. It is, in printing, purely a question of custom at what weight the use of hoists and trolleys to transport the forme is introduced.

Units of work (hay bales, cement sacks) are political in their design. Capitalists with work-study in mind and men with an interest in the male right to the job both have a live concern in the bargain struck over a standard weight or size. But the political power to design work processes would be useless to men without a significant average superiority in strength or other bodily capability. Thus the appropriation of bodily effectivity on the one hand and the design of machinery and processes on the other have often converged in such a way as to constitute men as capable and women as inadequate. Like other physical differences, gender difference in average bodily strength is not illusory, it is real. It does not necessarily matter, but it can be made to matter. Its manipulation is socio-political power play.

Above everything, a skill embodies the idea of wholeness in the job and in the person's abilities, and what this 'whole' comprises is the subject of a three-way struggle between capital, craftsman and the unskilled. The struggle is over the division of labour, the building of some capabilities into machines (the computer, the robot), the hiving off of some less taxing parts of the job to cheaper workmen, or to women. Craft organization responds to capitalist development by continually redefining its area of competence, taking in and teaching its members new abilities. Wholeness has become of key significance to the compositors' union as electronic technology has trivialized and shifted the pattern of the individual tasks. Socio-political organization and power have become of paramount importance as the old tangible physical and intellectual factors have been scrapped along with the old hardware.

■ Control of technology

Capitalists as capitalists and men as men both take initiatives over technology. The capitalist class designs new technology, in the sense that it commissions and finances machinery and sets it to work to reduce the capitalist's dependency on certain categories of labour, to divide, disorganize and cheapen labour. Sometimes machinery displaces knack and know-how, sometimes strength. Yet it is often the knowledge of the workers gained on an earlier phase of technology that produces the improvements and innovations that eventually supersede it. For instance, in a radical working men's paper in 1833, claiming rights over the bosses' machines, the men say: '*Question:* Who are the inventors of machinery? *Answer:* Almost universally the working man' (Berg, 1979: 90).

In either case, it is overwhelmingly males who design technological processes and productive machinery. Many women have observed that mechanical equipment is manufactured and assembled in ways that make it just too big or too heavy for the 'average' woman to use. This need not be conspiracy, it is merely the outcome of a pre-existing pattern of power. It is a complex point. Women vary in bodily strength and size; they also vary in orientation, some having learned more confidence and more capability than others. Many processes could be carried out with machines designed to suit smaller or less muscular operators or reorganized so as to come within reach of the 'average' women.

There are many mechanized production processes in which women are employed. But there is a sense in which women who operate machinery, from the nineteenth-century cotton spindles to the modern typewriter, are only 'lent' it by men, as men are only ' lent' it by capital. Working-class men are threatened by the machines with which capital seeks to replace them. But as and when the machines prevail it is men's hands that control them. Comps now have twice adopted new technology, albeit with bad grace, on the strict condition that it remain under their own control. They necessarily engage in a class gamble (how many jobs will be lost? will wages fall?) but their sexual standing is not jeopardized.

The history of mechanized typesetting offers an instance of clear sex bias within the design of equipment. The Linotype manufacturing company has twice now, in contrast to its competitors, adopted a policy that is curiously beneficial to men. A nineteenth-century rival to the Linotype was the Hattersley typesetter. It had a separate mechanism for distributing type, designed for use by girls. The separation of the setting (skilled) from dissing (unskilled) was devised as a means of reducing overall labour costs. A representative of the Hattersley company wrote 'it would be a prostitution of the object for which the machine was invented and a proceeding against which we would protest at all times' to employ *men* on the disser (Typographical Association, 1893).

The Linotype machine on the other hand did not represent the destruction but merely the mechanization of the comp's setting skills as a *whole*. In fact, the LSC congratulated the Linotype Company Ltd. 'The Linotype answers to one of the essential conditions of trade unionism, in that it does not depend for its success on the employment of boy or girl labour; but on the contrary, appears to offer the opportunity for establishing an arrangement whereby it may be fairly and honestly worked to the advantage of employer, inventor and workman' (Typographical Association, 1893). While Linotype were not above using male scab trainees when driven to it by the comps' ca'canny, they never tried to put women on the machines and indeed curried favour with the LSC by encouraging employers who purchased the machine to shed female typesetters and replace them with union men.

Ninety years on, Linotype (now Linotype-Paul) are leading designers and marketers of electronic composing systems. Most present day manufacturers, with an eye to the hundreds of thousands of low-paid female typists their clients may profit from installing at the new keyboards, have designed them with the typewriter QWERTY lay, thus reducing Lino operators at a single blow to fumbling incompetence. Linotype-Paul is one of the few firms offering an optional alternative keyboard, the 90-key lay familiar to union comps. Once more, they seem to be wooing the organized comp as man and in doing so are playing, perhaps, an ambivalent part in the class struggle being acted out between print employers, craftsmen and unskilled labour (since employers would profit more by the complete abolition of the 90-key board).

Now, electronic photocomposition is an almost motionless labour process. The greatest physical exertion is the press of a key. The equipment is more or less a 'black box'. The intelligence lies between the designers, maintenance engineers and programmers and the computer and its peripherals. Only the simplest routine processes and minimal decisions are left to the operator.

Two factors emerge. It is significant that the great majority of the electronic technical stratum are male (as history would lead us to expect). Male power deriving from prestigious jobs has shifted up-process leaving the compositor somewhat high and dry, vulnerable to the unskilled and particularly to women. In so far as he operates this machinery he has a 'female' relationship to it: he is 'lent' it by men who know more about its technicalities than he does.

The NGA, faced with a severe threat to composing as a craft, has been forced into innovatory manoeuvres in order to survive as a union. It is widening its scope, radically redesigning and generalizing its apprenticeship requirements, turning a blind eye to the fact that some of the new style comps it recruits 'on the job' come in without apprenticeships (and a handful of these are now women who have graduated from typing to simple composers). It is seeking to recruit office workers, a proportion of whom will be female typists who are seen as a weapon employers may try to use against comps. They are to be organized in a separate division within the union and thus will be under supervision by the union but not permitted to invade the area of existing comps' work.

■ Conclusion: men's power and patriarchy

This study has been of the workplace. Marxist theory proposed the workplace as the primary locus of capitalist exploitation, while women's disadvantage was seen as having its site in the property relations of the family. The corollary of this view was the belief (disproved by the passing of time) that women would evade their subordination to men when they came out into waged work (Engels, 1972). Feminists have shown on the contrary that the family, as the throne of 'patriarchy', has its own malevolent effectivity within capitalism and capitalist relations; it pursues women out into waged work (Kuhn, 1978; Bland, 1978).

Many women, however, are relatively detached from conjugal or paternal relationships. Many are single, childless, widowed, live independently, collectively, without husbands, free from fathers. Can 'the family' satisfactorily account today for the fact that they hesitate to go to the cinema alone, have to call on a man to change a car wheel, or feel put out of countenance by walking into a pub or across a composing room floor? Our theories of the sexual division of labour at work have tended to be an immaculate conception unsullied by these physical intrusions. They read: women fill certain inferior places provided by capitalism, but do so in a way for which they are destined by the shackles of family life. The free-standing women, the physical reality of men, their muscle or initiative, the way they wield a spanner or the spanner they wield, these things have been diminished in our account.

The story of compositors, for me, throws doubt on the adequacy of the explanation that the sexual relations of work can be fully accounted for as a shadow cast by the sex-relations of the family. It seems to me that the construction of gender difference and hierarchy is created at work as well as at home – and that the effect on women (less physical and technical capability, lack of confidence, lower pay) may well cast a shadow on the sex-relations of domestic life.

In socialist-feminist thought there has been a clear divide between production (privileged site of class domination) and the family (privileged site of sexual domination). The patriarchal family is recognized as adapted to the interests of capital and the capitalist division of labour as being imprinted with the patterns of domestic life. They are conceded to be mutually effective, but are nonetheless still largely conceived as two separate spheres, capitalism holding sway in one, patriarchy in the other.

Yet the compositors' story reveals a definable area of sex-gender relations that cannot be fully subsumed into 'the family', an area which has tended to be a blindspot for socialist-feminist theory. It is the same as that spot within the class relations of wage labour and capitalist production, invisible to Marxist theory, in which male power is deployed in the interests of men – capital apart.

In our analysis we can accommodate men as 'patriarchs', as fathers or husbands, and we can accommodate capitalists and workers who are frequently men. But where is the man as male, the man who fills those spaces in capitalist production that he has defined as not ours, who designs the machines and thereby decides who will use them? Where is the man who decorates the walls of his workplace with pin-ups of naked women and whose presence on the street is a factor in a woman's decision whether to work the night shift?

It was an incalculable breakthrough in the late sixties when the sexual relations of private life came to be more generally recognized as political. But somehow those sexual relations have remained ghettoized within the family. Only slowly are we demolishing the second wall, to reveal in theory what we know in practice, that the gender relations of work and public life, of the factory and the street, are sexual politics too.[11]

It is in this sense that the prevailing use of the concept of 'patriarchy' seems to me a problem. Some feminists have argued, I think rightly, that it is too specific an expression to describe the very diffuse and changing forms of male domination that we experience, and that it should be reserved for specific situations where society is organized through the authority of fathers and husbands over wives and offspring and of older men over younger men (Young and Harris, 1976).

Such a 'patriarchy' would usefully enable us, for instance, to characterize certain historical relations in the printing industry: the archaic paternalism of journeyman-apprentice relations, the handing of job from father to son, the role of the 'father' of chapel in the union, etc. But these practices are changing in printing – just as Jane Barker and Hazel Downing have shown that patriarchal relations of control in the office are being rendered obsolete by the new capitalist office technology (Barker and Downing, 1980).

Do we then assume that male supremacy is on the wane in the workplace? I think not. The gap between women's earnings and men's in printing has widened in the last few years. What we are seeing in the struggle over the electronic office and printing technology is a series of transformations within gender relations and in their articulation with class relations. The class relations are those of capitalism. The gender relations are those of a wider, more pervasive and more long-lived male dominance system than patriarchy. They are those of a sex-gender system[12] in which men dominate women inside and outside family relations, inside and outside economic production, by means which are both material and ideological, exercising their authority through both individual and organizational development. It is more nearly andrarchy[13] than patriarchy.

Finally, in what practical sense do these questions matter to women? Seeing bodily strength and capability as being socially constructed and politically deployed helps us as an organized group in that we can fight for the right to strengths and skills that we feel to be useful. On the other hand, where we do not see this kind of power as socially beneficial, our struggle can seek to devalue it by socio-political means in the interests of a gentler world (or to prevent our being disadvantaged by what may turn out to be our few remaining innate differences).

Identifying the gendered character of technology enables us to overcome our feelings of inferiority about technical matters and realize that our disqualification is the result not of our own inadequacy, nor of chance, but of power-play. Understanding technology as an implement in capital's struggle to break down workers' residual control of the labour process helps us to avoid feeling 'anti-progress' if and when we need to resist it. Understanding it as male enables us to make a critique of the exploitation of technology for purposes of power by men – both over women and over each other, in competition, aggression, militarism.

Unless we recognize what capital is taking away from some men as workers, we cannot predict the strategies by which they may seek to protect their position as men. As one technology fails them will they seek to establish a power base in another? Will they eventually abandon the de-skilled manual work to women, recreating the job segregation that serves male dominance? Or will the intrinsic interdependency of keyboard and computer force a re-gendering of 'typing' so that it is no longer portrayed as female? As men's physical pre-eminence in some kinds of work is diminished will they seek to reassert it heavily in private life? Or is the importance of physical effectivity genuinely diminishing in the power relations of gender? Can the unions, so long a socio-political tool of men, be made to serve women? We need to understand all the processes that form us as workers and as women if we are to exert our will within them.

■ Notes

This article appeared in *Feminist Review* No 9, 1981. The arguments are developed more fully in *Brothers: Male Dominance and Technological Change,* Pluto Press, 1983.

1 The article is based on a project in progress in 1981, 'Skilled printing workers and technological change', funded by the Social Science Research Council and carried out at The City University, London. The

paper was first given at the annual conference of the British Sociological Association in 1981.

2 The fact that a mode of production and a sex-gender system are two fundamental and parallel features of the organization of human societies should not lead us to expect to find any exact comparability between them, whether the duo is capitalism/'patriarchy' or any other. In the case of a sex-gender system there is a biological factor that is strongly, though not absolutely, predisposing. This is not the case in a class system. The historical timescale of modes of production appears to be shorter than that of sex-gender systems. And the socio-political and economic institutions of class seem to be more formal and visible than those of gender – though one can imagine societies where this might not be the case.

3 Michèle Barrett's recent book reviews in detail the progress of this endeavour (Barrett, 1980). An important contribution to the 'appropriation of patriarchy by materialism' has been Kuhn and Wolpe (1978).

4 I adopt here Michèle Barrett's useful re-assertion of the distinction between ideology and 'the material', in place of a simplistic fusion 'ideology is material'. She cites Terry Eagleton, 'there is no possible sense in which meanings and values can be said to be 'material', other than in the most sloppily metaphorical use of the term ... If meanings *are* material, then the term 'materialism' naturally ceases to be intelligible' (Barrett, 1980: 89-90).

5 Heidi Hartmann's definition of patriarchy is novel in including 'hierarchical relations between men and *solidarity among them*' (Hartmann, 1979b).

6 For instance, children whose families' low income entitles them to free school milk are shorter than the average child (demonstrated in articles in *The Lancet*, 1979). More information relating to class and stature should be available from Department of Health and Social Security 'Heights and Weights Survey', 1982.

7 Griffiths and Saraga (1979) have argued the same of sex difference in cognitive ability.

8 A fuller account exists in Cynthia Cockburn (1980) 'The Losing Battle: Women's Attempts to Enter Composing Work 1850-1914', Working Note No. 11, unpublished.

9 I have traced the course of this technological development in 'The Iron Comp: the Mechanization of Composing', Working Note No. 10, unpublished.

10 For an interesting discussion of 'dexterity' versus 'skill' in relation to gender, see Ramsay Macdonald (1904).

11 A sign of change in this direction was Farley (1980), concerning sexual harrassment of women at work.

12 Gayle Rubin's term (Rubin, 1975).

13 Rule by *men* as opposed to rule by fathers or male heads of household or tribe, cf. androgynous, polyandry, andro-centrism.

New Office Technology

Janine Morgall

The most frightening reactions to technology one can encounter in today's office are passivity, helplessness and resignation. At union meetings, courses, secretary groups, study groups and in offices one meets these reactions all too often. I've yet to talk with anyone who believes that the new office technology can be stopped in the long run. Most people feel that it is unavoidable, and in many offices defensive measures are being taken, such as demands for a certain number of rest periods, special glasses for working at Visual Display Units (VDUs) and specifications for office furniture. In other words except for individual attempts at passive resistance, there is a basic acceptance of the new technology as it is marketed by manufacturers, and clerical workers are trying to make the best of it.

What is lacking in my opinion is:

1 a pooling of the collective experience of office technology so far;
2 a review of the state of art by those who have actually operated these new machines;
3 a creative offensive.

New technology should be met with ideas and feasible plans for its utilization, not by unchallenged acceptance.

For women the realities of today's clerical labour market are harsh. Its characteristics are a division of labour by sex segregation, low paying dead-end jobs, and a double work role because of their responsibility in the family. These are indeed realities but must not be *excuses* for lack of collective response to the restructuring of their profession.

My interest in office technology stems from my many years as a clerical worker, private secretary, shop steward and most recently as a student of sociology. I feel more and more burdened by what I see as an inevitable and almost irreversible course which the technology is taking.

The purpose of this article is to look at office technology from a women's perspective and to discuss what I consider to be the most serious problems and some realistic suggestions for avoiding them.

■ Introduction

Technology is neither neutral nor value-free. Technological innovations reflect the political, social and economic conditions of the societies which create and put them to use. Technology can be used to eliminate inequalities in society or to exploit them further, depending on the motives and goals of those in power.

In the clerical sector, where women have traditionally held subordinate positions, technology *could* be used as a tool to liberate women so that they can play a more active and responsible role in their work place.

Women stand only to gain from the liberating potential of office technology. There are, however, no signs of this occurring, and this is not surprising when one considers the past relations between technological innovations and women clerical workers.

The new microprocessor-based technology is coming into offices where there is already a division of labour characterized by sex segregation. Far from eliminating the differences between 'men's' and 'women's' work, it appears that technology can now reinforce these barriers and make them more rigid.

This article begins with a short description of the feminization, rationalization and mechanization of office work in the United States. It will attempt to show how the creation of new occupations and changes in the organizational structure resulting from technological innovation have been used to widen the gap in the sexual division of labour, rather than minimize it. The typewriter and computer will be used as examples. The word processor will then be singled out as an example of the new technology showing how management can exploit it in order to further the division of labour and how these machines can be used by clerical workers to break down existing divisions.

The benefits of the new technology will be discussed, and in the conclusion I will suggest ways of realizing the benefits of the new technology for women clerical workers. It is not only a case of avoiding disastrous consequences for women, but also of improving their position on the job market. I do not have any answers, only suggestions.

This article is about women clerical workers ... share it with them!

■ The feminization of office work

During the last decades of the nineteenth century many US corporations underwent a period of rapid growth, marked by the development of monopoly capital. This was a time when a large part of the country's capital increasingly became concentrated into the hands of a few entrepreneurs, who used it to enlarge enterprises (Braverman, 1974). As a result, there was a demand for an expanded office structure, and a sharp increase in the amount of general office work (note: this was not a proliferation of the small offices of the nineteenth century where capital was not so concentrated but an entirely new structure). To fill this need in commercial concerns for literate labour in large numbers, employers turned to the great untapped pool of educated female labour.

Three interesting developments helped American women to break into office work:

1 the shortage of male clerical workers due to the American civil war.
2 the discovery that women worked for less pay than men.
3 the general acceptance in the late 1890s of the typewriter (Davies, 1974).

There was a fear that women would take work away from men. In 1900, an article appeared in the *Ladies Home Journal* warning women that the physical strain of office work was too much for them. As the need for low-paid office workers increased, a shift in ideology occurred condoning women office workers so long as they knew their place, and that place was 'at the typewriter' (Davies, 1974). It is an interesting fact that the profession of typist was sex-neutral but very quickly became identified as women's work.

As clerical work became more and more a female occupation, its function and status declined (Hagerty and Tighe, 1978). Women were relegated to the low-paying routine tasks, while a new, exclusively male managerial layer developed and continued to grow. With groups of five or six female typists working under one male supervisor, the pattern of male supremacy was clearly reinforced in the office hierarchy. Women did not step into the jobs previously held by men. Instead office work was adjusted so that women performed only the routine and subservient functions (Benet, 1973).

Modern office work became the process of acquiring, storing, transforming, presenting and sending information. It became women's work to transform, store and send information and men's work to acquire information, assimilate and manipulate existing information and generate new information.

Women did not improve their position in society by entering into office work. They were paid less than men, there was no career ladder for them and they were given the routine and less responsible tasks. Their position in the office became a reflection of the patriarchal society they lived in.

■ The rationalization of office work

With an increase in the volume of work and the number of employees came a need to systematize and control office work. In the early twentieth-century books on office management, the message was clear: the purpose of the office was to control the enterprise; the purpose of office management was to control the office (Braverman, 1974).

Rationalization or 'scientific management' was originally used to analyse and eventually control the work process in the factory. This method used time and motion studies to break tasks down into their smallest components. These components were then measured for length of time and extent of movement. Once the smallest units were identified, ways were found to cut down the time and the movement needed. Rationalization helped speed up the work process and reduced the amount of decision-making left to the workers, thus increasing the amount in the hands of management.

These techniques were soon applied to office procedures. As long as offices were small in relation to production, clerical work was more or less self-supervising. As offices expanded, the need to make office work more efficient gained importance. Under scientific management, decision-making and judgement on how work should be carried out became centralized in the hands of the office manager.

Every office process was studied closely. Daily records were kept on the production of each clerk. Every office employee became the object of interference from management. Once all phases of office procedure had been studied, management set out to rationalize the work process. The figures arrived at by the metering of all procedures were in many cases used as the statistical base for piecework payments. Clerical operations became standardized.

It is important to note that mechanization in the late nineteenth and early twentieth century was taken as given (the typewriter and early versions of adding and dictating machines) and no great advances in technical development were expected.

In the early part of the twentieth century the office layout was given much attention. In order to 'save time away from the desk' offices were designed with all necessary facilities, i.e. water coolers, toilets etc., in close proximity. Thus was born the sedentary tradition of clerical work. All motions or energies not directed to the increase of capital were considered 'wasted' or 'misspent' (Bravermen, 1974). Office work proved easier to rationalize than factory work.

Scientific management in the office meant that planning and decision-making became concentrated into fewer and fewer hands. Mental labour was further subdivided into conception and execution. The elimination of thought from the work of office labour took place as a result of:

1 the reduction of mental labour into a repetitious performance of the same small set of functions and
2 an increase in the number of clerical categories where nothing but manual labour was performed.

Second and third generation office managers reduced work into abstract labour. They viewed all human labour, both factory and office, as simple motion components; a finite motion of hands, feet, and eyes. Efficiency and fragmentation of jobs led to white collar alienation (Popkin, 1975).

▩ The mechanization of office work

The mechanization of the office occurred in three stages:

1 early mechanization consisting of the typewriter and adding machines,
2 punched card data processing and
3 computers

Rationalization combined with mechanization resulted in the regimentation of office work. Jobs became more standardized to meet the requirements of the machine (Hagerty and Tighe, 1978).

With the introduction of machines, machine-pacing became available to the office and was a method used by management to increase productivity in the office, as it once had been applied in the factory. The standardization of office work into small units provided management with an automatic accounting of the size of the workload and the amount done by each operator (Braverman, 1974).

Mechanization made possible new organizational models such as typing and steno pools; as early as the late 1880s there were typing pools in England (Delgado, 1979). Organizing work in this way contributed to a more efficient use of machines and to centralization of the work process which increased management's control over the workers (Hagerty and Tighe, 1978).

Many offices instituted the use of conveyer belts to move the work from one station to the next. A segregation of functions and an impersonal atmosphere developed. Offices began to resemble factories. Office workers were no longer considered skilled workers, they became as interchangeable as factory workers. An example of this is evident in the growth in agencies which market temporary office workers.

During the Second World War the first operational computer (the ENIAC) was used to perform some of the complex calculations required by the Manhatten Project (the wartime effort to design and build the first nuclear weapons). The programming task was considered 'clerical' and a group of one hundred young women were hired to do what was considered 'women's work'. The women designed the programme necessary for the bomb calculations in a few months by 'crawling around the ENIAC's massive frame, locating burnt-out vacuum tubes, shorted connections, and other non-clerical "bugs" ' (Kraft, 1979).

Programming became 'men's work' from the time it was recognized as intellectually demanding and creative, and that a broad knowledge of abstract logic, mathematics, electrical circuits and machines was required.

It is one of the ironies of programming that women pioneered in the occupation, largely by accident, only to make it attractive to men once the work was redefined as creative and important. The further irony, however, as we shall see, is that the men who followed women pioneers – and effectively eased them out of the industry – eventually had their work reduced into something that was genuinely like clerical labour. It was at this point that women were allowed to reenter the occupation they had created (Kraft, 1979: 4-5).

In the early 1970s, due to an increased division of labour accompanied by fragmentation, standardization and deskilling, women re-entered the field of programming. In the US in 1970 approximately 20 per cent of computer programmers were women, but the polarization of the occupation is obvious when one considers that men dominate in the most skilled sub-occupations.

There was never any doubt about the sex of keypunchers. Keypunching was immediately recognized as a job for the 'girls' because it was a keyboard machine. In most instances women lacking formal education did this work. Keypunching is a dead-end occupation which rarely leads to advancement. Keypunching has remained women's work.

Computers have increasingly created higher-level clerical jobs, both within and without the electronic processing unit. The higher-level jobs of computer operator, programmer and systems analyst became men's work, and the lower-level jobs of keypuncher, sorter and coder became women's work.

■ The new technology

The heart of what is known as 'the new technology' is the microprocessor – a miniature electronic circuit no bigger than a postage stamp. With the development of the microprocessor, computers which previously required several rooms can now be made to fit into a briefcase. The microprocessor has cut the cost of computer 'memory' a thousandfold since 1970. Pocket calculators and electronic watches are products of this technology.

One major trend in the use of microprocessors is in the development of new types of office equipment. The tendency is to eliminate paper as a medium of document storage and communication, by integrating word processors and data processors into local and global communication networks.

There are four reasons for the push towards implementation in the new technology in offices:

1 rising cost of clerical personnel.
2 low productivity in the office.
3 decreasing costs of microelectronic-based technology.

4 massive marketing campaigns to sell the new office technology
(launched by major multinational companies).

While office costs have almost doubled over the last decade,
productivity has remained almost stagnant. US estimates say that
office productivity has increased only four per cent while in the same
ten-year period industrial production nearly doubled (CIS Report,
1979). In the UK wages account for nearly 80 per cent of all office
costs. On the other hand, the price of office automation equipment has
been declining annually by 10 per cent and the performance of
computers has increased 10,000-fold in fifteen years (Markoff and
Steward, 1979).

*Microprocessors are expected to cause a revolution in office work
within the next ten years similar in impact to the industrial revolution.*
What will this mean for the female-dominated secretarial profession?
The changes in office work that will most affect secretaries will
primarily be a result of word-processing machines. Secretarial work
will never be the same again. Some secretaries have already been
affected by this, while others are not even aware of what is happening.

It is projected that the introduction of office automation will be
uneven and affect primarily women, urban areas and the public sector
(Barron and Curnow, 1979).

Word processing machines

Most word processing machines consist of:
- a microprocessor-based logic system (a computer)
- a storage facility (usually 'floppy discs')
- a keyboard
- a visual display unit (VDU)
- a printer

A word processing machine is a computerized machine similar to,
but more advanced than, a typewriter. Most word processors are
equipped with a VDU, a miniature television screen on which the text
being typed appears. Word processors can be coded so that text can
be set, centred and tabulated automatically. When a draft document
needs correction – e.g. if a paragraph needs to be added, deleted or
rearranged – it can be done in many cases by pressing a button. No
more cut and paste jobs, no more correction fluid, no more retyping
entire pages.

Word processing machines have a printing speed of up to 425 lines
per minute and a memory which can store basic drafts and letters for

later use. There are a number of devices available for storing information typed on the keyboard. One of these is the 'floppy disc', a single one of which can hold up to 100 pages of text. By typing in the correct code, the text is brought up onto the screen so the operator can revise and edit it. IBM estimates that the use of word processors could increase typists' productivity by almost 150 per cent. In many cases word processing equipment is creating factory-like conditions in the office, but they *could* be used as a tool for saving secretaries and typists from boring routine tasks.

Word-processors as a tool for management

Word processors can be used as a tool for management to increase control of the work force (in this case women) and further widen the gap between 'men's' and 'women's' work by deskilling qualified female clerical workers.

Secretarial work can be divided up into two parts: typing and administrative routine. In an attempt to rationalize and cut costs the trend is to divide these tasks, the typing work being taken over by typing pools equipped with word processors, and the administrative tasks being taken over by 'administrative support centres' which handle secretarial functions such as filing, answering the telephone, making plane reservations, typing chores of a personal and confidential nature, etc. The expected ratio is four to eight principals to one secretary – which involves tremendous cut-backs in the clerical labour force (Braverman, 1974).

Estimates from Germany suggest an overall decrease in clerical jobs by 1990 of 40 per cent, and in France a cut-back of 30 per cent is expected in the financial sector within the next ten years (APEX, 1979). In Denmark the office workers union (HK) expects 75,000 office jobs to disappear within the next few years as a result of word processing (*Aktuelt*, 1979).

Word processors will require typists, but the total number of jobs on the market may decrease. The need for highly skilled typists will decrease as programmes for the layout of tables and text are devised and stored in the machines' memory.

Some reports claim that word processors will create more jobs than they destroy. This is a fallacy. It depends on how these machines are used and what the purpose of installing them in the first place is. In other words if the goal is to eliminate boring and repetitive tasks and increase productivity, using the time saved for more qualified work then it could be imagined that both new skills and therefore new jobs will be created. If however the goal is to centralize the work process, quantify and monitor work increasing productivity and using the time saved to increase the work load, and intensify the work process, the result will most likely be a drop in the total number of jobs.

Some manufacturers claim that word processors will require highly skilled operators, thus bringing about an increse in the skill-level of typists. The contrary is true. It takes a trained typist about a week to learn how to use the machine and about six months to reach top efficiency. These machines deskill those who are required to work full-time on them, performing monotonous tasks and who are denied physical mobility and involvement in their work. Once the machine's 'memory' is developed with standard paragraphs and letters, word processors can reduce typing to an almost completely mechanical task.

Word processors can be used to increase managerial control over the work process itself. These machines can be programmed so that when one typing job is finished the next will come up immediately on the screen. The device which makes this possible is called a 'prompter'. These machines can be equipped with counters that register the number of key depressions per day, they can also be used to collect information on the speed and/or accuracy of individual workers. When a word processor enters the office an automated time and motion man may come along with it.

In order to capitalize on their investment, management may decide to increase shiftwork and speed up the work process. A piece rate system may be introduced which, as we have seen in industry, leads to competition, alienation and a continuous struggle over what a 'fair' rate is. The introduction of involuntary part-time work (breaking down full-time jobs into part-time jobs) is a serious and very real threat for female clerical workers.

In Scandinavia today more than 50 per cent of all women are active in the labour market. *One half* of these women are working part-time and the trend is continuing especially in the clerical sector. In the Danish Shop and Office Workers Union 37 per cent of the women members as opposed to 1 per cent of the male workers work part-time. This trend is very significant at this critical time of increased office automation.

Because of the occupational health hazards caused by sitting full-time at word processors with visual display screens, the unions are asking that a maximum of four hours per day be the limit for any one operator. Instead of filling the rest of the day with diversified clerical tasks an employer may be tempted to divide full-time jobs up into two part-time jobs. This will give the advantage of a fresh work force twice a day. The disadvantage being that these jobs are women's jobs and will in most cases weaken women's commitment to the labour market and to union activities.

Among feminists in Denmark there is a fear that this will lead to further splits in the already sex-segregated work force – full-time work = men's work and part-time work = women's work – thus putting women at an obvious disadvantage for promotion and the possibility for more responsible tasks. A movement for a six-hour day with full salary compensation of *both* men and women is mobilizing.

One result of the introduction of word processing equipment is that many secretaries and typists complain of an unnecessary increase in their workload. It appears that persons initiating work are becoming less orderly in their thinking as a result of the ease with which their secretaries can make corrections. These persons overestimate the productivity gains and there are cases where they 'create' additional work for the clerical staff.

The present level of light-weight portable terminals makes it possible for computer terminals to communicate with large central computers via telephone which makes work at home a reality. The potential for pushing women back into traditional roles would be disastrous, not to mention the destruction of the labour unions and the opportunity for management to have absolute control over the work process.

How word processors could be used

Word processing machines can assist secretaries and typists in their daily work. They can increase productivity and bring about a shorter work week. Word processors will save secretaries and typists time in correcting and editing documents. That time should then be used for more responsible and challenging administrative tasks, for the training in new skills and for union activity. Word processors should be a tool in liberating women office workers from low-paid dead-end jobs. *Women must insure that it is their brain-power and not their manual dexterity that is drawn on.*

The first step in introducing word processors should be an analysis of the needs of the office to determine whether a word processor would really expedite the work to be done. A common pitfall is an enchantment with the 'new technology' disregarding actual needs. Envisaged savings can in fact quickly be eaten up by concomitant usages to which the machine is put which are not strictly necessary. A good example of a machine creating the need is the photocopy machine. Whereas twenty years ago one or two carbon copies were often sufficient, today most documents are photocopied in many more copies than is absolutely necessary.

Word processors should not be allowed to create typing pools where none existed previously. They should be the tools of the clerical staff to be used when needed, integrated with other office duties.

No one should be made to sit at a word processor all day because:

1 it can deskill clerical workers and undermine their education and training;
2 it can lead to shift work, speed-up and a piece-rate system;
3 it will cause health problems as it creates monotonous, sedentary, fast-paced work.

As many of the office staff as possible should learn to operate the machine. No one should be made to work at a machine if not properly trained. Management often (in an attempt to save time and money) may send only one person on a training course and then expect that person to educate the others. This is a burden to the one sent on the course and unfair to those who have to receive 'second hand' instructions. Free instruction by the manufacturer for all potential operators should be a condition of the purchase.

The workforce should be kept together. 'Natural wastage' should not even be a consideration since it gives management an incentive to force people out. As positions become vacant they must be filled again.

It must be clear that anyone who is not able to work on word processing equipment for medical reasons (there are cases of eye problems and allergic reactions to the screen) must not be fired or laid off. This goes especially for older workers with weakened eyesight. Some industries in England have specified that persons over forty-five should not use VDUs (Harman, 1979). This approach sorts out people rather than eliminating occupational hazards. It is the machines that must adapt to the needs of people not vice versa.

■ The benefits of new technology

It must at all times be remembered that the *reasons*, the *goals* and *ideology* which support the introduction of technology are the basic underlying factors in determining whether the consequences will be harmful or beneficial for women clerical workers. For the new technology to have beneficial effects for women presupposes an active participation from them.

New jobs

It is projected that since microelectronic-based technology will increase productivity, it will lead to economic growth and also new jobs.

In the past, rapid technological advancement has generally been accompanied by high rates of job creation. When new technology poured forth after the Second World War the number of jobs increased and unemployment hit low levels in the industrial economies (Norman, 1980). New technology will make it possible for us to handle and exploit more information than now. This can increase jobs in the field of information usage.

New options for relocating industry and employment become possible because it is now technically feasible and sometimes economically profitable to decentralize the processing. It could create new employment opportunities in sparsely populated areas and in areas with high unemployment.

New skills

Computers have increasingly created higher-level clerical jobs both within and without the electronic data-processing unit. Lack of software skills is already seen as a bottleneck in the application of microelectronics and demands for these skills will probably increase (Hult, 1980).

Data bases and retrieval systems will require clerks to page through routine files and data banks to build up dockets of information relevant to particular problems for which their principals are engaged. This is a new form of creative and imaginative work requiring a higher calibre of staff than is needed in most clerical jobs today (Sleigh et al, 1979).

Many word processors can do much more than simple editing, for example sorting and mathematical programs can be performed. Exploring and utilizing the machines to capacity could lead to more qualified and interesting work, upgrading the operators and increasing their knowledge and control over the work process.

New organizational models

There is now the possibility of job sharing and reduced work hours for *both* men and women due to the productive gains expected from the new technology. Part-time and flexitime work for men will give them the opportunity to take a more active part in family life and will improve women's opportunities on the labour market.

Eliminating the drudgery of routine and monotonous jobs creates the possibility for a new division of labour whereby responsibility and decision making can be dealt with collectively. New systems of work organization such as small work groups will be possible.

How to realize the benefits of the new technology

It is essential that women participate in the debate and decision-making process with regard to new technology. This can be done at work, through unions and in women's groups. Women clerical workers must break their dependence on leaders to do all the thinking, and push for co-determination in the office. These goals should include the right to make decisions about how work is set up, staffing and personnel politics.

When technology breaks down traditional demarcation lines at work it is a time to suggest ways of redistributing occupations on non-sexist lines. Word processors can hook up to large central computers and can communicate with computer terminals. As the barriers between word processing and computer programming lessen women should seize their chance to get into programming and systems analysis, and take advantage of any available courses in advanced functions.

Encouraging male clerks to learn to operate word processors could be a step in the redistribution of the existing work. If previously non-typing male clerks began typing some of their own correspondence (or first drafts of manuscripts) this could be a time saver for female clerks. Such a move is extremely individual and the implications are dependent on the factors present in each separate work place.

An important step is to insist on the establishment of and participation in ad hoc committees with the task of evaluating all new technology. These committees can make suggestions for eliminating the negative results of the introduction of new equipment and for how best to exploit the benefits with special consideration for women. Training programmes should be provided in order to learn new skills which can help break down labour divisions and counteract the dead-end nature of most female clerical jobs.

Unions, although necessary in ensuring certain basic rights, support management's right to organize and distribute work. This limits what they can do. They can be counted on to help minimize the employment implications and to support health and safety measures, but must be pressured into challenging the authority of existing office hierarchies.

Permanent committees dealing with trends in technological innovations must be established in the unions. Again women must make their presence felt. The union is an excellent place to tap the collective experiences of its members, and thus discover the positive and negative applications of new technology.

Unions can be used to exert pressure on the computer industry. Manufacturers have the technology and the resources to develop safe equipment and to stop production of monitoring devices and 'prompters'.

Unions and women's groups should begin to criticize manufacturers and distributers for their sexist advertising. The majority of brochures for word processing equipment contain photographs of women *sitting down* at word processors and men, with documents in hand, *standing over them* instructing and pointing. On the other hand more advanced computer equipment inevitably features men as operators.

Technology agreements (made between unions and employers regarding guide-lines for usage of new equipment) are important tools for ensuring co-determination at the work place, they can ensure the right to information about new technology in the planning stages; participation in determining new organizational systems; and the possibility for appointing data shop stewards for this extremely important area.

Because women as a group will be disproportionately affected by the new technology it may be necessary for governments to develop policy measures for the labour market and compensatory education to help women overcome the difficulties (Hult, 1980).

■ Conclusion

Due to the rising costs of labour, the falling prices of office equipment and the supposed low productivity in the office sector, the new microprocessor-based technology is expected to change the organizational structure of the office. Women as a group will be disproportionately affected, because (except for managerial posts) clerical work is predominately women's work.

What is desperately needed now is for female clerical workers to become aware of their subordinate position on the labour market as a reflection of their position in society and the family, and to make every effort to change both.

In deciding how best the technology can help women's position in the clerical sector, female office workers cannot expect help or guidance from the firms designing the equipment, from their employers or from their unions. The technology being introduced in offices today incorporates the values and expectations of an already functioning and accepted division of labour based on sex segregation. The new technology will at best retain the status quo but threatens further to limit women's career possibilities in the office of the future. The new technology can be used in centralizing, monitoring and machine-pacing work. It could also be used to improve women's place on the job market.

Even if one is committed to finding ways of developing the liberating potential of technology, there are no existing structures or models to look to. The struggle that lies ahead requires a re-evaluation of the uses of the new technology, together with a formulation of an occupational/political ideology which will free women from boring and repetitive work in the office, instead of creating factory-like conditions which further limit the possibilities of breaking down sex segregation at work. It is fundamental for the struggle ahead that women believe that they can make an impact. The direction technology is taking today is neither unshakable nor irreversible.

> There is always a range of possibilities or alternatives that are delimited over time – as some are selected and others denied – by the social choices of those with the power to choose, choices which reflect their intentions, ideology, social position, and relations with other people in society. In short technology bears the social 'imprint' of its authors (Noble, 1979: 18-19).

Women must be made to see that they can be the 'authors'.

■ Notes

This article appeared in *Feminist Review* No. 9, 1981.

The article was originally published in Swedish as 'Med tangentvalsen mot friheten eller Kan den nya kontorstekniken frigöra kvinnora?' in *Kvinnovetenskaplig tidskrift* nummer 1-2 1981, Arg 2, Lunds Universitet.

Studies of Women's Employment

Veronica Beechey

It is now about ten years since the publication of some of the first classical texts of contemporary feminism and an immense amount of new feminist work has been accomplished in a whole number of spheres. In this article I want to look at some of the recently published studies of women's employment, and within the limited scope of what is primarily a review article, to make some assessment of how far we have progressed in developing a feminist theoretical understanding of women's place in the world of paid work. Writings on women's employment have taken a variety of forms over this period. Some experiential accounts of paid work have been published, although, given the experiential emphasis of much feminist thinking, especially in the early years of the women's liberation movement, these have been rather few in number. Statistical analyses of women's employment, many of them undertaken under the auspices of the Equal Opportunities Commission and the Department of Employment, have become more widely available. Although these are by no means adequate, as a number of critics concerned with women's employment have pointed out, they are indispensable for understanding the overall patterns of women's employment: changes in women's participation rate in the world of paid work; the distribution of women across industries and occupations; and evidence about rates of pay, hours of work and so on.

The bulk of 'mainstream' feminist writings on women's employment falls into three categories: political and educational books and pamphlets, theoretical writings and empirical case studies. Of the wide variety of broadly 'educational' material available, much of it is devised for women trade unionists: material on employment legislation, on women's place in the workforce and on women in trade unions. The more academic writings about women's paid work have veered between theoretical analyses and empirical case studies. In the early years of feminist analysis many feminists (myself included) engaged in largely theoretical work. We felt that it was necessary to clarify what concepts and theories were appropriate for a feminist understanding. We tried to use and transform the concepts which Marxists and radical economists were developing to analyse work in general, for example, the labour process, concepts of value, deskilling, the industrial reserve army of labour and the dual labour market. We also developed our own specifically feminist concepts, for example, patriarchy, production and reproduction, domestic labour and wage labour. It is still concepts derived from Marx and from radical economic analysis which form the basis of theoretical analyses of women's employment, although some writers have tried to 'marry' these with an analysis in terms of patriarchy (Hartmann, 1976 and 1979). Conceptual analysis is an indispensable part of feminist analysis, as indeed of any other kind of social enquiry, and our endeavours to clarify our concepts and theoretical frameworks were a necessary step in developing a feminist analysis of women's employment. But we may have been hampered by our preoccupation with developing a 'correct' theoretical understanding, and by our endeavours to constitute our concepts with little reference to concrete evidence about women's employment.

Over the past five years or so the prevailing emphasis of feminist studies of women's employment has shifted, and a number of case studies of women's work in particular industries, occupations and workplaces have been carried out. In this paper I discuss some of these recent studies of women's employment: Ruth Cavendish's account of assembly work in West London, *On the Line*, Anna Pollert's study of tobacco workers in Bristol, *Girls, Wives, Factory Lives*, and Judy Wacjman's analysis of the Fakenham Cooperative, *Women in Control*. I also discuss, rather more briefly, some of the essays in Jackie West's edited collection of essays entitled *Work, Women and the Labour Market*. My aim in this article is not to review comprehensively each of these texts but rather to discuss some of the empirical evidence produced by the studies and to analyse the relationship between this evidence and their more theoretical arguments. I hope through this process to begin the task of assessing some of the prevalent arguments which appear in feminist writings on women's employment, and to interrogate critically some of the concepts which are in common currency. In the concluding part of the article I shall briefly discuss two questions which are addressed in different ways in the texts: women's consciousness and occupational segregation, both of which are extremely important to any political analysis of women's employment, yet very tricky to analyse in theoretical terms.

■ On the Line

On the Line is about women's unskilled work in a car components factory. It is not an academic study of work but a kind of autobiographical account of Ruth Cavendish's experiences working on the assembly line of a London car components factory in 1977-78. Ruth Cavendish tells us that she decided to do this for mainly political reasons, one of them being to discover whether the central issues in the women's movement were relevant to working-class women. The book contains a graphic account of what it is like to do unskilled factory work, richly illustrated by Ruth Cavendish's own experience and by the contrasts she draws between her life as a white middle-class woman and the lives of the women she works with. She is well aware that her short spell of factory work and the choices open to her meant that her own experiences were quite different from theirs. We are told that the women on the line were very welcoming to Ruth, although they thought she was a bit odd to be doing assembly work when she could clearly have got a better job. Libel laws prevented Ruth Cavendish from disclosing the factory she worked in, so she has had to change the name of the factory and other details which would enable it to be recognized, to transpose it into a different section of the London labour market and to adopt a pseudonym. She comments wryly in the preface that in writing the book she learned the hard way how the libel laws in Britain inhibit freedom of speech.

UMEC, as the firm was renamed, employed about 1800 people, about 800 of them on the shop floor. Ruth Cavendish worked in the main assembly area doing assembly work. The division of labour in the assembly area follows a familiar pattern. The assembly work was highly labour intensive and was done entirely by women. The only men in the assembly area worked as chargehands, supervisors, quality controllers and progress chasers, all jobs which escaped the tyranny of the production line and which enabled the men to stand up or walk around. Women were all in the same grade as semi-skilled assemblers, except for one training woman, one woman chargehand and a few women at the lowest level of quality control. The men, in contrast, were spread throughout the grades and divided from each other by differences of skill and pay:

> You could see the differences so clearly on the shopfloor: everyone who was working was a woman, and the men in their white coats were standing around chattering, humping skips or walking about to check the number of components. It was obvious that the only qualification you needed for a better job was to be a man. (p. 79)

Even in the machine shop where both women and men worked, the women were paid at a lower rate on the grounds that they were unable to lift heavy coils of metal and had to use the services of labourers with trolleys. There was a clear division between young women and men. If you were a sixteen-year-old boy you would automatically be trained as a chargehand, whereas girls were not given the choice. The women assemblers had absolutely no prospects of moving on to other kinds of work:

> If you were a woman you could walk into the factory on your sixteenth birthday, get a job on the assembly line and stay there till you retired at sixty. There was no promotion off the line, so the highest position you could hope for would be 'reject operating', filling in when another woman was away, and mending the rejects. (p. 76)

It is hard, in a brief summary, to convey the vividness of Ruth Cavendish's description of life on the line, how the 'speeds and feeds' were set, how the machinery was organized, and to give a sense of the noise, the pace of work, the strain, the pain of learning a new job and the boredom of becoming proficient at it. The following is just one example of many vivid passages in the book:

> Differences between the jobs were minor in comparison with the speed and discipline which the line imposed on us all. We couldn't do the things you would normally not think twice about, like blowing your nose, or flicking hair out of your eyes; that cost valuable seconds – it wasn't included in the layout so no time was allowed for it. In any case, your hands were usually full. We all found the repetition hard to take; once you were in command of your job, repeating the same operations over and

over thousands of times a day made you even more aware of being controlled by the line. You couldn't take a break or swap with someone else for a change – you just had to carry on; resisting the light or the speed only made the work harder because the trays kept coming and eventually you would have to work your way through the pile-up. If you really couldn't keep up with the line, you were out. (p. 41)

At UMEC women ran the line but were mere appendages of it, and their views were never taken into account in changing the line – new designs and machinery were introduced with no regard for those working them. Discipline was imposed through the light, the conveyor belt and the bonus system, and women were slotted in like cogs in a wheel.

The book explores the question of class and the nature of divisions within the working class, and a major emphasis is on divisions of gender, race and ethnicity. The assembly area was largely comprised of immigrant women – about 70 per cent were Irish, 20 per cent were West Indian, and the remaining 10 per cent were Asian, apparently from Gujerat in the west of India. Practically all of them had immigrated into England, and they had usually got their jobs at UMEC through personal contacts, and frequently through relatives.

Ruth Cavendish was also interested in the culture of the workforce. She portrays this as a culture almost entirely separate from men, both at work and outside. Almost the only contact between women and men at work was through supervision and the authority structure and this took a highly sexist and patronizing form with the men calling the women 'dear' and 'girls'. Relationships between the women were generally friendly and supportive. The women would help each other when someone got behind with her work, and there were strong friendships which cut across ethnic groupings. The women discussed the newspapers and television, and topics like marriage, abortion, and children. The UMEC women saw family and home as the most important things in their lives. Ruth Cavendish interprets this 'familial' orientation in narrowly materialist terms. She argues that the women had no choice but to get married as their wages were too low for a single person to support herself. Most of the married women depended upon their husbands for a basic living and the single women had to take a second job like cleaning or working in a bar which they could do after work in the evenings.

The UMEC women were negative about the union's activities in the factory. There was a closed shop operating, but the women said they never knew what was going on and that they only learned about decisions after these had affected them. Union officials were seen as part of the firm's authority structure, alongside management, and as equally remote from the women. Most of the women were in favour of the union, sometimes saying that they, the women on the line, *were* the union. They were reluctant to take up a shop steward's post as they feared sticking their necks out and being let down by everyone else. In a dispute about a productivity deal which occurred while Ruth Cavendish was working at the factory, there was apparently immense solidarity among the women, but the eventual defeat due to the divide and rule tactics of the management left the women demoralized.

What to make of it? In her concluding chapter Ruth Cavendish reflects on what she learned about class and about women's employment from working in the factory. She argues that class should be understood as a relation between labour and capital, but that within the very broad category called 'labour' there are immense divisions. At UMEC there was no *common* experience of shop floor work. There was a division between those who ran the line and those who were run by it which was reinforced by divisions of sex and race. Ruth Cavendish argues that the most prominent division was that between men and women workers, and that the differences between women and men seemed to over-ride the similarities. There were ethnic divisions among both male and female workers. Relationships between the women of different ethnic groups are portrayed as congenial and non-conflictual although we are told that in the period of increased intensity of work after the dispute the women divided into their different ethnic groupings, and blamed each other.

Ruth Cavendish also addresses the question of politics. She argues that the women's movement has been relatively unable to appeal to women like those at UMEC because of its emphasis on 'alternative' lifestyles and conceptions. For the UMEC workforce it was hard to change anything when the nexus of work, low pay and home remained so tightly linked. She suggests that more practical demands are necessary to meet the immediate needs of women at factories like UMEC, like shortening the working week, better nursery provision, shops staying open later, fighting equal pay cases, demanding job opportunities for girls. She also argues for a new relationship between intellectuals and the working class, something which she clearly attained, at least momentarily, on the line at UMEC.

In assessing *On the Line* it is important to bear in mind that Ruth

Cavendish is not claiming to provide a general analysis of women's employment, but rather to make sense of her own experiences at UMEC. Nevertheless, several of her arguments about women's employment warrant closer examination as they raise more general questions.

The book's major theoretical argument is concerned with analysing divisions within the working class. Ruth Cavendish asserts that everyone was part of the working class in the sense that they sold their labour power in exchange for a wage, but the different groups were in different relations to production according to their place in the division of labour. This, she suggests, has implications for the ways in which surplus value was extracted from them. The basis of these differentiations lies in the conditions in which different groups sell their labour power. According to Ruth Cavendish women and immigrants sell their labour power under much less favourable conditions than skilled white men. Women have fewer formal skills to offer and a less valuable sort of labour power to sell due to their responsibilities for childrearing and for domestic labour. They are also less available and less mobile than men. People entering the labour market from overseas, she suggests, also have fewer skills to offer and their labour power is less valuable because they often have not been educated and trained in skills which they could use in England. Ruth Cavendish's principal argument is that the division of labour within the production process presupposes the existence of different types of labour power with different degrees of skill and training, and the production process is based upon, and reinforces, these divisions. She makes the very important point that there was no *inherent* need for the assembly work at UMEC to be labour intensive, but suggests that because there was an available supply of people (women and immigrants) who would work for low wages there was little incentive for UMEC to modernize its production process. I think this is an important argument because it suggests that the tendency (which, as Peter Armstrong's essay in *Work, Women and the Labour Market* tells us, is quite general in British manufacturing industry) for women to work in unskilled, labour-intensive and low-paying occupations is not inevitable.

The question of *why* women work in such occupations then becomes a problem to be explained. The literature on sexual divisions within the labour market is quite sharply divided between those which emphasize employers' demand for different types of labour power, and who therefore lay stress on the demand for labour, and those which emphasize labour supply. Despite the fact that most of *On the Line* concentrates upon the division of labour and women's experience of work within the production process itself, Ruth Cavendish ends up, in her more general theoretical chapter, by emphasizing that women (and immigrants) sell their labour power on the labour market in different conditions from those in which white men sell their labour power. She thus emphasizes the question of labour supply. This, in my view, is problematic. It renders the analysis of sexual divisions within the production process close to being tautological because it explains the situation of women workers almost entirely in terms of the fact that women's labour power is different from men's because of women's familial responsibilities. Thus, women's absence from skilled jobs is explained in terms of women's lack of skills. Curiously, I think that Ruth Cavendish's own analysis of the production process is weakened because, in placing so much weight on the conditions in which women sell their labour power, she pays insufficient attention to the construction of women's and men's jobs *within the production process itself*.

Ruth Cavendish's analysis of ethnic and racial divisions within the labour force is also problematic because it is couched solely in terms of the situation of immigrants and the disadvantages they suffer in entering the labour market. At a superficial level this formulation is legitimate because Ruth Cavendish tells us that she didn't meet any Black British women at UMEC. However, I think there are some problems with this formulation which I want briefly to indicate.

First, I think Ruth Cavendish is mistaken in talking about 'immigrants' as an undifferentiated category in her theoretical chapter. It would have been better if she had analysed the specific situation of immigrant women and if she had discussed whether the conditions in which they sell their labour power are different from the conditions in which immigrant men and non-immigrant women sell their labour power. Second, while it may be legitimate in the case of UMEC to analyse ethnic differences in terms of the situation of immigrant workers, this framework is not appropriate for analysing ethnic divisions more generally, because many Irish, West Indian and Indian women have been born and educated in Britain. Any more general framework for analysing race and ethnicity would need to discuss the ways in which the situation of different groups of British women is similar, and the extent to which it is different because of the operation of institutional racism which operates both within the labour process, and in the education system, training schemes and so on.

This brings me to my final point which concerns Ruth Cavendish's analysis of the women's consciousness. She cites evidence in *On the*

Line that the UMEC women saw themselves primarily as housewives and mothers, and she interprets these familial orientations as a result of the women's low wages which make marriage an inevitability, on the one hand, and as a response to the alienating nature of the women's work on the other hand. This interpretation differs from most feminist interpretations in two important respects. First, whereas most feminist writings emphasize the role of ideology in determining women's consciousness, Ruth Cavendish emphasizes material factors. Second, while many feminists assert that women's consciousness is determined by the family (whether this is defined in ideological or material terms) Ruth Cavendish emphasizes the role of the production process in determining the women's consciousness. In part I think Ruth Cavendish is right in emphasizing the material basis of the women's experience, and her insistence on the tight link between women's employment, low pay and the sexual division of labour in the family is a welcome corrective to studies which analyse women's consciousness solely in terms of ideology. In part, however, I think the absence of any analysis of ideology in her writings is problematic because she is ultimately unable to explain why the women's consciousness took a familial form rather than some other form. As I hope will become evident in the course of this paper, feminist studies of women's consciousness of themselves as workers are still in their infancy, and we have hardly begun to develop the conceptual framework which might help us to explain this.

I do not wish these critical comments to detract from the importance of Ruth Cavendish's book. *On the Line* is an interesting, vivid and perceptive analysis which is a significant contribution to our understanding of women's factory work. It is instructive to compare both the analysis and the evidence with the next study I want to discuss, *Girls, Wives, Factory Lives*, which is concerned with unskilled manual work at Churchmans tobacco factory in Bristol.

■ Girls, Wives, Factory Lives

In 1972 when Anna Pollert did her research Churchmans was part of the Imperial Tobacco Group. Like Ruth Cavendish, Anna Pollert spent some months at the factory, but she did not work on the line. She describes her research strategy as 'interventionist research', which involved arguing with and challenging the workers as well as observing work and interviewing the women and some of the men. She contrasts this with the more detached participant observation commonly used by sociologists. Anna Pollert wanted to explore the similarities between women and men when both are selling their labour power to a capitalist employer, and also to explore what is distinctive about women's wage labour and to examine how women's gender socialization and specific oppression enter into their experience of exploitation. She decided to study women factory workers because she thought that women's and men's experience of factory work could be directly compared and the effects of gender oppression on women's working experience examined.

A familiar picture of occupational segregation sets the scene. The Churchmans women worked in labour-intensive jobs – weighing, packing, stripping and spinning – while the men worked in highly mechanized jobs like moisturing, blending and cutting. Women and men rarely worked alongside each other on the same jobs, or even in the same department. Like so much women's factory work, the Churchmans women did work which was deadly monotonous and required competencies which escaped classification as skilled, for example weighing:

> Straight-line weighing needed finger tip precision and flying speed. Credited with manual dexterity, yet not qualifying as skilled; fiddly, delicate, women's work, somehow an attribute of femininity. (p. 30)

Despite the introduction of a common grading structure for women and men in 1972 and a timetable to achieve equal pay by 1975, the majority of women at Churchmans were in the four lowest job groups, and three-quarters were in the lowest three. Every job had its prescribed rate, and to keep up with this required perfect economy of movement.

Two-thirds of the Churchmans women were young single women. Of the remaining third who were married, about half had school-aged children and the rest were in their forties and fifties and had worked for Churchmans for a long time. Only two of the women had children under school age. Anna Pollert ascribes the relatively small numbers of married women (especially those with young children) to the absence of part-time work.

The atmosphere was steeped with male stereotypes about women, held both by the men and by the women themselves, and in Part Two Anna Pollert explores the women's 'commonsense' in some detail. These chapters are in my opinion the best in the book. First she considers men's attitudes towards women. The men generally thought that the women's place was in the home, or perhaps in a 'feminine' job like nursing. As factory workers the women were considered awkward, superfluous, or downright problems. The men had firm ideas as to what constituted women's work in the factory: it was routine, repetitive, fiddly, low-grade work. They thought the women should be paid less because they had babies, and were inferior, and because they worked for pin-money and didn't really need adequate wages. The women's consciousness is represented as fragmentary and contradictory. The women rejected the myth that their place was in the home, and were fully aware that the reasons they worked were primarily financial. Yet they thought of themselves as dependent upon a man, and conceived of their pay a marginal to a man's – this despite the fact that two thirds of the female workforce was young and single! The women did not think they had a right to a job. They did, however, have a strong sense of their place in the sexual hierarchy at work. They were angry at male mechanics who visibly sat around but who earned twice as much as they did, and insulted those who suggested that they enjoyed doing boring work or were stupid. The book deals separately with the consciousness of the young women and older married women, and I found the analysis of young women's consciousness particularly illuminating. Anna Pollert argues that low status unskilled manual work confirms the deprecatory self-perception of women as patient, passive and inferior, fit only for the mundane tasks of assembly work and housework. Unlike young men who, as Paul Willis has shown, (1977), can turn the prevailing cultural values on their head and transform manual work into a culture of machismo, the young women could only treat unskilled manual labour as an affirmation of their own worthlessness. They therefore sought refuge in romance, and looked to a career in marriage as a total alternative to the daily grind of being treated as a factor of production. The older women, crushed and split between home and workplace, still felt themselves to be primarily housewives. Even if they worked throughout their lives, they sympathized with the young women's focus on marriage as a life solution and reinforced the young women's identification with the roles of housewife and mother. A shared female identity along the continuum of stages in the lifecycle is thereby revealed.

Anna Pollert was on the look-out for signs of resistance, and found some against sexual oppression at work: escape, bending the rules, mucking in, laughs, sexy bravado and biting wit. There was defiance, particularly among the older women, who openly challenged their superiors. She suggests that the older women treated their male superiors in primarily familial terms:

> Playing at turning the tables, being intimately personal as they might be with their sons, or husbands, were the older women's style of self-assertion. (p. 154)

However, she goes on, they did not really alter the power relations:

> even if they could be taken seriously as 'more mature' and 'responsible' than young girls on one level, at another their criticisms could be patronizingly interpreted as no more than the nagging of housewives. Once more they were assimilated into the patriarchial ideology of conciliatory permissive management – but luckily, without the stranglehold of sexual conquest. Their collusion of course, was with the role of housewife, not that of sex object. (p. 154)

The study has a number of interesting accounts of the ways in which relations between (male) supervisors and (female) assemblers took a patriarchal form.

Anna Pollert found little evidence of shopfloor organization and control. Churchmans did have a union and 90 per cent of the workforce was unionized. The women's relationship to their union was similar to the UMEC women's: membership was purely formal, the union was bureaucratic and inhospitable, and the shop stewards were all men. Here again the description of the women's attitudes is the most interesting. The women were not anti-union, but they expressed the anti-union prejudices of a right-wing press. They were dissatisfied with their own union, yet hostile and resentful towards better organized workers (dockers and car workers in 1972). Anna Pollert suggests that the women's experiences of trade unionism confirmed their sense of belonging to another (female) world. The younger women were unlikely to engage in activity which they saw as generationally and sexually alien, while the older women received a stream of conflicting messages. On the one hand they were told they were second-rate workers who should really stay at home, and on the other that they should be better trade unionists. Caught between the two, they blamed themselves. Anna Pollert interprets the women's alienation from trade unionism as a combination of passivity and fatalism, which she sees as a common class sentiment, and the extra exclusion from public life which women experience due to their association with the home. There were brief flashes of activity when the women tried to fight the introduction of a new productivity scheme, when confronted with redundancies, and in a one-day company-wide strike over a national wage claim. When the strike failed, apparently due to lack of rank and file involvement and control, compromise by union leaders and eventual betrayal, there was confusion and demoralization and a deepening of disillusion. The women fell back on to common scapegoatist beliefs about Blacks, the unemployed, dockers, scroungers and layabouts.

Girls, Wives, Factory Lives is an interesting study of women's factory work, and the analysis of the women's consciousness is particularly illuminating. There are some major theoretical and political problems with the book, however, which I shall briefly discuss. First, there is a serious hiatus between the book's theoretical arguments and the detailed empirical research. This is a common problem with empirical research as it is difficult to provide a nuanced account of the social world and at the same time make hard and fast theoretical propositions about it. It is, however, a particularly serious problem in this study, with the result that the evidence I have so far discussed has little bearing on the theoretical propositions advanced. One area which is theoretically problematic is the analysis of exploitation and oppression, in order to separate out the distinctiveness of class and gender components of women's experience as workers. It does not, however, succeed in this aim. Anna Pollert adopts a conventional Marxist conception of male workers, assumes that men's experience is different because of the effects of oppression, whose roots lie in the home and which 'follows women to work'.

I think there are two problems with this formulation. The first is methodological. Anna Pollert did interview some men workers at Churchmans, and she makes occasional comments about the ways in which men, too, can be family-centred. However, the main emphasis of *Girls, Wives, Factory Lives* is on the distinctiveness of the women's experiences, which Anna Pollert often describes and interprets very interestingly. It is this emphasis on the distinctiveness of the women's experiences, however, which creates problems for Anna Pollert's analysis, because she never systematically compares the experiences of the men and women workers. This means that, in the end, she is unable to tease out the effects of exploitation and oppression.

My second objection is conceptual. Anna Pollert never actually defines what she means by exploitation, but I assume that she refers to the process by which surplus value is extracted at the point of production. She outlines what she means by oppression in the following passage:

> the roots of women's oppression lie in their segregation and isolation as mothers outside the social relations of production. Today this is expressed in their sexual oppression and their economic dependence in marriage – which is reinforced ideologically and by the state. (p. 3)

Thus, according to Anna Pollert, oppression is rooted in structures outside the production process, and ultimately in the family, whereas exploitation has its foundation in the production process. I think this formulation is problematic because it pays no attention to the ways in which gender divisions are constructed within the production process itself.

Furthermore, while it may be analytically possible to distinguish between exploitation and oppression I personally do not consider this to be a very useful strategy for analysing either women's or men's paid work. It seems to me that both women and men enter the labour market and sell their labour power as gendered beings, and both are set to work within labour processes in which men's and women's occupations are clearly demarcated. If we want to analyse the similarities and differences between women's and men's work, as Anna Pollert does, we need to use the same model for both sexes and to ask questions about gender with respect to both men and women workers.

Churchmans closed in 1974. The workforce was given the option of redundancy money or redeployment. According to company records about half the workforce opted for redundancy money and half for redeployment. Anna Pollert tried to trace the Churchmans workforce in 1979. She found that of the forty women whom she managed to trace, twenty had left, either to marry or to find other 'short-term' jobs before the voluntary redundancy scheme was introduced, and of the remaining twenty, ten went for redundancy and ten were redeployed at Wills (although five of these left after three months to take redundancy pay and two to get married). This, she argues, is evidence that the women workers comprised an industrial reserve army of labour.

The industrial reserve army thesis has often been used by feminists to analyse women's employment, but this too is problematic. This is partly because the theory is often imprecisely specified *qua* theory and partly because it is hard to operationalize it so that it can be used in empirical research. In a useful article on the industrial reserve army of labour, Irene Bruegel (this volume) points out that Marx developed his industrial reserve army thesis to show how the expansion of capitalism inevitably drew more and more people into a labour reserve of potential, marginal and transitory employment. Many feminists, she points out, have given the thesis a somewhat different meaning. They have used it to suggest that women workers are more disposable than men, particularly in periods of recession ('the hypothesis of greater disposibility') and to suggest that women are therefore functional for capital. Two recent articles by feminists (Perkins, 1983 and Mayo, 1983) have criticized aspects of this version of the industrial reserve army thesis. Teresa Perkins questions whether women are among the first to leave the labour force in periods of recession because of their reserve army status, while Marjorie Mayo argues that employers use a variety of different strategies to restructure the labour process in periods of recession. It is beyond the scope of this paper to go into a general discussion of the industrial reserve army thesis, and of the ways in which it may or may not be useful for feminist analysis. For the moment I wish to focus upon the disposability thesis because this is the meaning which Anna Pollert gives to the industrial reserve army concept.

In my view Anna Pollert's arguments are not substantiated by the evidence which she discusses. At one level she is suggesting that women comprised an industrial reserve army of labour for Churchmans as a firm because the women lost their jobs, and many left the labour market. This, however, cannot be taken as evidence that women are more disposable than men because when the closure occurred *both women and men* were affected and both were offered redundancy or redeployment. There is no sense in which the *women* as a special group were selected for redundancy, as has happened to part-time women in some companies. Anna Pollert also suggests that women comprise a reserve army of labour at the level of the economy in general. However, neither her evidence nor the evidence of Irene Breugel (on which she bases her arguments) supports this claim (as Irene Bruegel herself is well aware). It is clear that the loss of women's jobs in manufacturing industry was greater than the loss of men's between 1951 and 1976, but this was compensated for by an increase, both absolute and relative, in women's jobs in the service sectors of the economy. Anna Pollert suggests that this pattern may well be reversed by public expenditure cuts and the introduction of new technology in the office, but she does not provide evidence to support this claim. For the period she is primarily concerned with (up to 1978) the available evidence does not support the claim that women as a group were disposed of to a greater extent than men within the economy in general, although they may have been within particular manufacturing industries. Anna Pollert also argues that it is part-time workers who conform most closely to the model of the industrial reserve army of labour. Here she relies upon Irene Breugel's evidence that part-timers have been made to bear the brunt of the decline in employment. However, Irene Breugel's arguments are disputable if the distribution of women part-timers within the economy as a whole is taken into account. While part-time women were clearly disposed of in preference to men in certain manufacturing industries (for example, electrical engineering) in the mid 1970s, this was not the case in other industries (for example, professional and scientific services, miscellaneous services and public administration) nor in the economy as a whole, where part-time employment has increased, becoming, in Teresa Perkins' words, 'a new form of employment' (1983). Here again, I think Anna Pollert is using a theoretical framework which is not appropriate for the evidence she describes.

A similar tendency appears in the political conclusions to the book which many feminists would disagree with. Anna Pollert asserts that the Churchmans women need to develop 'good sense' in place of the 'common sense' which she has described in the book. By 'good sense' she means

> a coherent view of the world arrived at through a socialist critique and self-activity; for the working-class majority of women, both a feminist and a working-class view. (p. 231)

I think this statement embodies a crude (and therefore inadequate) way of thinking about ideology, and an unsatisfactory way of thinking about politics. One of the strengths of Gramsci's conception of 'commonsense' (a conception which Anna Pollert seems to be adopting in her concrete chapters) is that it draws attention to the fact that 'commonsense' is 'an ambiguous, contradictory and multiform concept' (Gramsci, 1971), rooted in the practicalities of everyday life. It is an oversimplification of Gramsci's view to assume that this can be juxtaposed to a coherent 'correct' form of thought called 'good sense'. It is also bad politics. Just as Gramsci argued that people had to be 'won' to socialist politics, it is critical for feminists to try and 'win' women to feminist politics. It is curious that *Girls, Wives, Factory Lives* provides a lot of evidence of the separate spheres of women and men, and of the familial orientations of the women, and yet concludes by arguing that 'a separate women's movement offers [the women] no solutions' (p. 240), and that struggles at the point of production are all important. Like *On the Line*, Anna Pollert's study contains some interesting empirical evidence and many perceptive analyses. Its general arguments are marred, however, by their lack of relationship to the evidence she discusses and to the more specific interpretations developed throughout the book. I shall return to some of her more general arguments about consciousness at the end of this article. Meanwhile, I want to discuss Judy Wacjman's analysis of her Fakenham Co-operative, *Women in Control*.

■ Women in control

Given the evidence from studies like Ruth Cavendish's and Anna Pollert's that women are inadequately represented by trade unions, I was pleased to discover that Judy Wacjman's book on the Fakenham Co-operative had been published. Since co-operatives are popular among both Tories (who think of them as another form of small business) and the left (who variously see them as experiments in industrial democracy, prefigurative forms of work organization, or full-scale workers' control) I was glad of the opportunity to learn a bit more about one group of women's attempt to form a co-operative, and I picked the book up hoping that a different story of women's consciousness and of their endeavours to change their situation would emerge.

Women in Control is the story of a Norfolk shoe factory which became a co-operative through the collective action of the women who worked there. Judy Wacjman spent several months doing participant observation at Fakenham, 'helping out', observing the work organization, talking to the women and conducting formal interviews with the women and their husbands. An early chapter in the book provides a history of the co-operative movement which is indispensable to those who are as ignorant about co-operatives as I am. It is also important in understanding the specific history of Fakenham.

Fakenham is a small Norfolk country town, in a highly agricultural area which has little industry and has low-paying jobs for both women and men. Most women need a job and a wife's income is indispensable to the family. Yet, there is little choice of available jobs and a severe shortage of part-time work. With little industry and a contracting labour market, high unemployment has been an ongoing part of

Fakenham's history, and job insecurity a recurring theme. Most of the women at Fakenham Enterprises (as the co-operative was called) had a history of low-paid, irregular and unpleasant work either in factories (in food-processing plants, clothing or shoe manufacture) or as shop assistants, waitresses, domestic servants or agricultural workers.

Fakenham Enterprises was set up in 1972 when the workforce of a satellite factory of a Norwich shoe firm was closed down because it was not profitable. Judy Wacjman lays great emphasis on the economic situation of the factory when it closed and she argues that this is crucial to understanding its subsequent history. The salient facts are that it was an unprofitable factory in a declining industry. It had never produced whole shoes, but had been predominantly the 'closing' room for the main factory. The women at the factory had used sewing machines to close the shoe uppers, and the machines were geared only to this single stage of shoe manufacture. The Fakenham factory was totally dependent upon the Norwich factory for its existence. Shoe uppers were delivered from Norwich pre-cut and returned there for completion. Furthermore, the administrative, managerial and marketing sections and machine repairs were all housed at Norwich.

Much of *Women in Control* is a narrative account of the history of Fakenham Enterprises after the company had closed and the workforce was threatened with redundancy. It is impossible even to summarize this account here as it is both detailed and complicated. Some of the important points to emerge are the following. The women working at Fakenham decided to occupy the factory when another company took over Sextons, the parent company, but not the Fakenham factory, and the union (the National Union of the Footwear, Leather and Allied Trades) accepted this. Despite being under severe pressure from NUFLAT and the employment office, a fluctuating core of twelve women maintained the occupation for eighteen weeks. They made substantial attempts to democratize the workplace, made real changes towards more collective decision-making, and shared skills and work tasks. The co-operative had difficulties finding adequate finance, a marketable product and competent management, and had to depend on external finance, imported management, and contract work. There were conflicts between the women and outsiders and among the women themselves, and tensions grew as the financial situation worsened. Eventually, the co-operative collapsed and Fakenham once again became a factory doing outwork.

As well as telling the story of Fakenham Enterprises, Judy Wajcman analyses the women's relationships to their work at the co-operative.

She argues that the Fakenham women could be divided into two groups, those who worked part-time (six hours a day) and those who worked full-time (eight hours a day), and that the workforce was polarized between these two groups. They were all paid wages at the standard rate and they all did the same kind of work, yet the two groups had very different kinds of commitment to the co-operative.

The eight-hour group was able to play the most active and central role in the co-operative. The women in this group were single, or if married, were either childless or had children who were economically independent: they were thus free from childcare and relatively free of financial pressures. Judy Wacjman suggests that this group needed to work but could survive periods of low pay with less hardship than the others (although I doubt whether this is true of the single women). Work, she asserts, played an important part in this group of women's lives and they identified with the factory, frequently making sacrifices and working extra time without pay. They saw the six-hour group as being uncommitted to the co-operative, ignoring, it is suggested, the constraints operating on mothers of young children. The six-hour group, in contrast, had been unable to take part in the original occupation. The women in this group had a very different kind of commitment to the co-operative as it was the only kind of work which allowed them to fit their work in with children's school hours and school holidays, and which enabled them to bring their children to work. At a certain point when pressure was put on them to work full-time they were torn between their need for part-time work and the likelihood that Fakenham would collapse if they refused to work full-time. Their potential for fuller involvement, it is suggested, was circumscribed by the combined constraints of children and financial strain.

These different kinds of commitment are interpreted in *Women in Control* as a result of what is broadly called 'the domestic economy'. This is different, according to Judy Wajcman, at different stages of the lifecycle. She suggests that in families with young children the financial pressures were strongest, yet children placed limits on the women's capacity to participate in the labour force. In families whose children had left home, in contrast, both kinds of constraints were less. I think that Judy Wacjman's emphasis on lifestyles is extremely important. It suggests that women's involvement in the labour force is subject to material constraints which lie outside the labour process. Judy Wacjman also asserts that in both kinds of family the husband's wage packet was seen as providing subsistence while the wife's wages were regarded as supplementary, an ideology which she suggests was reinforced by the common allocation of money within the family.

Like Anna Pollert, Judy Wacjman examined the women's consciousness. She wanted to find out how far their experience of the co-operative affected their consciousness of themselves. She shows that the women's consciousness of themselves as workers was fairly contradictory. The founding members identified with the co-operative, seeing it as a bit like a family business, while those who joined later treated it more like any other job (although one whose flexible hours were appreciated). All the women were union members but the union never had much of a presence within the factory and never took the occupation seriously. The women were largely disenchanted with the union, but, like the Churchmans women, their views about unions in general were contradictory. They were ready to mouth clichés about unions having too much power, causing strikes and being responsible for inflation, yet they nearly all agreed with their husbands' view that 'workers need strong unions to fight for their interests'.

On a broader front, the Fakenham women generally shared the belief that women's primary duty is to the family and they fully identified with motherhood. Interestingly, despite having established close and loyal friendships at work which did not find expression outside the workplace, the women viewed their fellow workers as wives and mothers – a view which was reinforced by their husbands' attitudes towards their wages. One consequence of this ideology of domesticity, according to Judy Wacjman, was that the women's experience of working at Fakenham didn't profoundly alter relationships within the family. It also didn't alter their wider political attitudes which remained generally conservative.

Judy Wacjman concludes that the Fakenham women were doubly oppressed, as women and as workers, yet they seemed to subscribe to opinions which justified their oppression. She criticizes the view that this resulted from false consciousness, and the widely-held dominant ideology thesis, for implying that people carry around a fixed and coherent set of ideas in their heads. Dual consciousness theory, she argues, goes some way towards explaining the apparently contradictory nature of the women's consciousness *vis-à-vis* male domination. However, this too emphasizes attitudes and values and fails to deal adequately with social and practical experiences, she suggests. In developing her own theory of consciousness Judy Wacjman shifts the focus on to the women's powerlessness. Like Prandy (1979) she suggests that 'it is those who exercise least control over their lives [who] are most likely to adopt an attitude towards society of its national "givenness".'

The question of control becomes central to Judy Wacjman's analysis, and her principal argument is that the problems the Fakenham women faced did not lie within their control. They tried to transform a business failure in a harsh economic environment. From her analysis of Fakenham she suggests that women, the most exploited members of the working class, are constrained in their participation in the world of paid work by the domestic economy, and that their experience of employment makes them particularly unsuitable for running a co-operative. Her conclusions are deeply pessimistic, both about the effects of the experience of Fakenham on the women's consciousness and about the possibilities of co-operatives providing a satisfactory alternative to capitalist forms of enterprise. Sadly, the story of Fakenham (fascinating as it is in Judy Wacjman's account) is not more optimistic about the possibilities of change than the other studies I have discussed in this paper.

I want to conclude by mentioning three problems with the book. The first is that the numbers of women in Judy Wacjman's study were tiny. The core group of the occupation was only twelve women, and even the whole group was not really large enough to provide a basis for the generalizations Judy Wacjman makes. The second problem is that Judy Wacjman interprets the women's experience of the co-operative and their conflict with each other in entirely familial terms. It is difficult to judge from the evidence presented whether the conflict could have been interpreted in other terms – for instance in terms of different views about how best to survive in a harsh economic climate – but I would have liked to see this question of alternative interpretations discussed (even if ultimately discounted). My third point concerns the book's analysis of the women's consciousness. Here again I think Judy Wacjman is making general theoretical claims which are not really justified. Like Anna Pollert, she cites interesting empirical evidence. She shows that the women's consciousness was fragmented and contradictory, that some of the full-time women were affected by their experience of working in the co-operative, and yet their consciousness of sexual divisions more generally and of wider social and political questions was hardly touched, but her theoretical arguments do not grasp the complexity of consciousness which she describes. I think Judy Wacjman is right when she criticizes the dominant ideology and dual consciousness theses for overemphasizing attitudes and values and for failing to deal with practical experience.

However, in emphasizing the ideology of domesticity and in giving weight, within her theory, only to the women's experiences within the family, she loses sight of the contradictoriness of the women's work consciousness, and of the ways in which (as she says herself) some of them *were* affected by working in the co-operative.

Two themes run through the texts which I have discussed in this article. The first concerns women's consciousness of themselves as workers. The second is occupational segregation. In the remainder of this article I try to draw together some of the arguments I have made, and to raise some questions about feminist analysis of these tricky issues. At certain points in the argument (where relevant) I shall also discuss some of the essays in *Work, Women and the Labour Market*.

■ Women's work consciousness

The question of women's consciousness arises in one way or another in each of the texts I have discussed, and all the studies have produced some very interesting evidence about women's consciousness. There are certain similarities between the studies. All the studies represent women's consciousness as being fragmented and contradictory. They all reveal elements of what might be called a work consciousness among the women, but in every study this is shown to co-exist with a primarily familial definition of the women's consciousness.

Ruth Cavendish, for instance, describes a strong culture operating among the women at UMEC and a strong commitment to the union. This co-exists, according to her analysis, with a strongly familial orientation. The Churchmans women, too, are depicted as having contradictory consciousness, on the one hand hostile to men's privileges within the workplace and resentful at their paternalism, and on the other hand escaping into romance and strongly committed to marriage and domesticity. Similarly the Fakenham women (or at least the full-time ones) seem to have been affected in their work consciousness by their experience in setting up the co-operative but, according to Judy Wacjman, their consciousness of the sexual division of labour and their wider political consciousness did not seem to have been affected. They, like the Churchmans women, seem to hold contradictory attitudes towards trade unions.

Despite the extremely interesting concrete discussion in each of the texts, I do not think that any of them has a satisfactory theoretical framework for analysing the women's work consciousness. Furthermore, I think that the theoretical concepts used tend to oversimplify the question of consciousness rather than grasping the complexity of the women's consciousness at the level of theory. Thus Ruth Cavendish discounts the role of ideology in structuring the women's experience, since she sees experience as a direct product of the material conditions of the women's work. Anna Pollert does not take cognizance of the women's contradictory consciousness within her broader theoretical framework, and she seems to think that the women's consciousness is somehow deficient. And despite her endeavours to develop a more sophisticated analysis of the women's consciousness, Judy Wacjman, too, loses sight of its contradictory nature in her general theoretical arguments because she places so much weight on the ideology of domesticity.

We have hardly begun to develop an adequate conceptual framework for analysing women's work consciousness, and I cannot pretend to have got very far in thinking about this question myself. Nevertheless, I want to conclude this section by making a number of general observations. The first thing to note is that feminist studies of women's employment, like Marxist studies of employment more generally, have placed a lot of emphasis on the question of consciousness. This is for obvious political reasons, for it is assumed that if women are to act to change their situation they need to understand that the present state of affairs is unsatisfactory, and that things could be different.

My second point is that I think that feminist analysis is in danger of setting up an 'ideal-type' feminist consciousness, and assuming that if women do not express this themselves, then their consciousness is somehow reactionary. This is precisely what Anna Pollert does in juxtaposing 'good sense' to 'common sense', but the problem also exists more widely. Just as Marxist studies of class consciousness which set up an 'ideal-type' model of class consciousness often overlook ways in which workers may have a limited and fragmentary consciousness of themselves at work, so feminist studies which adopt a similar approach are in danger of missing important aspects of women's consciousness which may well be positive but which do not fit neatly into the theoretical model which has been constructed.

Third, I think there exists a tendency in a number of feminist writings to see women's consciousness as entirely separate from men's, and to think of women's consciousness as being rooted in the family while men's consciousness is rooted in the labour process. Marilyn Porter's extremely interesting essay in *Work, Women and the Labour Market* is a good example of this tendency. She summarizes her basic argument in the following passage:

This paper shows how the ideas that women have about work and collective action are currently related both to their ideas and to their experience of the material reality of their place in the family. Class consciousness is constructed within the specific context of people's experience. This means, among other things, that we cannot 'read off' women's position, ideas or consciousness from men's. Women's experience of work is significantly different to that of men, and I want to suggest that that difference rests upon a sexual division of labour rooted, outside work, in the family. (p. 117)

This simple proposition, however, raises a number of questions which need to be addressed. What do we understand by the term 'consciousness'? Is there such a thing as 'women's consciousness'? Is women's consciousness essentially the same as men's or different from it? If women's consciousness is different from men's, how can we account for the differences? How can we develop a framework for analysing consciousness which is appropriate to women?

In the rest of her paper she analyses the consciousness of a group of married women with dependent children, none of whom had full-time jobs and all of whom were dependent on their husband's wage. She shows how the women's consciousness of themselves as workers is mediated through their role as housewives, and in a particularly interesting passage suggests that women also relate to their husband's work as housewives. I found Marilyn Porter's analysis extremely interesting. It shows how one group of women experienced both their own and their husband's paid work and it shows how the women's consciousness is rooted in the practicalities of their everyday lives. As a general framework of analysis, however, it is problematic. There are two reasons for this. The first is theoretical. I think it is wrong to accept unquestioningly the distinction between the public and private spheres and the association of men with the public and women with the private which is constructed within the dominant ideology. We need instead to allow for the possibility that both women's and men's consciousness of themselves as workers is affected by both their workplace and their familial experiences. This is not to say that women's and men's consciousness is the same. Far from it. But it is to say that we need to use similar concepts to analyse both women's and men's consciousness, and not to use 'familial' concepts to analyse women, and 'workplace' concepts to analyse men. Only then will we have a sound theoretical basis for analysing both the differences and similarities between women's and men's consciousness.

My second objection to Marilyn Porter's analysis is primarily methodological. Marilyn Porter asserts that her group of women constitutes the 'paradigm situation of all women in capitalist society' (Porter, 1982: 118). Yet it is clear from a footnote that her sample is quite specific. For a start it is part of a sample of couples drawn from a fibreboard factory in Bristol where all the men worked, and is thus drawn from the *men's* place of work. Furthermore, the group of women has quite distinctive characteristics. They are all married, they all have dependent children under sixteen, they are all dependent on their husband's wage and none of them works full-time. Given the ways in which the sample was drawn and the social and demographic characteristics of the women in question, it is hardly surprising that Marilyn Porter found extensive evidence of domestic ideology. It is quite possible, given the evidence from the other studies I have discussed, that Marilyn Porter's conclusions would have more general validity. It seems equally possible, however, that women's work consciousness varies at different points in the life cycle, as Angela Coyle suggests in her book (1984) on women's unemployment. I think we need to be cautious about making generalizations about women when we are actually studying quite a specific group.

The general methodological point I wish to make is that our studies need to have a much sounder empirical basis. If we wish to analyse the similarities and differences between women's and men's consciousness, we need to study women and men, using the same concepts and asking the same questions. If, on the other hand, we want to look in more detail at women's consciousness, we need to stop thinking about women as a unitary category and to consider the differences among women, which the books I have reviewed all discuss. Ruth Cavendish, for instance, pays a great deal of attention to ethnic and racial difference while Anna Pollert distinguishes between young women and older women and Judy Wacjman emphasizes the importance of the women's different positons in the lifecycle. However, these distinctions are not always carried through satisfactorily in the books' discussions of consciousness. Anna Pollert's theoretical analysis, for instance, is not informed by the awareness of age and marital differences shown in her more empirical chapters. Since it is clear from aggregate statistical evidence that women's participation in the labour market follows a definite pattern, and that most women have at least one interruption in their working lives, and many women work part-time when they have young children or other dependants to care for, we need to investigate empirically how women's consciousness differs at different points in the lifecycle, and to ascertain whether it varies according to different household structures, racial and ethnic groups and social class.

■ Occupational segregation

A second theme running through the texts is occupational segregation. This is a very important structural characteristic of women's work in contemporary Britain, as Catherine Hakim has emphasized (1981) and is a major reason why the Equal Pay Act has proved virtually useless in rectifying inequalities between women and men. It seems likely too that occupational segregation has had a major impact on women's relationship to trade unions, but very little work has been done on this to date.

From studies like Anna Pollert's and Ruth Cavendish's we are beginning to get quite a clear picture of how occupational segregation is experienced in particular workplaces. It is also clear from these studies and from studies of particular industries like Angela Coyle's of the clothing industry (1982) and Cynthia Cockburn's of printing (1983) that women's concentration in unskilled and semi-skilled occupations stems as much from the social construction of men's jobs as skilled as from the exclusion of women from skilled jobs. In his essay in *Work, Women and the Labour Market*, Peter Armstrong makes the further point that in the footwear and electrical goods factories which he studied, female labour was associated not only with unskilled labour but also with labour-intensive forms of labour process.

In this section I want briefly to consider how far we have got in explaining occupational segregation. As in my discussion of consciousness in the preceding section, my aim is to raise some questions about theoretical approaches to occupational segregation rather than to provide any definitive statements. There are two prevailing approaches to occupational segregation within the literature, and both have been heavily used by feminists. The first is the Marxist argument, developed most cogently by Harry Braverman (1979), that women have been drawn into unskilled low-paying jobs in the course of capital accumulation. According to this argument the advantages which accrue to employers from hiring female labour are that they provide a cheap and unskilled labour force, and women's position within the labour force is to be understood in terms of the process of deskilling. Feminists have criticized these arguments on a number of grounds: for ignoring the role which trade unions and men play in the process of deskilling (Hartmann, 1976; Rubery, 1980); for failing to recognize the advantages which accrue to trade unions and to men when employers hire female labour (Hartmann, 1976; Rubery, 1980), and for neglecting to mention the role of ideology. One of the central arguments which some feminists (myself included) have levelled against Harry Braverman is that he does not manage to explain why women constitute a reserve of cheap and unskilled labour because he does not consider the family and the impact of the sexual division of labour in the factory or the sexual division of labour within the production process within his theory (Beechey 1977 and 1982).

The second explanation of occupational segregation which is commonly used is dual labour market theory (Barron and Norris, 1976). This asserts that women constitute a secondary sector workforce which has been drawn into secondary sector jobs; these are characterized by low pay, lack of promotion prospects, insecurity, etc. Classical dual labour market theory does not provide an analysis of the positive advantages which accrue to employers when they hire female labour. It analyses the positive advantages which hiring white men have for primary sector employers, and asserts that because they lack those characteristics which would make them a preferred primary sector workforce, women inevitably end up in secondary sector jobs. Dual labour market theory has been criticized for being ahistorical, for lumping all women together in a 'secondary worker' category which is defined primarily by its difference from the masculine norm, and for failing to provide a theory of the positive advantages which accrue to employers from hiring women (Beechey, 1978). Like Marxist theory, it has also been criticized for neglecting to analyse the role of trade unions and of men in maintaining a segmented labour market (Hartmann, 1979; Rubery, 1980).

Although I have in the past argued that a Marxist-feminist variant of Marxist deskilling theory – one which includes the family within its framework of analysis – can be used to analyse female wage labour, I do not think that this framework can be used to provide a *general* analysis of occupational segregation. Neither do I think that dual labour market theory is adequate for analysing occupational segregation. I think there are a variety of reasons for this, some of them historical and some of them theoretical, which I am only beginning to work out.

The major historical reason is that occupational segregation was evident under feudalism, as a number of writers have pointed out

(Middleton, 1979; Kenrick, 1981). Although the deskilling thesis, unlike the dual labour market theory, locates the employment of women as cheap unskilled labour within an historical framework, it sees the employment of unskilled labour as primarily a by-product of the development of industrial capitalism, thereby failing to recognize the extent to which occupational segregation existed before the development of industrial capitalism (and, indeed, before the development of capitalism).

A second, and related, problem is that both the deskilling thesis and dual labour market theory see women's employment as a by-product of the dynamics of capital accumulation and capital restructuring. While it is clearly true that capital accumulation and restructuring works on existing gender divisions and constantly transforms them, I do not think that either theory is adequate for analysing occupational segregation because it is not centrally concerned with analysing gender divisions. I think therefore that we need to develop a theory whose central concerns are occupational segregation, and which does not see this as a merely a by-product of employers' strategies to maximize profitability.

I think there are two elements to such a theory which need to be analytically distinguished. First, we need to analyse the conditions under which women sell their labour power which, as Ruth Cavendish points out, tend to be different from the conditions in which men sell their labour power. In this context the construction of women as a particular category of worker within the family, the education system and training schemes is crucially important. It is also important to distinguish between the role of familial ideology, which asserts that a woman's primary responsibilities are those of housewife and mother, and the concrete constraints which caring for children and other dependants impose upon certain women. Second, we need to analyse the construction of gender within the labour process itself, and to explain *why* women are employed in particular occupations and men are employed in others. In some manufacturing industries women's occupations can clearly be explained in terms of the deskilling thesis. Angela Coyle's excellent study of the clothing industry (1983), for instance, shows quite clearly how the concentration of women in unskilled and low-paid jobs results from management strategies designed to cheapen labour and trade union practices in which skilled male workers have struggled to differentiate themselves from unskilled female labour and to preserve pay differentials. In other industries, however, women's employment and occupational segregation requires a different kind of explanation. In the public sector, for instance, a major reason why women have been employed in 'caring' occupations (for example as home helps) is because this work has been constructed as an extension of women's domestic role. What I am suggesting, then, is that we need further studies (both historical and contemporary) of women's employment and occupational segregation in particular industries. We can then go on to analyse how the process of capital accumulation and restructuring and the development and restructuring of state employment affect the patterns of occupational segregation without seeing this as simply a by-product of the development of industrial capitalism.

The shift which I am advocating has major implications which should be stressed. It suggests that we need to analyse occupational segregation and the processes of gender construction within the labour process itself. Women's position within the occupational structure cannot simply be 'read off' from an analysis of the sexual division of labour within the family, as a number of feminists (myself included) have suggested in the past.

Clearly the possibilities open to employers when they are restructuring the labour process will be affected by the kinds of labour which are available, as Ruth Cavendish points out, and labour can be 'called forth' on to the labour market by the availability of jobs. Women, for instance, may simply not think of themselves as 'seeking work' if there are no 'women's jobs' available in their area. What I do want to emphasize, however, is the need to analyse gender construction within the labour process itself as well as within the family, the education system, training schemes, and so on. This is something which a number of feminist studies have actually done (for instance in analysing the association of gender and skill) but we have not yet managed to incorporate the insights from these studies into our more general theoretical frameworks.

■ Conclusion

My remarks about consciousness and occupational segregation are fairly tentative. They grow partly out of a critical reading of the studies I have discussed, and partly out of a long term interest in the theoretical analysis of women's employment which has itself been modified by the experience of doing empirical research on part-time work. I have throughout this article criticized some of the general theoretical concepts which are commonly used in feminist studies of women's employment, and in feminist discourse more generally. It has not been my intention to argue against theoretical analysis *per se*, but rather to object to theoretical arguments which do not take sufficient account of empirical evidence, and which thereby oversimplify the questions with which they are concerned. I have developed this argument in some detail because I think we are at times in danger of developing a feminist 'commonsense' which makes assertions which are questionable and which have unfortunate implications not only for feminist intellectual work but also for political practice.

◼ Notes

This article appeared in *Feminist Review* No. 15, 1983.

Many thanks to Catherine Hall and Ann Marie Wolpe for discussing earlier drafts at great speed and for helping me with this article.

Women and
Trade Unions

Nicola Charles

At national level in recent years the Trades Union Congress (TUC) has passed resolutions and adopted policies towards women workers which are progressive in terms of women's equality within the trade union movement.[1] These developments are the result of years of struggle on the part of women within the labour movement and as such are an important gain; however, resolutions are not necessarily translated into practice. On the contrary they often represent a token commitment which bestows upon the unions concerned the appearance of supporting women's struggles, while masking the continued existence of practices within the unions which operate very much against the interests of women workers. While not wishing to belittle the importance of such resolutions, it is certain that passing a resolution is infinitely easier than transforming practices within the trade union movement. Thus, while the trade union leadership may pay lip service to the cause of women's liberation, the practices of the union at local level often bear little or no relation to policies at national level. For instance, it is national trade union policy that 'the protective legislation concerning women's employment should not be repealed but strengthened and its provisions extended to men' (Private correspondence). However, at local level there are women working permanent nights in bakeries, despite national policy *and* despite the fact that night work is viewed by many trade union officials and shop stewards as something wholly unsuitable for women, particularly married women. On the other hand, it *is* seen as acceptable for *men* and is regarded by many trade unions as an unpleasant but unavoidable fact of working life. The distinction made between men and women in this context is supported by the view that if a woman takes up paid employment, it must fit in with her prior domestic commitments; such opinions constitute part of familial ideology. The conflicting and co-existing ideology of sexual equality, which manifests itself most clearly at the level of national policy, is also present but in a much weaker form at local level and has so far failed to take root, either within the practices of the trade unions or within the attitudes and practices of the women themselves.

In this article we explore the attitudes and practices of local shop stewards, union representatives and union officials towards their women members together with the views of the women concerned. We argue that familial ideologies remain dominant over egalitarian ideologies at local level primarily because the material conditions of existence within which men and women live, particularly sexual divisions of labour at work and at home, reinforce familial rather than than egalitarian ideologies. Secondly, the strength of this familial ideology indicates that, so far, despite official policy statements and conference resolutions, the unions concerned have largely failed to change opinions and practices at grassroots level.

Before attempting such an exploration it is important to define the concept of ideology which is here being used. Ideology, as Althusser (1971) has argued, does not only exist in the realm of ideas; on the contrary it has a material existence in the form of practices, and these practices give rise to 'theoretical' ideologies or ideas and systems of belief. It is important to stress that ideologies are rooted in and reproduced by material practices, thus they have a material existence. Althusser also argues that ideologies are class ideologies and are therefore crucial to the maintenance of state power.

Michèle Barrett has argued that the social division of labour within the British social formation has been constituted by ideological struggle which is inseparable from economic and political struggle, and that economic struggle always takes place within and around specific ideological formations (1980). Thus, although at a certain level of abstraction the social division of labour can be seen as the necessary outcome of the development of capitalist relations of production, this analytical concept relates to a concrete historical process in which capitalist relations of production exist in articulation with historically specific ideological and political configurations which form the *conditions of existence* of capitalist relations of production. In the context of the historical development of the British social formation, the sexual division of labour characterizing the workforce has arisen through ideological class struggle – the struggle for a family wage, for a reduction in the working day, for the exclusion of women and children from extreme forms of exploitation (Barrett and McIntosh, 1980; Humphries, 1981; Charles, 1979) – and thus ideological divisions along male-female lines have been constituted within the working class. These divisions exist materially in the form of the sexual divisions of labour at home and at work, and reproduce ideologies which in turn reinforce the already existing divisions. It is these processes of reproduction as they occur within the workplace and particularly within the trade union movement at a local level which we are concerned to describe and analyse.

■ The research

During the course of a research project exploring the ways women experience shift work, the strength of familial ideology and the extent of its persistence despite the 'equality' legislation of the last decade became increasingly obvious. One hundred and sixty women working different shift patterns and their eleven union representatives and officials, four of whom were women, were interviewed at seven different workplaces during the spring and summer of 1980. The shifts and workplaces were as follows: a permanent night shift in a bakery; a double day shift in a packaging factory; a twilight shift in an electrical components factory; double-day shifts including weekend working at a motorway services and bus company; and double-days, three-shift rotating or twelve-hour day/night shifts in two computer firms.

In most of the workplaces there was a marked sexual division of labour and women were usually employed on work which was considered to be 'women's' work. Thus, in the packaging factory women operated the machines which packaged the plastic bags while the men performed all the other jobs, which ranged from labouring jobs involving heavy lifting to highly skilled jobs in the extrusion department. Most of the women at the bakery were employed as packers on the production line and in the electrical components factory women were assembling the tiny parts. There were only two workplaces where women were working in jobs which were not considered to be 'women's' work and where women were not in a majority; these were the bus driving and conducting jobs and the computer operating jobs.

We first describe the attitudes and practices of the local shop stewards, union representatives and officials towards women as workers and then compare their views with those of the women themselves. The ideologies which these views express are related to the actual situations in which most of those interviewed, women and men, find themselves. We then look at the practices of specific unions within the workplace as seen through the eyes of their female members to show that, in the women's opinions, the unions not only fail to take into account the specific needs of women workers, but also, in many cases, operate against the interests of the workers.[2]

■ Women's work: the views of the unions at local level

The sexual division of labour which was characteristic of most of the workplaces, and the accompanying pay differentials between men and women workers, were not seen as problematic by the union representatives at local level. In the words of the Transport and General Workers Union (TGWU) shop steward at the electrical components factory:[3]

> There's been a great increase in humdrum jobs like the jobs here, that you wouldn't get a man doing ... But the women can sit at a bench eight hours and pick up little fiddly screws and put them in. I think it's fantastic, and they can go for week in week out, you know – but you'll never get a man doing it, so that's why you need ... women working.

The view that women were 'naturally' more suited to work that was fiddly, repetitive, monotonous and requiring dexterity was commonly heard and this work was always considered to be less skilled than the work the men were doing.[4] A consequence of this ideological valuation of 'women's' work, which the unions and management held in common, was that women working on women's work were paid less than men working on different, 'men's' jobs in the same factory.

At the motorway services young men worked alongside women in jobs that were clearly regarded as women's work and were paid accordingly. The Union of Shop, Distributive and Allied Workers (USDAW) shop steward commented:

> this sort of work is no good to a man ... the wages aren't up to standard ... When I was in the mines and at M......n I used to have nearly as much as that as pocket money.

There was a clear view on the part of the union representatives of the **type** of work and accompanying pay that were appropriate for women. All those interviewed felt that most women who went out to work were earning a secondary wage and that therefore the fact that they were paid less than their male fellow workers was not a problem. There was some recognition that this secondary wage was often necessary to the family budget but this state of affairs was regretted. An Amalgamated Union of Engineering Workers (AUEW) shop steward said, 'I've been in the happy position where my wife's never worked ... she was at home with the two kiddies all the time'. But he added that now with mortgages to pay 'these women have got to find that little bit extra'.

In the packaging factory where the women were working a double-day shift and where a relatively high proportion (17 per cent) of women were supporting families on their own, there was some recognition on the part of the union representative that the women's wages were not adequate:

> Some of the women on here who live alone or who live with their mothers, and they've got to run a house and they're the only people who are working, the mother's ill or something like that, and you know if you've got to run a house ... the pay is nothing after they've paid the rent or the mortgage, you know, they've got nothing for it, just enough going for food.

However, even here there is the assumption that the wages would be adequate for women who were living with a husband or partner who was in work.

One of the TGWU shop stewards attributed absenteeism amongst women to the 'fact' that their wages were too high for their needs as secondary wage earners:

> Usually it's a second wage so four days is ample, and so the fifth day they have off and they do it regular ... the women can live on four days but a man's got to work five usually, and some of the women will work five if they haven't got a husband earning.

There is clearly a dual standard in operation here which is in contradiction with the notion of equal pay for women and also conflicts with the rhetoric of equality at a national level.[5] Although this particular shop steward, and indeed most of those spoken to, agreed that equal pay for women was only fair – *if* they were doing the same work as a man – there was a much stronger feeling that actually women didn't *need* such a high wage as a man because their wages were nearly always of secondary importance to the family income. This view conforms to familial ideology and indeed has its roots in material practices within the family. Recent research has shown that many families budget on the basis that the wife's wage is secondary and temporary and that the husband's wage, which is regarded as a family wage, is permanent and must pay for the daily running of the household (see for example Hunt, 1980). Thus pay differentials between men and women both reinforce and are justified by the sexual division of labour within the family. Conversely, ideologies of equality are not reinforced by the sexual divisions of labour at work and in the home.

There was considerable feeling that ideally married women should not need to go out to work and that a family wage should be paid to men. One of the TGWU shop stewards clearly voiced this opinion:

> Fifteen, twenty years ago women working was unheard of – not that I'm against women working – and it was not because they didn't want them to work but there was no *need* for the housewife with kiddies to work, but because of the way the whole system's gone ... they've got to work to survive. I mean I would never allow my wife to work and allow my child to be left with a baby minder, that's one of the reasons my wife didn't work. But even with my beliefs my wife had to go out to work on a twilight shift, and for the area I'm supposed to earn a good wage ... I'd like to see the companies paying a decent living wage and then there'd be no need for part-time working, twilight shifts, whatever you like, plus the unemployment figures would be better as well.

An USDAW shop steward voiced this opinion bluntly:

> The man's the breadwinner isn't he so therefore if there's any jobs going it should be for a man ... I've always said a woman's place is in the house ... I've been married twenty-five years and my wife worked twelve months just after I got married and she's never worked since.

There was clearly a feeling that the best situation to be in, for a man, was one where the husband earned enough so that his wife did not need to go out to work. However, as Barrett and McIntosh put it:

> If the demand for a family wage were actually realized and married women no longer went into paid employment, married couples might possibly be as well off in purely financial terms;

> but the women would not necessarily get their share, and if they did it would be under conditions of subordination to their husbands. And single women, especially mothers, would be at an acute economic disadvantage. Hence, if the men of the working class struggle for a family wage, they do so in opposition to one of the central demands of the women's movement and against the interests of working class women (Barrett and McIntosh, 1980: 62).

These comments point to another important effect of the relative wage earning potential of men and women and that is the power that is conferred upon the male breadwinner within the family by his ability to earn a higher wage than his wife. This relation of power is alluded to in the first quote when the shop steward talks of 'allowing' his wife to go out to work and is revealed more starkly when the relation is reversed, as was the case with one of the women working nights at the bakery whose husband was unemployed. She said that going out to work had made her feel independent and had affected her relationship with her husband:

> I think 'It's me going out to work. I've had to take it off you (husband) when you was working and I was at home so now you can take it from me ... I'm the gaffer in the house.' And to me I think I am, cos as I say there's only my wage coming in and everything's got to rely on me ... to me when a man's working he's the man of the house, but when he's unemployed and then the wife goes out to work it changes it.

■ Attitudes towards hours of work for women

The union representatives and officials were asked their opinion of shift work for women and from their responses it became clear that they had very firm ideas of the hours of work that were appropriate. In this sphere local attitudes and practices bore more relation to national union policies in so far as part-time work was considered to be one of the best options for a married woman with children who wanted to work outside the home.

Strong opinions were often expressed about women working shifts. The union representative at the packaging factory whose female members were working on weekly alternating double-day shifts (6 a.m. to 2 p.m., 2 p.m. to 10 p.m.) said, 'If my wife did shifts I'd break her neck, well not her but the bloke's that tried to get her on to them.' He expressed his major reasons for thinking shifts so unsuitable for women:

> I can't see a reason why a woman should have to work four or five hours at home and come to work for eight hours and come home and do a couple more hours. Shifts for a woman – what a life – she has two days a week off but she doesn't get two days off cos she gets Saturday and Sunday and that's when she has to do her washing and her ironing and all the rest.

Although he appreciated that women who work outside the home have two jobs, he did not see any need for a redistribution of domestic tasks. In fact only one shop steward thought that a change in the traditional division of labour was important. He was in the Association of Scientific, Technical and Managerial Staff (ASTMS) and represented the computer operators, perhaps significantly an area where young women had only recently (mid-seventies) been employed on work which had previously been exclusively male. He said:

> I do think that married women on principle – that we should have industrial set ups that allow married women with children to work ... if they want to work they should have the opportunity to work.

He went on to say that the way to facilitate this was to increase the availability of childcare provision. But for the other male shop stewards, married women working was seen not only as undermining the privileged position of men within the family but also as a threat to their position in the workforce. A TGWU shop steward clearly saw women working shifts, or even working at all, as a threat to men's jobs and one of the causes of male unemployment:

> Women working on nights ... would put more people [read men N.C.] out of work and the unemployment situation would obviously get worse and there's women that would be attracted back into the industry ... the ones that couldn't work twilight or days but could work nights. What I say with unemployment is ... if the same percentage of women were working today that were working in 1965 I don't think you'd have 400,000 unemployed – do you understand what I mean?

However, the main reason expressed for thinking that women should not work shifts was the role of women within the family. It was felt that most shiftwork makes it difficult for women to fulfil their prior commitments to children and husband. The solution to the very real problem that confronts women in combining paid employment outside the home with bearing and rearing children was seen in terms of providing hours of work for women (usually part-time) which would fit in rather than conflict with their domestic responsibilities. For instance, one of the women shop stewards of the Electrical Electronics Telecommunications and Plumbing Union (EETPU) at the electrical components factory said, 'for the married woman I think nine to four is ideal' and the union representative at the packaging factory said: 'I don't reckon women should stay at home. I reckon a woman should have a job to suit herself, just a few hours a day *if* she wants one.'

This position was not only held by union representatives at shop floor level but was shared by full-time union officials. A local USDAW official said that they recommended that their women members at the motorway services should have the choice of working permanently on one shift, either the morning or the afternoon in a double-day shift system, in order to fit in their employment with family reponsibilities. He went on to describe the tendency in retailing towards employing only part-time workers. He said that one of the reasons for the success of this was that it 'gives women a break as much as earning money'. He also thought that it would be a good thing to introduce a thirty-hour working week for women while maintaining a forty-hour working week for men precisely because it would enable women to combine work outside the home with their family commitments. There was no understanding of the way such policies would work to segregate further the labour market along male-female lines and reinforce the inequalities and lack of opportunities that women suffer in the workplace.

Trade unionists at shop floor level often regard part-time workers as secondary to full-time workers and it is difficult to say whether this is because part-time workers are seen as a threat to full-time workers or because most part-time workers are women. The following quotes from shop stewards in industries where part-time workers are employed illustrate this point. An USDAW shop steward said, 'We'd sooner have a full-time worker than part-time or anything like that.' He was working at the motorway services where 56 per cent of the workforce was female and 12 per cent of it part-time. An AUEW shop steward at the electrical components factory where a twilight shift was employed said, 'The general view is that they [the union] don't want twilighters in there cos they prefer people to be full-time.' And a woman shop steward in the same factory said that the union, in this case the EETPU, accepted the twilighters (who were all women) 'as long as it doesn't interfere with the full-time employment'. None of the three unions in this particular factory had any twilight workers as members. Another shop steward thought that one full-time job given to a breadwinner, assumed to be male, was preferable to two part-time jobs: 'I'd sooner a man that needs a full wage got a job instead of two part-timers who need the extra money'. He went on to say that during periods of full employment part-time work was acceptable but otherwise work should be reserved for full-timers; the implications of this are obvious given that most part-time workers are women.

As we have argued elsewhere (Charles and Brown, 1981), certain hours of work in themselves tend to discriminate against women with responsibility for young children. However, although the difficulties women face in combining full-time paid employment with family responsibilities were recognized by the trade unionists, the 'solution' of part-time work that they put forward, far from solving the problem, actually ensures that it remains untouched and that women with domestic responsibilities continue to be excluded from most full-time employment. This advocacy of part-time work for women is firmly rooted in familial ideology and therefore retains intact the sexual division of labour both within the family and within the workforce. By leaving these sexual divisions unchallenged the unions are in fact accepting them and so contributing to their reproduction. A clear picture emerges that, with only one exception, all the union representatives interviewed thought that women's and men's roles were clearly defined and were different, and ideally women should be able to stay at home with their children while their husbands went out to work to support the family. The notion of a family wage, earned by the man, governs their assessment of men's and women's work and men's and women's wages. In these circumstances it is hardly surprising that women's low pay is not seen as problematic by the unions at this level. It only becomes a problem if and when it is seen to affect men's pay because, after all, women's continuing low pay reinforces the superior position of men both within the workforce and at home as the main breadwinner.[6] Egalitarian ideologies such as that of equal pay, on the other hand, tend to undermine this position and do not have a material basis, as does familial ideology, in the 'traditional' sexual division of labour within the family.

■ The women's views

The strong adherence to familial ideology expressed by most of the shop stewards and union representatives interviewed was not only voiced by the *male* shop stewards and does not arise from simple prejudice against women or a type of 'false consciousness'. Their views are shared by a large proportion of the women workers they represented and can be seen as arising directly from the material reality of their daily lives.

On the issues of women's work and women's pay, many of the women shared the men's view that men were not suited to repetitive or 'fiddly' jobs and needed a job with a prospect of promotion. One of the machine operators in the packaging factory said that the youths put on to the women's jobs 'don't stick to it and you can't really blame them – I mean, it's a very boring job, it's not really a job for a man with prospects is it?' And one of the telephonists said: 'I think it's more of a woman's job than a man's job unless they are handicapped in any way ... I know my husband couldn't do it, I don't think he would have the patience.' However, although the women agreed that some jobs were more suited to women then men, they did not agree with the men that women did not mind being bored. One women doing assembly work in the electrical factory said:

> I found it terrible when I first came ... and I never thought I would stick it then, and I thought the monotony would drive me round the bend, but I think you just get into the routine and then you can forget about work and just chat away to each other.

This comment underlines the fact that work does enable women to get out of the isolation of the home and mix with other women for at least part of the day; this compensates for some of the disadvantages of their jobs.

The existing divisions of labour between men and women within the workforce and at home, together with the complete lack of childcare facilities, reinforce familial rather than egalitarian ideologies. The contradiction between the notion of equal pay for equal work and the different needs of men and women which arise from the very real division of labour within the family was brought out again and again. One of the telephonists supported the principle of equal pay for equal work but when talking about her own wages compared to a man earning the same wages said, 'I think the pay for shift work for a woman who is not the breadwinner is good. But you see if you're going to be the breadwinner then I don't know.' Many other women echoed this view and several felt strongly that men *ought* to earn more than women. At the packaging factory one of the women said 'a man should bring in more money than a woman.' However, ambivalence was often expressed. For example, one telephonist said:

> I'm of the opinion that men shouldn't get the same wage as a woman anyway, I think a man should always get a little bit more, I don't know, cos when you're working with them they don't do any more than you ... they are actually the breadwinner.

And another woman at the packaging factory said:

> I don't think a man should be paid any more than a woman for the same job – no, if you're doing the same job as the man I don't see why he should be considered to have more wages than you.

In the bakery where the women were working permanent nights one woman, who was herself supporting a family and invalided husband, said:

> I don't think it's very good for a man cos I mean he's got a family to keep, hasn't he? I know *I'm* keeping a family but at the same time now me husband is getting a little bit of money with him being on invalidity for the rest of his life while he gets on to pension age. But I mean, obviously a man working has got nothing, *only* his wage.

Even on the buses where the women constituted 5 per cent of the workforce and were working in a so-called man's job, there was clearly a different standard in operation for the assessment of men's and women's wages. One woman said:

> Well I suppose it's twice as bad for a man really, because he's got a family to support. I know a lot of the men on here, their wives do go out to work, but that's not married life is it, their having to work as well. I know some of them, they work six or seven days every week ... to take the money in.

The examples are endless and, despite the ambivalence described earlier, the number of women advocating a higher wage for a male breadwinner was very much greater than those who thought men and women should receive equal pay for equal work regardless of their family situation.[7] One of the women even put forward the idea that married women should stay at home: 'I don't think married women should have to work, they should give them an allowance from the government.'

This espousal of familial ideology where wages are determined by the supposed family position of the worker was also expressed in the views on the hours of work thought to be suitable for women with children. Several women felt that part-time work would be more satisfactory if they could afford not to work full-time, and others thought that a working day the length of a school day would suit them best. These views reflected both the desire to spend enough time with their children, which was not felt to be possible with a full-time job, and the need to carry out all their domestic tasks. Many also felt that it was better that they and their partners share childcare and arrange their hours of work accordingly rather than send their children to a day nursery or child minder. There was also some recognition that part-time hours and family commitments meant that women were disadvantaged in the labour market. One woman working a twilight shift said:

> A married man can mostly adapt in the day to his job, but a married woman has not only got her job to think about, she's got to think about home and everything ... perhaps a single girl could get on as a married man, but I don't think a married woman could.

A significant number of the women thought that childcare provison for pre-school age children and school age children out of school hours and in school holidays would be a definite advance for women with children who wanted or needed to go out to work, and there was some recognition of the fact that many women were unsupported mothers and therefore needed to earn a full-time wage. However, alongside this view went the belief that most married women had husbands to support them and therefore did not need to earn as much as men did.

This view was clearly reinforced by the material circumstances of their lives. Of the 146 women interviewed, eighty-four of the 107 working full-time were either married or living with their boyfriend. When asked whether their partners earned more than they did, sixty-four said that they did and fifty-four said that they considered their partner to be the main breadwinner in the family. The situations of the majority of women therefore conformed to the traditional division of labour within the family. As Donzelot (1980) has argued and demonstrated, this family structure, and the familial ideologies that go with it and reinforce it, have been constructed as an important means of social control, particularly of the working class. It should not be surprising, then, to find that working-class men and women accept and live familial ideologies both materially and in terms of their ideas and beliefs. It also indicates the magnitude of the problem faced by any agent attempting to transform these sexual divisions and inequalities. The higher earning capabilities of most of the women's partners clearly mean that, if one partner is required to stay at home to look after children because there are no childcare facilities available, that partner will be the woman. Thus the ideology of the male breadwinner and the secondary nature of the woman's wage, however important that second wage may be for the family, has a basis in and is reinforced by material reality.

As has been pointed out above, the egalitarian ideology of equal pay for equal work and the notion of an individual wage not only conflict with past trade union practice but are seen to conflict with the perceived need of *men* to earn a family wage to support their wives and children at home. And this need is not only perceived but at a certain stage in the lifecycle actually exists in fact, and is something which most of the women interviewed had experienced for themselves. Of course, this is not the whole story. Reality is not monolithic but contradictory and many working men do not support families while many working women do. However, it remains the case that for most of the women and men spoken to, familial ideology gains its strength from their material conditions of existence and is not an invention of men, adhered to by them alone. Those women who were sole supporters of families often thought themselves to be abnormal. Familial ideology in these cases was more effective than their own experiences and rendered the latter abnormal rather than the former invalid. In addition there was an awareness on the part of the women of the contradiction between the notion of equal pay for equal work, which was accepted in principle by everyone spoken to, and the notion of a family wage. Most of them also felt that work outside the home was essential not only for the finances of the family but for their own sense of independence and self-respect. One of them summed it up:

> You've heard of bored housewives haven't you? I've got one friend told me off yesterday cos I haven't been for a couple of

days and she said that she went to bed cos she was that bored, and the baby was asleep, and she was so *bored*, and I can understand how she feels cos I was the same before I started work. It is boring being at home if you've got nobody coming to visit you and nobody to talk to, I mean you've got the children there to talk to but it's not the same as talking to an adult is it?

This view, common amongst the women, differed from the views of those male shop stewards and union officials who thought that ideally men should earn enough to enable their wives to stay at home.

In general the women showed a greater awareness of the problems they faced in combining paid employment with childrearing than did the men, which is hardly surprising. Some women also, despite the strength of familial ideology, put forward more imaginative and challenging solutions and seemed to be more aware of the contradictory nature of social reality and ideologies to which it gives rise. We are thinking particularly of the desire for different and more flexible hours of work and increased provision of childcare of different forms. Perhaps, as Safiotti (1978) has argued, because of women's marginalization as far as the world of work is concerned, they are by definition less integrated into its practices than are men and are therefore more able to imagine alternative ways of doing things. Thus, even though we have argued that familial ideology is reproduced by practices within the workforce and within the family, the contradictions experienced by women workers and the problems they face in combining paid work outside the home with family commitments can open a space for change.

■ Women as trade unionists: the views of local trade unionists

Several of the shop stewards and union representatives felt that women were just as good (or bad) as men as far as attendance at union meetings and interest in the union was concerned. However, they thought that there was a difference in the attitudes of men and women towards industrial action, particularly strikes. The woman shop steward in the electrical components factory said:

You'll always find if there's going to be a strike situation, the men will be all for it but not the women. Most of the women, you won't get them coming out on strike, not here.

The AUEW shop steward in the same factory thought that women in general were against taking strike action. The woman shop steward put forward as an explanation for this: that 'the women always seem to think on the money side of it, and the men are always thinking about what they're going to gain after'. An USDAW shop steward at the motorway services said of the older women:

> They just turn round and say, 'Well it's no use me joining the union cos I'm too old' which they are at that age really. I mean if you had a walkout here it would take you all your time to get them out cos they wouldn't stick together.

An USDAW official said that in his opinion women treated unions as an insurance policy rather than as a cause to be fought for and would only go to a union meeting if and when they had a particular grievance; this was not the case for men. He also thought that union activity was restricted for women because of their family commitments and because of this they would go to union meetings in working hours but not otherwise.

The majority of unions studied had no regular branch meetings for the membership. The exceptions were the bakery where meetings were held monthly on Saturday mornings which was seen as not very convenient for anyone, the computer operators where ASTMS held regular branch meetings on a weekday evening, and the EETPU which was one of three unions at the electrical components factory and which also held meetings on a weekday evening. At the motorway services the USDAW shop steward was waiting for management to convene a regular shop stewards' meeting with the result that none had been held since the union was established there; no meetings had been held with the membership either. Most shop stewards communicated with their membership by word of mouth or by putting up notices and meetings were called only as and when an issue needed to be discussed with the membership. Under these circumstances participation by members, whether male or female, is almost guaranteed to be minimal. No facilities to enable women with children to attend meetings, such as creches, were mentioned, and a TGWU shop steward who had tried to initiate regular branch meetings in the lunch hour reported that this had failed 'for one good reason, that they [the women] do their shopping in the lunch hour'. In the packaging factory where meetings were held during working hours, a good attendance on the part of the women was reported. Little concern was expressed by the unions about attendance at meetings and virtually no attempts were being made to involve the membership more fully in the unions. This situation puts rather a different light on the TUC 'Charter for Equality for Women in Trade Unions'. Although two of its clauses relate to union meetings they seem to bear little relation to practices at local level:

> Where it is not practicable to hold meetings during working hours every effort should be made to provide childcare facilities for use by either parent.
>
> Childcare facilities, for use by either parent, should be provided at all district, divisional and regional meetings and particularly at the union's annual conferences, and for training courses organized by the unions (TGWU, 1980).

▣ The women's experience of unions

The majority of the women spoken to did not conform to the picture presented by their union representatives. Most were interested in unions and, with the exception of some of the telephonists, supported the principles of trade unionism. This, however, did not prevent them from being critical of their own union both in terms of its effectiveness as a union and in terms of its practices towards its women members. One of the women on permanent nights said:

> I'm all for the unions cos we wouldn't survive without the unions. I know these are not much cop but it's the only one we've got ... If you take striking action away from the working class what have they got – they're nowt but slaves again.[8]

At the motorway services where there was a weak union presence, considerable interest was expressed in the union and many women who were not members would have joined had they been approached. Several of the women on the twilight shift, none of whom were union members because the unions refused to recruit them due to the administrative difficulty of dealing with temporary employees, would have preferred to belong to a trade union.

The only workplace where a significant amount of apathy towards trade unions was expressed was that of the telephonists. Their work situation was unusual in our sample because there was a very strong union presence and the union was actively involved in all aspects of work organization and conditions. The need for a union can be lost sight of in such a context precisely because the union is already strong enough to ensure that the interests of the workforce are always taken into account by management. The comments below were fairly typical: 'If you'd got the choice I wouldn't particularly be in the union, but I mean I am and I go to the meetings and that.' These women in general had few complaints about their work or their union. One of them said:

> We should have regular meetings but we don't stick to it cos quite honestly there's so little griping in this job it just isn't worth it. And when I was on day staff it was the same, you couldn't get people to meetings cos there was nothing they wanted to moan about you see and then all of a sudden perhaps they would. So we find it better to call them as and when rather than say there's one once a month type of thing.

In the other work places, apart from that of the computer operators, there were more criticisms, both of the unions and of the jobs. In two factories in particular, the bakery and the packaging factory, the women criticized their unions for being too much on the side of management. One of the women at the packaging factory said:

> I've never really bothered with the union, I mean I would ... if it was a decent union, you know, I'd perhaps take up interest, but with these, they just don't bother, they're more for the management than for the work people.

One of the women in the bakery gave an example:

> I don't think they're for the workers, they're for the management ... we were in a dispute once ... and we were supposed to be on a work to rule, and all the members voted to have it, and to me a work to rule is just doing your normal hours and that's it ... we wanted to ban overtime as well ... but of course the shop stewards didn't want to ban overtime. They wanted to carry on with overtime and still work to rule, but I don't think you can do that ... cos every time they've got you working overtime and there's no point in working to rule as far as I can see. But you see we voted that in, but they got it, you know, voted back so that we were working to rule and still doing overtime.

Another of the women at the bakery who had previously been a shop steward there, said: 'I was a shop steward. And that was one of the reasons I came out, cos this union's got to do what the management tells them and that's it.' At this particular bakery the women were working permanent nights, which is against the policy of the Bakers Union nationally. However a management representative told us that there had been no opposition from the union locally to women working this shift. In fact the baking Industry (Hours of Work) Act 1954 prohibits employers from keeping men on night shifts for more than twenty-six weeks every year. They get around this prohibition by employing women on an exemption order. It must be said that at a *national* level the union is aware of, and worried by, this development:

> Over the years we have been concerned with the ease by which employers have been able to get exemption orders to allow night working for women. Not being able to work men on nights without agreement with the Union we believe that employers are using the exemption orders to undermine the unity of the Union as well as exploiting women. We know of several such cases where such exemption orders have been abused and where women have been forced onto nights, the alternative being to lose their jobs (Private correspondence).

Women in six of the workplaces were unionized and in four of these the unions were felt to be ineffective. One of the women on the buses said:

> If Moss Evans or anybody like that come down here he'd have a heart attack because they just don't fight for anything ... instead of saying we're all Transport and General it's garage against garage.

And at the motorway services complaints of the union's ineffectiveness were legion. The shop steward was so little in evidence that many of the women did not really believe there was a union presence at all. One of them said that the union (USDAW) was 'not very effective at all. I've been here nearly a year and nobody from the union approached me, I had to go and ask them for the forms.' Another woman described the lack of contact between the union and the workforce:

> The union man came up here the other day and he says that he comes up here when there's new ones and asks them if they want to be in the union. Well I've been here two months and I only just heard about the union when this rise was coming up and he hadn't been and asked me if I wanted to be in the union – I

didn't even know there was a union till the rise came up – so he can't come up and ask all the new girls whether they want to be in a union, cos we didn't even know there was one, hadn't heard of it, and didn't even know who the rep was.

At the packaging factory it was felt that the union had not acted effectively in the interests of the women when double-day shifts had been introduced a few years previously. The introduction of shifts meant that women who had previously been working days were given the option of changing to double-day shifts or being given the sack. The union had also failed to negotiate a satisfactory shift allowance:

> I brought this up … as I say, we don't get paid shift allowance and I went and asked why, and when the company were wanting an agreement with the union over going into working the shift system … and they said we would get so much for shifts. And, to me, the union made no attempt to say 'Well you should pay them such and such' and fight. And I'd brought it up beforehand and they said 'Now don't go on about that again, it's been explained and it's the agreement the company went into and we can't alter it now' and I'm sure they could if they'd a mind to do it.

Her criticisms were clearly justified. The flat rate for those women working double-day shifts included a shift allowance which meant that they were paid $1\frac{1}{2}$ *pence per hour* more than those women working days: hardly an adequate shift allowance. The same union was also criticized for being undemocratic:

> I don't know how they say that it's what the people want and it's what the workers vote for because since I've been in the union we've had no say in nothing, the *union* tell you what they're doing, and the union tell you what rises you'll accept, you know.

It should be said at this particular factory the union representative who had been newly elected was popular with the women and shared their criticisms of the union. Both here and at the motorway services there was a lot of feeling that they were in the wrong union, that it was not effective, and that the TGWU would have been more appropriate. Also at these two workplaces there was a feeling that women union representatives or shop stewards would have been more effective than men, particularly when dealing with women workers. Several of the women would have been prepared to become representatives if they had had the chance. When asked if she would consider becoming a union representative one of the women said: 'I'd like to because there's so many underhand things done ... I'd be on the workers' side.' Thus many of the women criticized the unions from the point of view of the support, or lack of it, that the unions gave them as workers. They were also critical of the unions' attitudes towards them as women.

The unions and women's interests

Most of the women, apart from the telephonists, felt that the unions did not take enough interest in women or in issues that were important to women. One of the women at the packaging factory said·

> They're on about equal rights and all that, but they don't seem to fight as much for the women as they do for the men, you know, the man's still the domineering person ... they don't stick up for the women as much as they do for the men.

And another one said: 'I don't think they're interested in women's opinions and they just try to fob you off, and they just think you're complaining all the time.' These criticisms were made of a union whose membership is over 50 per cent female. At the bakery the union was felt to favour men's promotion at the expense of women's:

> I don't think they're for the workers enough over here – and they're not for the women ... like I say, over the jobs, I think if it were left to the union they'd get precedence, men get higher thought on you know.

Even at the computer firm where the stop steward was more aware of the problems faced by women at work, one of the computer operators said:

> I think you find at a place like this where there aren't many women, nobody really thinks about women having separate problems, and even if there are it isn't seen that way, it tends to be – everything is a general issue, so everyone ends up being one of the boys.

There were several issues which had been specifically raised as women's problems that the unions had not considered important or else thought it inappropriate for a trade union to concern itself with, such as menstrual problems and the problems of combining full-time work outside the home with looking after a family. These problems were remarked on by several of the women, particularly those at the bus company, and illustrate the problems facing women at work when equality is defined in men's terms and allows for no differences. One of the women at the bakery described the lack of understanding exhibited by the union:

> I don't think they understand the kind of problems a married women has, it's more or less 'forget about it and get on with your work' ... same as if a woman – one of her children are really ill and she has to have time off, now if you have two days off here in a month you get a warning ... regardless of the reason unless you have a sick note ... as they say on one of the plants, 'If you can't do a full shift or you can't do a full week, then you're no good to me', and that's the end of the matter.

At the bus company and in the computer firms the women felt that they should be entitled to a day off a month if they suffered from menstrual problems. One of the women on the buses said:

> Where I used to work they allowed you one day off a month for that type of thing, periods and all that, and they actually paid you for it, you got sick pay for that day.

They had raised the issue with the union, the TGWU, but they had received no support from the male shop stewards. One woman described the problem:

> Some days in the month I'm crippled up, other months I'm completely alright, but there's no concessions there. There's no way a man's going to have a period pain and they can't understand it, you get no concessions.

Another woman said:

> This day off per month for periods, and things like that, they're just not interested, if you go to them and try to tell them they just don't want to know. They say, 'If we give you a day off a month the men'll want a day off a month' ... you know, that's the way they look at it here.

Another said, 'I do think they forget we're women' and another commented, 'Well, you're classed as a man so I would say you're all the same, you know, you're all classed as brothers.'

■ Conclusions

The women thus criticized their unions on two counts: one that the union worked too much with management and two, that they protected men's interests and paid little attention to issues of importance to women. The attitudes expressed by the trade union representatives confirmed the latter point. As far as they were concerned, if women wanted 'equality' at work, they should behave as if they were men. If they did not, then they did not deserve to be treated as equals of men. This view automatically excludes such problems as menstruation and childcare from the agendas of trade unions. They are defined as something 'private' which is external to the world of work and is the concern of women not men. Given these views, it is not surprising that women, apart from the case of the bus drivers, had not raised these issues with their unions even though they felt them to be important. Judging from the reaction of the TGWU to the women bus drivers' menstrual problems, it seems likely that other 'women's' issues would have been given equally short shrift. Clearly the trade unions, along with the world of work in general, are structured to cater for the interests of men, and women's specific interests fall outside what has until now been defined as the proper concerns of the trade union movement. While this is beginning to change at national level, the structures at local level are still not able to incorporate the interests of women.

The views of the women clearly showed that their particular unions, whatever their national policy, were failing either to take seriously issues which were important for women workers or to involve women at local level. Meetings, if they were held at all, were with one exception held outside working hours, in evenings or at weekends, and did not have any creche provision, thus making it extremely difficult for women to attend.

This failure on the part of the unions is a consequence of the dominance of familial ideology at local level both in terms of attitudes and in terms of the lived reality of the workforce and the family. That this ideology is not simply prejudice on the part of sexist men is clear; it also structured the views and perceptions of the women interviewed. This was the case despite the fact that some women's own circumstances would seem to contradict the assumptions on which familial ideology is based. Ideologies of equality also exist at local level but in a much weaker form, although they were stronger amongst the women interviewed than amongst the men. We have tried to show that familial ideology gains its strength from existing practices, both at home and at work, and that it structures and makes sense of the lived reality of large numbers of working class men and women. It also reproduces the position of women as economically dependent on men within the family and as secondary wage earners in the workplace. Thus despite the 'equality' legislation of the mid-seventies, women are still viewed by the trade unions as being primarily concerned with the home and men's jobs are given priority. The world of work, which includes the trade unions, is structured according to the needs of capital in the first instance but also according to the interests of men. Thus women's interests are considered inappropriate for the trade unions and if women work alongside men they have to accept equality on men's terms. This clearly puts women at a disadvantage and highlights the urgent need for trade union practices to be transformed so that women's interests are as much part of their legitimate business as fighting the next wage round.

The marginalization of women's interests by the union not only reproduces the secondary position of women in the workforce but also weakens the *unions* because they lose potential support. Thus the divisions, although seeming to give advantages to working class men both at work and at home, in fact operate in the interests of the employers by allowing them to continue to use women as a source of cheap labour and by creating a situation where women remain in fundamental ways uninvolved in the trade union movement.

At a national level the trade unions have expressed concern about the lack of involvement of women and have introduced certain measures in an attempt to rectify the situation. But from the evidence presented here it is obvious that there is an enormous gulf between resolutions at national level and practices on the shop floor. Although egalitarian ideologies may be embodied in resolutions, it is familial ideology which has a material existence in practices at local level. We would argue that to increase the participation of women in trade unions and to make the unions more sensitive to women's interests, it is essential that this ideology is changed through the transformation of those practices which contribute to its reproduction. Positive discrimination at all levels of the trade union movement together with programmes of education for women workers and the implementation of measures such as crèches at union meetings and/or holding meetings during working hours, are important beginnings in this process. It is also essential, given the profound ignorance that we encountered among many of the union representatives at shop floor level, for the unions to educate their own officials and representatives, not only in bargaining practice (which is itself in need of transformation) but also on issues which are considered to be important by the unions nationally. This would perhaps make it more likely that some of the measures mentioned above would be implemented at local level.

Finally and most importantly, for any real transformation to take place in union practices it is essential that women themselves organize within the unions to formulate their own demands and to ensure that the unions at local level put into practice what is enshrined in policy statements and resolutions at national level. Obviously such organization is not easy, particularly given the dominance of familial ideology in the daily reality of most working women's lives. However, it is not impossible, as women from the Ford machinists to the Grunwick strikers have demonstrated. And, as we have shown above, the contradictory nature of the reality that women experience opens a space for change. This type of organization is not likely to be initiated by the trade unions themselves but is an important task for feminists within the trade union movement. Without such organization and pressure, there is little hope that the male-dominated unions will implement their fine-sounding rhetoric and begin to put into practice their at present largely theoretical commitment to the cause of women's liberation.

■ Notes

This article appeared in *Feminist Review* No. 15, 1983.

1 For instance, at the 1979 TUC a 'Charter for the Involvement of Women in Trade Unions' was adopted and in 1976 the TUC's 'Aims for Working Women' was redrafted to include a demand for abortion to be freely available as part of the struggle for women's rights.

2 This function of trade union bureaucracy of dampening down grassroots initiative and in effect allowing capitalism to operate more smoothly is vividly described by Amrit Wilson in her book *Finding A Voice: Asian Women in Britain* (1978).

3 Unless otherwise indicated all shop stewards and union representatives quoted are male.

4 As Diane Elson and Ruth Pearson (this volume) have pointed out there is nothing natural about the ability to do this type of work. Women are trained for it outside the workplace at home from their earliest years. Work that is in fact often highly skilled is not recognized as such because

the training does not take place within the workplace and is therefore conceived of as a natural ability which women possess and men do not.

5 This conflict exists throughout the trade union movement as Michèle Barrett and Mary McIntosh have pointed out: 'Recently ... the trade union movement has tried to have its cake and eat it too. While day-to-day bargaining has routinely used the argument of family needs, the official pronouncements of the TUC in relation to equal pay have tried to play down this consideration and emphasize the wage as payment for work performed. Thus, as Bea Campbell and Val Charlton (1978A: 32) so lucidly put it "The Labour Movement has managed to combine a commitment to equal pay with a commitment to the family wage; you can't have both"' (1980: 52).

6 At the bus company when women bus conductors were first employed the union insisted that they receive equal pay. This was not so much for the benefit of the women, but to ensure that pay levels for the men were maintained: 'During the war years when we started having conductresses because we couldn't get men, it was said even then that they'd be paid a man's wage, because if they don't pay a man's wage when the war finishes they won't employ the men because they're employing the women for cheaper rates. So I mean we've always had this thing on 'ere as far as conductors go of equal pay.' A comment from the AUEW shop steward at the electrical components factory indicates the effect that women's low pay can have on men's pay and points up the very real contradictions that exist between the interests of men and women workers: 'When equality came it was one of the worst things that happened actually as far as men in the X industry went because about 95 per cent of the people employed are women, and so instead of women coming up to the men's wages the men's wages were depressed.'

7 It is quite possible that with further discussion the women's initial reaction to the question might have been modified. Unfortunately due to the structure of the interview it was not possible to pursue this issue further. However, it is significant that their initial reactions on the wages issue were in the main in conformity with familial rather than egalitarian ideology.

8 This type of support was prevalent amongst those women working in the factories. The exceptions were often provided by women who had been in one of the Armed Forces. One of those who had been in the Army said: 'If you've got good management and things like that you can do without ... I mean the Army doesn't have a union and if things happen like that they still get sorted out just the same, so I can't see the reason for having them really.' However, women with this sort of opinion were in a minority and most of them were very much in favour of a principled union presence.

Black Women and
the Economic Crisis

Amina Mama

The available literature on Black women is extremely diverse. It is broadly divisible into the following four categories which are briefly commented on.

First there is the material produced by Euro-American women about Black women both here and in our countries of origin. This utilizes western concepts and approaches which can be seen to have varied applicability across the different women they purport to study. This applicability depends on a number of factors, the most significant being the degree to which Euro-American imperialism has succeeded in dominating the cultural, socio-political and economic arenas, and the manner in which such domination has infiltrated the lives and experiences of Black women. This applies particularly to orthodox anthropological and sociological frameworks, as well as to Euro-Marxist conceptions of class and Euro-feminist conceptions of gender, patriarchy and sexuality (see Amos and Parmar, 1984). The resulting texts are often held together by unspecified assumptions such as the universality of female oppression, or the transcendence of 'sisterhood' over existing differences (for example Cutrufelli, 1983). Many of these problems are typified in the compilation format employed in *Third World, Second Sex* (Davies, 1983). While this contains some rich texts by women from all over the 'Third World', and as such may provide reference material for some, it is deficient because one is left to wonder what assumptions operated to put such diversity within a single book cover (see also Jayawardena, 1982).

These criticisms also apply to some of the work by African women trained in western academic traditions, particularly those who have opted to remain within some of the more orthodox frameworks. Christine Obbo's 'African Women', for example, is actually about women in a particular part of Eastern Africa, and uses sociological theory which does not do justice to the data she collected (Obbo, 1980). In contrast to these is the seminal research conducted in Eastern Nigeria (Amadiume, 1983 unpub) which concentrates on one people to examine the changing status of women in the traditional (pre-1900), colonial and neo-colonial periods.

The third main source is the growing body of Black American literature currently forming a significant reference point for feminists in this country, perhaps to a greater extent than is merited by the general historical similarities that do exist between Black women in Britain and the US. Our specific histories are quite different, as are the political practices and ideologies that have developed out of these (Davis, 1981; Aptheker, 1982; Ladner, 1971; Cade, 1979; Joseph and Lewis, 1981; Hull, Scott and Smith, 1982; Hooks, 1981; Rodgers-Rose, 1980).

Finally there is the growing body of literature produced by organizations and individuals on Black women in Britain.[1] In the light of the reservations raised about the first three categories, a major objective of such work must be to develop appropriate conceptual tools and well-grounded theory. By this I mean grounded in the experiences and realities of the specific Black women concerned, and which incorporates the contingency of action on experience. Such grounding should enable us to transcend the assumptions underlying Euro-American (white dominated) thought, methods and practices. This is important because even Marxist and feminist theories have been produced out of histories and ideologies that reflect particular and oppressive relations to Black people, and particularly Black women. These in turn, generate 'knowledge' that is partial and particular, despite universalistic claims.

The diversity of the literature we have glanced at here raises the need for clarifying our terms and identifying the communities implicit in my usage of the term 'Black women'. This will be followed by a discussion of our relationship with the British economy as workers, and secondly of our relationship to the state as citizens. These relations are cast in a historical perspective which recognizes the significance of the changing forms of imperialism internationally and racism within Britain as integral to the relations examined. The manner in which gender textures relations of Black women to the economy and the state is also considered throughout.

■ Clarifying terms and identifying communities

The historical and political origins of the term 'Black' require particular attention in the light of the prevalent attempts to group all who are not white *and* English ('non-whites') together as 'ethnic minorities' or 'Third World' persons, thereby reducing us to an amorphous, homogeneously underdeveloped and oppressed mass. This negation of the validity of 'Black' traditionally comes from the political right, which fails to recognize racism. It has also come from 'Marxists', the most recent example being Anthias and Yuval-Davies (1983), ostensibly because they feel that:

> The notion of 'Black women' as delineating the boundaries of the alternative feminist movement to white feminism leaves non-British, non-black women (like us – a Greek-Cypriot and an Israeli Jew) unaccounted for politically.

It is interesting that we now have white women responding to Black women's historically rooted tradition of autonomous organization in this manner: first by seeing it as 'an alternative movement' and secondly that this somehow makes them feel 'left out' of things. We have also witnessed the extension of the term 'Black' to include all those subject to imperialist domination, so that 'Black' sometimes refers to 'white' people. Despite the glaring historical inaccuracy and political foolishness of the exercise, time has been wasted arguing whether or not to include Iranians, Palestinians, Filipino, even Irish, as 'Black'. In the US some American feminists have attempted to resolve the issue raised there by Hispanics, native Americans and others, by adopting the phrase 'women of colour', thus reserving 'Black' for Africans.

In Britain it is clear that Black refers to Africans (continental and of the diaspora), and Asians (primarily of Indian subcontinent descent). All have a shared history of oppression by British colonialism and racism. Only the Caribbean African (Afro-Caribbean) community have the specific history of enslavement. They share with fellow Africans elements of a Pan-Africanist consciousness ('Black consciousness'). Amongst the Asian communities, which include those from the Asian diaspora (the Caribbean, east and southern Africa (cf Tinker, 1974)), the political consciousness that includes self-definition as 'Black' is more recent. It has come from the superimposition of the experience of white racism on the experiences of indentured labour and colonial domination.

Historically, Black consciousness (Pan-Africanism) has its origins in two related sources. First on the African continent it was manifest in movements against settler colonialism in the south and east. These date back to the Khoisan attacks on the white settlers invading the Cape in the 1600s (Marks and Atmore, 1971), through to the 1906 Zulu rebellion in Natal (Marks, 1970) and Chilembwe's revolt in Nyasaland, 1915. Today we have a political movement and continuing liberation war against the scourge of apartheid (for example the Black Consciousness Movement of Azania).

In East Africa there was the Nyabingi protest movement (referred to as a 'Cult'), which immobilized the administrative efforts of three colonial powers for nearly two decades in South-Western Uganda, up until 1928. One of the most powerful and feared warrior leaders was a woman known as Muhumusa. Indeed Nyabingi was also female, as were most of her 'bagwira' (mediums or representatives). Male bagwira maintained their influence in part by adopting female patterns of dress. East Africa was also the site of the famous Mau Mau rebellion.

West African political consciousness developed somewhat differently. The Indirect Rule system employed in Northern Nigeria, for example, did not facilitate the polarization of class interests along the specific dimension of skin colour in quite the same way (for example, see Azikwe in Langley, 1979). However, it took numerous military campaigns to conquer each of the people and empires: Benin, Ashanti, Kebbi and Sokoto. Even after formal assumption of sovereignty over Northern Nigeria, for example, Lord Lugard had to wage successive campaigns to take over lands whose armies were supplied with arms by the Nupe kingdom (Bida and Kontagora, 1900; Yola, 1901; Bauchi, 1902; Kano, 1903; Sokoto, 1903, and Burmi, 1903).

The diasporean source of Black consciousness must be traced back to the earliest slave rebellions; for example the Maroon wars in Jamaica, the Haitian rebellions; and in post-slavery resistance. The reader is referred to the writings and practices of Blyden, M. Garvey, G. Padmore, A. Cesaire, W.E.B. DuBois, C.L.R. James.

'Black' therefore has a particular significance for African peoples. Those from the Indian subcontinent come out of their own history of struggle (see P. Trivedi, 1984).

Among Asians, two subgroups are additionally of interest. East African Asians had a particular relationship both with colonials (for whom they performed petit-bourgeois functions) and with the Africans (who rejected this role with the departure of the colonial masters). This is relevant to the status of this group today, who like the African elites enjoy a class position here which is often facilitated by links with capital 'back home'.

Amongst Indo-Caribbeans, the relation to Black consciousness varies between the different nations, depending on numbers, and the consequent extent of 'creolization'. In Guyana (where Asians are the majority) and Trinidad (where they are the largest single group) communities have remained largely distinct, and thus been less exposed to Africanist Black consciousness.

From this we can see that Black women in Britain are historically rooted in three different continents. It would be foolish even to attempt to summarize the diverse cultural, religious and socio-political histories out of which we have evolved. African women, for example, may come from any part of a continent so diverse that a single nation may have 250 languages reflecting cultural differences which include extremely diverse gender and status relations. To try to isolate the 'position of women' from any such cultural context is difficult yet necessary. To generalize for a whole continent borders on the foolish, and in respect of three continents must be the height of folly. Furthermore, Black women's experiences and struggles, apart from being rooted in so many different contexts are further complicated by the varying penetrations by and relations with British society. Black women here constantly identify with and politically support a range of movements, and accord varying priority to African national liberation struggles, African and Caribbean movements and events in Asia. There is also general political support for other anti-imperialist struggles such as the Latin American fight against Euro-American domination and the Irish liberation struggle against British imperialism.

From another angle we can be viewed as three 'generations'. First there are those who have inhabited Liverpool, Cardiff and London since the seventeenth century, who arrived either as slaves, or as the daughters of Black ex-slaves or of unions between Black sailors and native white women. The middle 'generation' of Black women came as migrants from the tropical reaches of the British empire. Most recent is the growing generation born and/or predominantly raised here, by migrant parents. This last group is influenced to varying degrees by parental cultures. It is noteworthy here that a substantial proportion of the 'non-white' population is of mixed origin – this ranges from 6 per cent in the West Midlands to 40 per cent in Merseyside (1981

Labour Force Survey). Most of us are urban: 40 per cent of the 'New Commonwealth and Pakistani origin' community lives in the GLC area (59 per cent of West Indians), 20 per cent in eight large cities and the remaining 40 per cent in smaller cities. Fifty per cent of the Black community are Asian, 30 per cent West Indian, with the remaining 20 per cent from 'Africa, the Far East and the Mediterranean' (Population Trends 28, 1982).

In addition to the various 'parent cultures', there are new cultural and political forms evolving out of the Black British woman's unique experience, textured as this is by contemporary forms of racial, class and sexual oppression, and the corresponding patterns of rebellion and resistance.[2]

Black feminism in this country reflects the diversity of origin and variation in geographical, historical and cultural reference points. The unity of Black women as Black feminists is a political phenomenon that seeks a coherent and co-ordinated rebellion against the varied manifestations of oppression. The priority given to Afro-Asian unity by African and Asian women's organizations such as OWAAD, is a fundamental aspect of the growing awareness of the need for a united front at a time when the British state is intensifying its discriminatory practices in ways detrimental to us all.

■ Black women and the economy

The relationship between the various organs of this state and its Black citizens has been discussed along with some of its many ramifications in the context of the economic crisis (Hall *et al*, 1978; Gutzmore, 1975 and 1983; Sivanandan, 1976; Solomos *et al*, 1982). The effects of this crisis on Black women at the levels of state and economy, and effects of the strategies of Britain's ruling class for dealing with the crisis on us, have rarely been discussed. These are addressed here. Throughout it is recognized that both the crisis and the strategies have both political ideological and economic manifestations, and that these amount to a regrouping, reformulation and restructuring by forces that have a history of domestic and international exploitation in the interests of capital. The apparatuses of the colonial state that maintained British supremacy at horrendously destructive costs to Black people on the African and Asian continents during slavery and colonialism continue to uphold the interests of international capital today by means which include the monstrosity of apartheid. At the same time there is an ongoing, many-pronged assault on all sections of the Black communities resident in the UK. It is the fact of racism in its changing forms in the contemporary British context (Lawrence, 1982) which underlies the economic strategies and crucially informs the ideological changes we are now witnessing.

Our relations to the economy are discussed here primarily with reference to the NHS and office work, and as such focus on African and Caribbean Black women, unless specified otherwise. It is argued that these relations are constructed along the dimensions of race and gender, to the detriment of Black women, and that the contemporary situation is one in which these divisions are being upheld and accentuated by the present government's strategies for dealing with the economic crisis, and by its policies and legislation in general.

The relations of Black women to the British economy should be considered in the context of Black people, but must in addition be analysed in terms of gender. This is because they are not equitable with or reducible to those of Black men, or subsumable to those of the Black community. It is not simply a matter of going into detail about Black women as a subgroup. There are qualitative differences along the dimension of gender and its meaning in British society which have implications for Black women, and have textured the economic relations of Black people in general. We have played a specific role in the rationalization processes of British capitalism.

To cast things in a historic perspective it is necessary to consider relations from slavery onwards, which have been documented (Philips, 1975; Shyllon, 1974; Gutzmore, 1975; Williams, 1944). In Britain 1764 saw some 20,000 slave workers in London alone, an estimate which discounted what must have been a substantial number of slaves, freed slaves and 'mulattoes', who must also have been workers of some sort (Rogers, 1942). In the same period, a certain John Fielding protested against bringing these 'poor creatures' over from the West Indies because they became intoxicated with liberty and started to expect wages and 'corrupt' Black servants with notions of freedom. He also connected those sent back to the Caribbean plantations with insurrections. The 'St. Giles black birds' were largely made up of Black men who had served the British Army in America and were discharged in London to become destitutes in 1783 (George, 1925).

Studies of the post-war period are often discussions of 'immigrants', and therefore collapse all of us into a single, and by implication recently arrived, generation. A second deficiency is that little of this material is gender-differentiated although there are a few recent publications on female immigrant labour (Foner, 1976; Phizacklea,

1983). Peach (1969) in *West Indian Migration to Britain* presumed female migration to have been a passive following of menfolk. He put the proportion of 'women and children' at over 40 per cent of the total between 1955 and 1964 (p. 45). A substantial proportion of the women are likely to have been single, since women were specifically recruited. Regardless of marital status, the vast majority of these middle-generation Caribbean women came to this country as workers. Concerning recruitment, the National Health Service and the then Ministry of Labour were in consultation with the Colonial Office as early as 1944, and the local selection committees constituting a centralized recruiting system had been set up in sixteen countries (including Nigeria, Sierra Leone, British Guiana, Trinidad, Mauritius and Jamaica) by 1948. Doctors and dentists were recruited primarily from the Indian subcontinent. It is notable that restrictive immigration did not hinder recruitment, since quota systems allowed the NHS to continue importing unskilled labour for ancillary jobs, and skilled labour was not restricted (Doyal *et al*, 1981).

The 1981 Labour Force Survey shows 47.2 per cent of white women to be economically active, as compared to 67.6 per cent of 'West Indian or Guyanese', 48.1 per cent of Indian women, 40.5 per cent of African women and 15.5 per cent of Pakistani or Bangladeshi women. This gives Black women an officially higher rate of 49.4 per cent. The location of Black women in the labour market reflects and compounds the dimensions of inequality intrinsic to British society. In accordance with racial differentiation, we are to be found in the lower echelons of all the institutions where we are employed (this in itself reflecting the patterns of a segmented labour market), where the work is often physically heavy (in the factories and mills no less than in the caring professions), the pay is lowest, and the hours are longest and most anti-social (night shifts, for example).

In accordance with gender divisions, Black women tend to be employed in particular industries (clothing and food manufacture, catering, transport and cleaning, nursing and hospital ancillary work). Jobs in the 'caring' professions (nursing, teaching, community and social work) exploit oppressive notions of 'femininity', and yet actually involve heavy labour as in the case of nurses, ancillary workers and cleaners (see Unit of Manpower Studies, 1976).

The National Health Service

The NHS is a major component of Britain's welfare state, which has been developed since the last war. Its birth was fundamentally a fruit of wartime class collaboration and social democratic consensus, and financed by the post-war boom. This was also a time when workers, like soldiers before them, were recruited from the colonies to staff the boom and facilitate white upward (and outward) mobility, while keeping wages to a minimum that would have been unacceptable to the increasingly unionized white working class. Black labour was allocated by the market to specific purposes as we have seen.

Nursing is where professional Black women are employed in the NHS, usually as State Enrolled Nurses (SENs) rather than as State Registered Nurses (SRNs), despite the fact that the lower status SEN qualification is unrecognized in many of our countries of origin. National data on overseas nurses in the NHS are not available, and the studies that have been done include the large and fluctuating proportion that have been recruited from Ireland, Malaysia and the Philippines. In the hospitals they studied, Doyal *et al* (1981) found 81 per cent of the qualified nursing workforce to be from overseas (within this, Irish and Malaysians were more often SRNs, ward sisters and nursing officers, while Afro-Caribbean and Filippino women more SEN or nursing auxiliaries).

With regard to ancillary and maintenance workers the same study found 78 per cent of ancillary workers and within this 84 per cent of domestic and catering workers, from overseas. The proportion of female overseas ancillaries was more than double the number of males, and within that 78 per cent of domestic and 55 per cent of catering workers.

For more detailed exposure of the stratification within nursing and the role of Black labour in facilitating the rationalization of the labour process both within the NHS and industry, the reader is referred to Doyal *et al* (1981). They argue that, in general, migrant labour has been used to enable changes in the organic composition of capital on terms more favourable to capital accumulation. In the case of the NHS immigrants are seen as having provided a crucial source of cheap labour, enabling the NHS to meet the demands of Britain's changing demography. The ever-increasing numbers of geriatric and chronically mentally and/or physically handicapped people has resulted in a growing demand for long-term care in unpopular areas; migrant labour has been used to facilitate caring for these people without dramatically increasing costs.

The economic crisis and its attendant legislative and political changes have affected Black workers disproportionately across the board. 'Restructuring' involves closing down old, declining areas in favour of new, expanding ones. It so happens that because of the historical role Black labour has played, it is exactly those sectors of the market that have employed Black people that are now closing down, while persisting discrimination ensures racist recruitment patterns in those areas being expanded and developed, which are exacerbated by unemployment. Racist redundancy policies must also be taken into account. While the NHS cannot close down overnight, as we have seen recently, it has been a focus of Tory cutbacks. The government strategy is to whittle away as much as possible while privatizing, and it is the areas where Black women work (ancillary services) that are going first. For workers, privatization means an intensified exploitation: longer hours, less bargaining power, lower wages and fewer people employed on these inferior terms. The laying-off and sacking has already provoked protests from Black women workers (see, for example, *Caribbean Times, 158*, March 1984).

The recent 'fishing raids' and deportation of Filippino nurses are evidence that the state is using immigration legislation to regulate Black women workers according to demand, much as the Ministry of Labour and the Colonial Office acted together in earlier recruitment strategies. The current context of high unemployment means that inferior jobs are becoming attractive to white British workers who previously enjoyed the luxury of regarding these as 'below' them.

Offices

Seventy per cent of all jobs in the GLC area are office jobs and 50 per cent of the Black community live in London. Recent years have seen some Black women employed in some office jobs. These have generally been low-skilled ones, in local government and welfare offices. Offices have been at the heart of the so-called 'technological revolution'. Emma Bird had this to say about it:

> women are disproportionately affected by the introduction of new technology. Not only are they more likely to lose their jobs, but they are also more likely to find that the quality of work has deteriorated in the jobs that remain. (Bird 1980)

Her estimates are comparatively low: 2 per cent (21,000) office job loss by 1985, rising to 17 per cent by 1990. In 1979, APEX predicted a quarter of a million job loss by 1983. Assessment of actual job loss is complicated by the fact that many are lost by 'natural wastage'. The West Yorkshire case study (Leeds TUCRIC, 1982) concluded amongst other things that new technology leads to job losses in all the areas of women's employment, that new jobs in scientific and technical areas will favour men, that there are disturbing increases in stress and new health hazards are evident (100 per cent increase in headaches, 77 per cent increase in eye troubles and 69 per cent increase in tiredness are reported) after the introduction of new technology. As in industry, restructuring has had the effect of decreasing certain areas while increasing new ones. Predictably by now, it is the less skilled secretarial jobs, where Black women tend to be employed, that are most affected. The areas currently expanding (banking, finance and telecommunications) are not those which have tended to employ Black women, and racist recruitment and selection for training in the new skills required is preventing proportionate representation of Black women in these areas. In short, what is bad for women is worse for Black women.

To conclude this section, it needs to be pointed out that the Black woman's status as a worker is particularly important because we are more often heads of families, and have more dependants than our white counterparts. Black women are also more likely to have unemployed menfolk, and when this is not the case, Black male wage levels are low. The Black woman's wage is therefore crucial to our communities, and changes to it affect all Black people.

We can conclude that the sexist and racist devaluation of Black female labour by Britain is not only historical but also a contemporary fact and that the situation, far from improving, appears to be deteriorating. In addition to this we have particular relations to the British state, firstly as workers to capital's needs, and secondly to the legislative apparatus, particularly through immigration legislation which is used to mediate this relation and keep it on terms that do not include our interests as workers. Finally, the present strategies for coping with economic decline/crisis are particularly detrimental to Black women workers, in the NHS and offices, and presumably in the areas not covered here. The overall picture is suggested by the Black female unemployment rate being estimated at three times the national average. Given the manner in which unemployment figures omit married or cohabiting women, the figure is probably higher, and this would further increase the twice the national average given for Black unemployment. The pattern, however, is not simple or uniform, as the case of the NHS illustrates; it varies with skill level and qualification levels, and is affected by recruiting from different countries at different times and in different areas of work.

■ The welfare state and Black women

The welfare state's primary purpose is the reproduction and maintenance of the nation's labour force. Apart from being workers in it, Black women have a second relation to the welfare state; that of residents and therefore consumers. Discussion will focus on the National Health Service and the Department of Health and Social Security. In addition to the staff cutbacks and hospital closures currently in evidence, all aspects of the welfare state are being increasingly policed in ways that particularly affect Black people. These changes affect us as women disproportionately, because, in accordance with our roles as wives and mothers, sisters and aunties, we come into more frequent contact with all agencies in our own right, as well as in accompanying our relatives. In our reproductive capacity we have to attend family planning clinics, antenatal clinics and hospitals for deliveries and post-natal care. I shall argue that the quality of healthcare provided for us by the NHS is mediated by historically rooted racism and sexism.

Looking at earlier periods, we can see that our reproductive abilities have fundamentally influenced our relationship to British society. In earlier centuries, Black female sexuality and reproductive powers were commoditized like anything else, and were therefore the property of the slave-owning class. It can be argued historically that Black female reproductive powers have been controlled according to the needs of the capitalist labour market. Black slave women, apart from being labourers themselves, also had the task of reproducing the Black labour force, particularly when legislation obstructed the wholesale importation, and particularly when the life expectancy of slaves was not very long. Angela Davis has elucidated this aspect of slavery for us (Davis, 1981). Contrary to a sexist mythology that slave women had an 'easier time' as a result of their sex, rape was an additional form of punishment and coercion. 'Breeders' were compelled to reproduce as fast as biology would permit but given none of the status or care associated with motherhood. Pregnant and mothering women had to work the fields and were subjected to the same maltreatment as everyone else.

> A woman who gives offence in the field and is large in any way is compelled to lie down over a hole made to receive her corpulency, and is flogged with the whip or beat with the

which has holes in it; and at every stroke comes a blister. One of my sisters was so severely punished in this way, that labour was brought on, and the child was born in the field. This very overseer, Mr Brooks, killed in this manner a girl named Mary. (quoted in Davis, 1981)

The racist myths about Black female sexual prowess undoubtedly developed and contributed to large scale sexual abuse; the proximity and intimacy that domestic slaves were forced to live in relation to their 'masters' would have facilitated regular and repeated abuse. In the nineteenth century, a certain J.J. Virey commented:

Negresses display no common proficiency in the art of exciting the passions and gaining an unlimited power over individuals of a different sex. Their African blood carries them into the greatest excesses. (J.J. Virey 1837, cited in Rogers, 1945)

The limiting of Black female reproduction, in stark contrast to the slavery period, is a recent phenomenon. It would be unrealistic to divorce this from the world economic situation. The slump in western metropolises, and the continued underdevelopment of our countries of origin agriculturally and economically, must be brought to bear on our reproductive relations with the British state, both here and abroad. One of Josué de Castro's central points is that starvation causes over-population, and not the reverse (de Castro, 1973). It is the reverse assumption that underpins the western approach to family planning both here and abroad.

Contraception is one area of the NHS which has not been cut back. Pressure is put on Black women, particularly young, single ones to have abortions and both start and continue using the pill. Disturbing evidence about the long-acting contraceptive depo-provera has provoked campaign action and protests from Black women, and even cries of 'genocide' from some quarters.

Childcare is another site at which our contemporary reproductive relation to the state must be considered. Inferior housing and financial situations, coupled with racist evaluation of Black homes and mothers, go some way to accounting for the high proportion of Black children in care. Financial difficulties and inadequate childcare facilities particularly affect the Black single mother. Recent legislation has further weakened the position of parents in relation to the social services and foster agencies. Unfamiliarity with the legal intricacies involved in retrieving children from the state agencies, and the racism

of officials involved in disputes that arise, give cause for concern, as do the problems that arise out of transracial adoption and fostering in a racist society.

Among the West African community, the same difficulties in housing and employment, along with the pressures of study that originally brought many of us here, and the lack and expense of daycare facilities, lead many to have children privately fostered. There is evidence of an undesirable tendency of outside observers to over-emphasize the role of 'West African culture' in this. Extended family systems purportedly make us prone to fostering out our children (Ellis, 1978). West African mothers are fully aware that sending young children to English foster families or institutions is not the same thing as sending them to live with a close and trusted relative (which, in any case, occurs when they are older). The suggested remedy is, predictably, to leave them 'back home'. This short-sightedness overlooks basic facts about West Africans in London; first that it is the desire to have children that inspires parents to have them. Secondly, many still desire an English education for their children as well as themselves. Thirdly, many of us do not return to West Africa for a good many years, and fostering is generally a short-term measure. Finally there is the fact that few West Africans have anticipated the actual level of hardship and hostility that is met here.

Goody's study on the delegation of parenting by Black families in the Caribbean, West Africa and London (Goody, 1978) found the reasons given for fostering in the British context to be quite different from those in West Africa, where sophisticated systems of kinship obligations and ties are involved, which implies that the two phenomena are far from culturally equivalent.

Misportrayals and misunderstandings compound the racism of social service officials, precipitating and sustaining the disputes over parental rights between the state or (usually English) foster parents, and real parents.

The psychiatric aspects of the welfare state are of particular concern to all Black people, given the fact that 40 per cent of all Black people in NHS beds are there as psychiatric patients (Black Patients and Health Workers Group, 1983). The historical relations of Black people to psychiatric medicine are relevant here. During slavery, for example, many were diagnosed as suffering from 'drapetomania', an incurable urge to run away (Thomas and Sillen, 1972). The subsequent pathologization of Black resistance has two notable ideological concomitants; first it discredits revolutionary or rebellious ideas and actions and secondly it conflates these with 'madness'. Today, as in the past, there are 'Black-specific' categories of mental illness: 'West Indian psychosis', while 'paranoia' and 'religious mania' feature strong. 'Marital psychosis', purportedly occurring in young Asian women, should be considered against the background of state intervention into Asian marital customs (see Trivedi, 1984). Littlewood and Lipsedge (1983) point out that the treatment of Black patients differs substantially from that received by white ones. Black people receive more physical treatments (electro-convulsive therapy, oral and injected drugs), and at higher dosages (or numbers, in the case of ECT). We receive less nonphysical treatment (therapy, counselling etc), and are less likely to see consultants or other highly qualified staff.

The pathologization of women also has historical roots. The burning of two million witches is regarded by many as the antecedent of modern psychiatry (Chesler, 1972; Szasz, 1970; Foucault, 1965). Other research suggests that both clinical psychologists and psychiatrists tend to see 'adult women' as more pathological than 'adult men' (Broverman et al, 1970). The epidemiology of depression shows women having higher rates (Brown and Harris, 1981).

Objections are being raised about the large-scale over-prescription of tranquillizers and anti-depressants to women across the class scale from suburban housewives to young mothers living on vast housing estates in appalling conditions. For Black women, the evidence has not been systematically gathered together. (For the Black American situation, see Carrington, Aldridge, in Rodgers-Rose, Chesler 1972.) White cultural stereotypes about what constitutes 'normal' behaviour for women, combined with the tendency of mental health professionals to pathologize what they do not understand or are unfamiliar with, give cause for concern.

In relation to the rest of the state, we are witnessing a growing encroachment of psychiatric expertise into the prisons and courtrooms. Magistrates more frequently demand psychiatric reports for Black defendants, especially if they have locks. Black people are disproportionately represented among the involuntary section of the persons receiving psychiatric treatment. Treatment may also be a condition of probation or eligibility for parole. The social services also utilize psychiatric reports in, for instance, child custody cases.

The Mental Health Act (1959 Review) allows the Home Office to deport any person receiving in-patient treatment if they do not have the right of abode (Section 90). The erosion of human rights that occurs once a person has been stigmatized psychiatrically is extensive.

Sections 135 and 136 give the authorities the power to 'enter premises' or 'remove a person from a public place' to a 'place of safety' (which may be anywhere from a police cell to a hospital). Various other clauses provide for involuntary detention (sections 25, 26 and 29), and extension of this (section 30).

In the context of the growing corporatization of the state it seems that psychiatry plays a particular role, since psychiatric expertise can be and is being called upon by different organs of that state. The relation of psychiatry to Black women is mediated by the dimensions of race and gender, whose effects have been briefly mentioned above.

In the case of the DHSS, legislated sexual discrimination renders married or cohabiting women unentitled to claim, thus forcing dependence on men regardless of the financial basis of the relationship. Social security investigators interrogate and spy on women in an attempt to ascertain the sexual habits of female claimants. The racist stereotype of Black people as social security scroungers promotes these forms of harrassment. The current government has increased and intensified the policing of these services.

The recent Nationality Bill has given hospital staff the role of enforcers, since proof of citizenship is required before receiving healthcare. Questionnaires are presented at hospitals. It is Black people who are most often required to prove citizenship, in case they are 'foreign', and it is this that has has provoked the 'No Pass Laws to Health' campaigns. Hospital closures and staff cutbacks have put added and growing pressure on the NHS, which manifests in the attempts to restrict access as far as possible.

■ Conclusion: the erosion of rights

Many aspects of our relationship to the British state in its current state of flux have been omitted from this discussion. For example, the overtly coercive aspects of the state the police force, courts and prisons have not been adequately considered, although the growing policing of the welfare state was discussed. Policing in particular is going through drastic changes; the Police and Criminal Evidence Act constitutes the most overt threat to civil rights in this country (see The National Campaign Against the Police Bill Bulletin 1983, and Christian, 1983).

However, even from this limited account several points emerge. Firstly, the complexity and multiplicity of our relations with the British state cannot escape comment. This is a result of our own historical and contemporary diversity as a group. It is also due to the numerical array and sophistication of the organs and agencies comprising what is loosely referred to as 'the state'. The term is still useful, particularly in the light of the manner in which these are increasingly linking up with each other (increased corporatization), as exemplified by the discussion of the NHS implementation of Home Office immigration controls. During the 1981 uprisings, NHS hospitals are reported to have turned casualties over to the police. The growing seepage of psychiatric expertise into the courts, schools and prisons suggests that psychiatry is playing a particular role in the corporatization process.

The economic crisis is being exploited by the government as a means to erode away the welfare state, and with it the right to health, education, housing etc. These measures are specifically affecting Black women in the ways mentioned.

The right to earn a living is being seriously undermined by the high levels of unemployment resulting from economic decline and industrial atrophy. Strategies being employed ostensibly to remedy this are actually exacerbating the situation particularly for Black women, as we have seen in the cases of the welfare state and office technological innovation. In short the quantity and quality of work available to Black women, already severely limited by historical and contemporary racial and sexual division of the labour market, is deteriorating as a result of the economic situation, but being even further eroded by the present government's policies.

As Black women we can draw courage from the fact that these are merely contemporary manifestations of old phenomena. Historically we have found ways to survive and resist the forces of class, racial and sexual oppression. There is no reason why we should not do so today. We must continue to evolve new strategies, organize more cohesively and effectively. We must consolidate the benefits of centuries of experience in order to move ever forward.

■ Notes

This article appeared in *Feminist Review* No. 17, 1984.

1 See for example FOWAAD (1979 onwards), produced by OWAAD OWAAD Conference Papers; SPEAK OUT, produced by the Brixton Black Women's Group; OUTWRITE, from number 1 March 1982 SPARE RIB numbers 101, 107, 110, 111, 123, 132.

2 See 'Black Women Organizing Autonomously' *Feminist Review* No. 17, 1984.

3 OWAAD: Organisation for Women of African & Asian Descent.

Equality and the
European Community

Catherine Hoskyns

■ Equality legislation and the women's movement

Over the last fifteen years there has been a steady development of policy and legislation at the level of the European Community on the subject of women's rights in employment. This parallels developments in the member states, and has the effect of generalizing policies, so that very gradually similar provisions are being adopted throughout the Community. In very broad terms, these developments at both the national and the Community level spring out of the increased involvement of women in the labour market, the social unrest of the 1960s which forced governments to pay more attention to disadvantaged groups, and the greater awareness and organization of women in the 1970s. The European legislation, however, was not fought for in any direct sense by women, and remains virtually unknown to the majority of those who are supposed to be its beneficiaries.

This development of policy and legislation at the European level raises in an even more extreme form questions which have already been the subject of some debate in the women's movement of the different countries with regard to national legislation. All of this legislation, whether supranational or national, is based on the idea of equality, and in general seeks to remove some of the barriers, particularly in terms of overt practice and written provisions, which make it difficult for women to compete freely in the labour market. But legislating for equality between groups which are unequal in their whole social situation has little substantive effect, unless strong supporting and implementing measures are also taken. The truth of this is clearly demonstrated in a recent article in which Nicola Charles discusses her survey of workplaces in one locality, and shows how little impact equality legislation has had on basic assumptions about family reponsibilities, which still determine both how work is organized and the attitudes of management, trade union representatives and most male and female workers (Charles, this volume).

Leaving aside the problem of implementation, however, many women in the women's movement have questioned, either explicitly or implicitly, whether equality in a man's world is really what women should be aiming at. Indeed, the formation of the women's liberation movement in many countries in the 1970s can be seen as an attempt to transcend the strategy of the more traditional women's rights movement, which did in general aim at equality, and to mount a challenge from the different and particular perspective of women to the whole of patriarchal society. To a large extent this has been done by developing alternative attitudes and actions, many of which are based on the 'difference' of women and spring out of the specific situation in which women find themselves.[1] A recent and compelling example of this kind of action has been the attempt of the Greenham women to project into the debate about defence, concerns and a style of protest which derive from the particular position of women in this society. Thus the women's movement in most European countries has tended to distance itself from the state, and to be suspicious of legislation – and particularly legislation about equality– as a solution to women's problems.

National equality legislation – and European legislation even more so – appears to be handed down 'from above'. In general, there has been little mobilization about equality (with the exception of campaigns in the 1960s about equal pay) and little concern except among élite groups about what form the legislation should take. This is in marked contrast to the situation with regard to divorce reform and abortion. Legislation on these issues has been deliberately sought and in a number of countries has led to massive mobilization by women. An example of this in this country is the very solid organization by women which has so far prevented the watering down of the 1967 abortion law. More recently, the issues taken up most strongly by the women's movement in this and other countries have had to do with combating male violence, and have led to the setting up of rape crisis and battered women's centres, the organization of 'reclaim the night marches', and involvement in the wider peace movement.

Issues like abortion and male violence relate directly to the situation in which many women find themselves. Clearly mobilization around these realities is much easier than around an abstract concept like equality, which may or may not be relevant to particular circumstances, and is in any case hard to enforce. This is not to say that resentment about manifestations of inequality at work does not exist. A recent study of women and employment in the West Midlands brought hundreds of complaints about unfair practices, discrimination and sexual harassment, all of which seemed to be intensifying in a situation of unemployment and recession (Low Pay Unit, 1984). Women faced with these circumstances, however, are not usually in a situation where they can organize effectively or apply equality legislation.

This paradox has led the women's movement in Scandinavia to coin the phrase 'state feminism' to describe equality laws which are neither mobilized for nor implemented by women, and which create rights on an individual basis. They see these laws as co-opting women into the labour market, without in the process creating any greater power or autonomy for women in a basically patriarchal system (Nielsen, 1983).

This, however, may be to go too far in minimizing the role of legislation. Even crude legal instruments can be important to weak and disadvantaged groups in society and can give them at least some purchase on the political process. Experience has shown that this is especially the case where the normal mechanisms and instruments through which pressure can be exerted, and where compromise is negotiated, are themselves conditioned by the practices and assumptions being challenged. This is certainly true for women, where patriarchy has already shaped the form and structure of trade unions, political parties, pressure groups and so on. In these circumstances, the existence of individual legal rights and the ability of individuals and small groups to take action, can be an important lever.

The Defrenne cases, brought in Belgium in the early1970s and referred to the European Court of Justice, are a good example of this.[2] These cases were brought by individual women against the advice of both the European Commission and leading Belgian trade unionists. Yet it was the Defrenne judgments that clarified the extent of the application of Article 119 of the Treaty of Rome on equal pay, and spurred the Community on to adopt a much broader policy on women's rights. More recently in this country, in the Clarke and Powell case, the bringing of a legal action supported by the National Council for Civil Liberties was successful in regaining rights for women to which they were entitled under the law, but which had been negotiated away by their trade union representatives.[3]

■ Formal and substantive equality

The lack of mobilization over both the adoption and implementation of equality laws has in fact been very disadvantageous to women. For the precise way in which these laws are drafted, and the extent to which the provisions which do exist are taken up and used, can make the whole difference between laws which assert a formal equality only, and those which begin to tackle the substantive problems which create inequality in the first place (Gregory, 1981).

In judging how far legislation has gone in this respect, the following criteria are important:

The scope of the definition – this can either remain at the level of prohibiting intentional discrimination only, or go some way towards tackling indirect discrimination by focusing on the discriminatory *consequences* of particular practices.

Positive discrimination – equality legislation can either ignore, allow, or actively encourage positive discimination, that is measures that favour or give special treatment to the groups affected by discriminatory practices. Since any effective measures in this direction are likely to be at the expense of dominant interests, such provisions can be extremely controversial.

The extent of derogations – the term 'derogation' refers to all the provisions in the law which make exceptions possible or in any way limit or minimize its effect. All equality laws allow for derogations for provisions to do with maternity and for sex-specific jobs; most make an exception for some kind of positive discrimination. Derogations can, however, go further than this in allowing protective legislation to be retained, and in introducing additional groups of excepted occupations – like the church and the army. There is a recent tendency also to allow certain discriminatory practices to continue, if they can be 'justified' by economic considerations or market forces. Though protective legislation presents a particular problem (since its abrupt removal without compensating measures can worsen conditions for the weakest categories of women workers) in general the extension of these kinds of derogations has the effect of undermining any real application of the laws.

Implementation – the 'seriousness' of equality legislation can to a large extent be judged by the measures adopted for its implementation. Particularly important are:

the type of administrative procedures established;
the persons, groups or institutions empowered to take action;
the resources available for information and support;
the measures taken to compel authorities to review and monitor
existing practice;
the sanctions and penalties imposed for non-compliance.

Legislation varies enormously in the procedures used for implementation, and national traditions and particular circumstances will largely determine what practices are effective. The most attractive statutory provisions can be easily undermined by inadequate or over-complicated mechanisms for implementation.

Favourable provisions in some or all of the categories listed above can turn equality legislation from a formal instrument into something which begins to touch on the real situation of women. Furthermore, since equality legislation deals mainly with employment, laws of this kind can provide some defence against attacks on the right of women to work, which are likely to be made in times of unemployment and recession. Given these circumstances, it is worth considering whether equality legislation, however imperfect and however derived, should not be accorded greater importance in the overall struggle to improve the situation of women. This may be the case both in the sense that better use should be made of the provisions that do exist and also that campaigning for improvement and extension should be given a higher priority.

There are some indications that this is beginning to happen. The amendment to the Equal Pay Act (1970) – on claims for equal pay for work of equal value – which the British Government has been forced to make to comply with a judgment by the European Court of Justice, aroused some publicity and extensive lobbying by interested groups. The resulting provisions (although still unnecessarily complicated) are somewhat better than they would have been otherwise, and in one of the first cases to be decided under the amendment, Julie Hayward, a canteen assistant at Cammel Laird's Merseyside shipyard, won equal pay (a rise of £31 a week!) with the carpenters and joiners who work on the ships.[4] This judgment opens up the possibility for the first time of basing equal pay claims on a comparison of the work of men and women who do *different* jobs. Similarly in France, the passing by the socialist government of new equality legislation, which both broadens the scope of existing provisions and provides additional means for enforcement, has opened up new possibilities for action. It has also had the effect of reopening debate on these issues within the French women's movement.[5]

In this context, the existence of policy-making and enforcement at the level of the European Community is extremely important. For the application of the European provisions involves a set of procedures which make steady demands on states to monitor, reform and adjust national legislation. This creates a situation of some movement which opens up possibilities for debate and pressure. So the coming into force in December 1984 of the European Community's Directive on Equal Treatment in Social Security (and the necessity for states to introduce measures to comply with it) focused attention on the dependent position of women within even the most advanced social security systems. It has also reinforced some of the suspicions about equality legislation in general, since it seems that as long as men and women are treated equally, it is quite in order for states to comply with the Directive by cutting benefits to everyone.[6] There is now, however, sufficient organization and awareness for women in the countries most affected – Ireland and the Netherlands – to have responded vigorously, and to have protested both nationally and at the European level.

One effect of the existence of a Community policy on women has been that women in the various member states have very gradually established links at both an official and an unofficial level. The first manifestation of this was when women civil servants and specialists in employment questions came together in 1974 over the negotiation of the Community's Equal Treatment Directive. Subsequently, the European Commission set up an advisory committee consisting of representatives from the semi-official bodies (like the Equal Opportunities Commission) which deal with women's issues in the different countries. Women members in the European Parliament have set up various formal and informal committees and some contact between women's organizations – mainly the better organized and more traditional ones – is maintained through the Women's Information Bureau in the Commission.

At a more feminist and grassroots level, the Centre for Research on European Women (CREW) has tried to bring together independent and autonomous women's groups with the aim of establising some kind of a women's lobby in Brussels. Interestingly, the women who came to the first conference, organised by CREW in January 1983, seem to have been more interested in establishing links and exchanging information on a permanent basis, than in reacting to developments in Brussels. In this they showed again the instinctive suspicion which the women's movement has of institutions, and made clear that they wished to determine their own priorities for action and not merely respond to Community initiatives. In the end the decision was taken to set up, not a Brussels lobby, but a European Network of Women, with the aim of creating links, initiating joint campaigns and exchanging information between women's groups in the different countries. There is now a British section of the Network (see box for address) and three further conferences have been held, in Brussels, in London and in Paris. The Network is currently campaigning on the application of the Community's Directive on social security and has sent a list of twelve demands to the Commission. The problems involved in this kind of organization, at a grassroots level and across national boundaries, are, however, enormous.

European Network of Women (ENOW)

ENOW is co-ordinated in Brussels by the:
  Centre for Research on European Women (CREW)
  38 Rue Stevin
  1040 Brussels, Belgium
  Tel: 010 322 230 51 58

CREW produces a monthly Bulletin, *CREW Reports*, which covers developments in the European Community of interest to women, and *Network News*, which covers developments in ENOW. Anyone interested in joining or working with the British section of the Network should contact:
  ENOW (UK)
  53/54 Featherstone Street
  London EC1
  Tel: 01 251 6575

At different levels then links are beginning to be made between women in the Community, and very gradually an awareness is growing of common problems and the existence of a common framework. In this situation, it is important that more information should circulate, and that some attempt should be made to analyse these new developments – from the point of view of women and taking the Community as a unit.

As a contribution to this, I will turn now to look at some aspects of the evolution of the Community's policy on women and its impact in member states, in the light of the points I have made about equality legislation and its implications for women.

■ Negotiating the European policy

There have been a number of constraints on the development of a policy on women at the European level. The Treaty of Rome is basically a document about economic structure, and although there is a wider intention implicit, this is left imprecise, while the provisions to establish a common market and liberalize economic activity generally are spelled out in detail. The Treaty does provide for a social policy – though an employment policy would be a more accurate description of what is covered (James, 1982). The main aims of this are:

> to promote the free movement of labour;
> to cushion some of the more adverse effects of change on workers;
> to attempt to harmonize the labour costs which affect fair competition among the member states; and
> in general to move towards a situation where the control and organization of labour operates at a level more commensurate with the new scale of economic activity.

The policy does have a more genuinely 'social' aim, which is 'to promote improved working conditions and an improved standard of living for workers' (Article 117) but again provisions to achieve this are not spelled out in any precise way. It is quite clear from all this that the social policy is intended to deal only with workers and the situation at work; any concern with the non-working population and with people in general is assumed to be the responsibility of the member states.

Clearly a policy on women fits rather uneasily into such a structure, and as the policy has developed there has been increasing pressure for it to be implemented, not just in terms of economic rationality and in the interests of harmonizing labour costs, but in the light of the social aims of Article 117. This was largely achieved in the judgment in the second Defrenne case (referred to earlier) where the European Court of Justice ruled that in applying Article 119 on equal pay, the social objectives of the Treaty should be seen as more important than the economic. More recently, attempts have been made to move beyond the confines of an employment policy, and to suggest measures which have relevance to the total situation of women. These attempts have so far met with little success, given the extreme reluctance of governments to allow the Community to assume new responsibilities or more into areas not clearly defined in the Treaty.

European legislation on women is firmly rooted in the concept of formal equality, starting with the provisions on equal pay (*égalité des remunerations*) and moving on to equal treatment (*égalité de traitement*). The term 'equal treatment' which was used once the policy moved beyond equal pay was already part of Community terminology, and represented one of the key concepts upon which the common market had been established. Legislating for equal treatment for women was therefore acceptable, and seemed in tune with the Community's basic aims of removing barriers and encouraging free circulation and fair competition. 'Restrictive practices' were to be removed so that women could compete freely on the labour market! This orientation helps to explain why it has been much more difficult for the Community to adopt the concept of 'equal opportunity' (*égalité de chances*) which implies some move towards positive discrimination and substantive equality. While *equal* treatment and the harmonization of provisions is part and parcel of Community practice, *special* treatment and measures which involve intervention and redistribution go against the general ethos, and can only be considered in particular and very compelling circumstances.

The central period for the evolution of the women's policy was 1972-6 when the Directives on equal pay and equal treatment were negotiated and adopted.[7] Of the two, the Equal Treatment Directive was the more significant. It represented in itself a big expansion of policy and also provided a framework within which further legislation could be considered. The process by which this Directive was negotiated reveals a great deal about the politics of Community decision making; it also gives some indication of where the final version of the Directive stands in terms of the criteria for equality legislation considered earlier.

Discussion about the development of new initiatives in the field of women's employment began in the European Commission early in 1973. This was after the Heads of State had decided at the end of 1972 to launch a whole new programme on social policy with the objective of giving the Community 'a more human face'. 1973 was in fact a traumatic year for the Commission. It started with the need to accommodate cohorts of new civil servants from Britain, Ireland and Denmark; it ended with the oil crisis which altered all the assumptions upon which plans for the future had been laid.

The Social Affairs Directorate (DG V) was particularly affected by the arrival of new personnel. The new Commissioner was an Irishman, Patrick Hillary, and various British civil servants arrived to take up senior positions. The new people seem initially to have been quite disconcerted by the limited definition of social policy which the Community had adopted, and in the early months clashes with the 'old guard' in DG V were not infrequent.

The person in DG V responsible in an overall sense for the women's policy was Jacqueline Nonon, a French career civil servant, who was now ready to push for a stronger line on women's rights. DG V had already commissioned a report on the problems of women's employment in the Community from a French sociologist, Evelyn Sullerot (1970). Other more detailed country studies had also been made. Drawing on this material, Nonon now proposed that the Community should take action to see that the concept of equality was applied to all conditions of work – not just pay; and to make easier the reconciling of family responsibilities with job aspirations. The actions to be taken under the second half of this proposal were not specified, but the linking of the two elements was clearly intended to move the Community beyond formal equality towards the taking of more substantive measures.

Although the reference to family responsibilities went rather beyond the strict definition of an employment policy, this formulation was accepted by the new Irish/British leadership in DG V. Indeed, the proposals were incorporated almost unchanged into the new Social Action Programme (SAP) presented by the Commission in October 1973.[8] In Action II (4) of the SAP, it was expressly stated that in creating a situation of equality in the labour market 'immediate priority could be given to the problems of providing facilities to enable women to reconcile family responsibilities with job aspirations'. Though this phraseology seemed to assume that it was only women who had family responsibilities, it nevertheless represented a considerable advance in Commission thinking. The SAP was adopted by the Council of Ministers in January 1974, by means of a Resolution which explicitly accepted the expansion of the policy on women along the lines suggested above.

■ The 'ad hoc group' and the draft Directive

Once these proposals had been accepted, an 'ad hoc group' was set up to advise the Commission on implementation. The normal procedure for setting up a group of this kind is for the Commission to request each government to nominate representatives, usually 'independent experts' or civil servants from appropriate departments. Nonon used her influence and contacts to ensure that as many as possible of those appointed were women – and genuinely involved in and knowledge-able about the problems of women's employment. In this she was largely successful: of eighteen members usually only four or five were men, and most of those appointed were actively involved in work on the issues being discussed. The group held four meetings between February and November 1974.

The group exchanged information, compared statistics, and created useful horizontal links between women dealing with the same issues in the different member states. Although most of the members were either working in or advisers to their respective Ministries of Labour, they seem for the most part to have discussed issues in terms of the needs of women rather than the interests of particular governments. Interes-tingly, they expressed the view that *special* as much as *equal* treatment for women was needed, and endorsed the emphasis on family responsi-bilities included in the SAP. At their third meeting, a draft for a Directive was submitted by Eliane Vogel-Polsky, a Belgian lawyer who had helped to bring the Defrenne cases. This gave equal weight to the concepts of '*égalité de traitement*' and '*égalité de chances*'.

Many of the proposals in the SAP were never taken up, largely due to the economic reversal expected as a result of the oil crisis. The new proposals for women were implemented, however, partly because of the extent of preparation already undertaken, and partly because it would have been impolitic to abandon these initiatives in the run-up to International Women's Year in 1975. The go-ahead was therefore given for two new Directives, one to clarify and reinforce the concept of equal pay, and the other to deal with wider issues.

At the end of 1974, Nonon was given the job of drawing up a draft for this second Directive, and for an explanatory Memorandum to go with it.[9] The Memorandum, which went through nine revisions, in its final form exhibits a note of caution. Although the situation of women in the family, it says, is crucial to their situation at work, the Community cannot deal with all aspects of this problem, and must for the moment confine itself to the particular problems of women working outside the home. The Memorandum, however, does not rule out the possibility of legislation over facilities at work – such as parental leave and child-care arrangements – which could benefit working parents.

The draft Directive also follows this narrower line of thinking, apparently on the advice of the Commission's legal service. It was better, the lawyers argued (and they were probably right in this) to aim at something effective for women within the employment situation, rather than attempt to go wider, and risk endless delay and discussion about whether the Community had the right to legislate in other policy areas.

The draft Directive, therefore deals with equal treatment in the areas of access to employment, vocational training, promotion, and working conditions (including social security). Equal treatment is defined as:

> the elimination of all discrimination based on sex or on marital or family status, including the adoption of appropriate measures to provide women with equal opportunity in employment, vocational training, promotion and working conditions.

Thus very deftly, the definition of equal treatment itself is broadened to include the idea of positive discrimination ('appropriate measures') which would make equality more of a reality. No mention is made, however, of indirect discrimination.

No mention is made either of derogations, and the implication is that protective legislation should be withdrawn where 'no longer justified'. States are required to make it possible for people who feel themselves victimized to take legal action, and they have to inform 'persons concerned' about the Directive. Nothing further is said about support for litigants, the monitoring of existing practices or penalties for non-compliance.

■ The Council working group

This draft was approved by the Commission and then went to the Council's social affairs working group for a detailed examination. This working group, which consists in the main of the social affairs attachés from the delegations in Brussels of the member states, represents the arena where real inter-state bargaining on social policy issues takes place, and where the effects and costs for each state of any proposal are carefully weighed.

In this case a certain urgency prevailed since it was hoped to approve the Directive during 1975 as a gesture to International Women's Year. Nevertheless debate was keen, since states with legislation in this area already (like Britain) were anxious to go not an inch beyond it, while states with virtually no provision (like Germany) were anxious to limit the potential damage. All the principal representatives in the working group at this point were men. Nonon, though present, was considered too junior to represent the Commission and found herself having to brief more senior Commission men who were neither so well-informed nor so committed.

The Directive emerged from this discussion – which went right on to a final full Council meeting in December 1975 – much amended. The particular points at issue were:

The definition – the attachés immediately jumped on the 'appropriate measures' reference, and asked what it meant. Very quickly they decided it was too vague and agreed to delete it. All mention of positive discrimination was thus removed, and it was only as an afterthought that a clause *permitting* positive measures was included (Article 2/4). As if to compensate, however, the basic definition was somewhat altered, and the concept of indirect discrimination was included, if in a rather ambiguous form, apparently at the suggestion of the British representative (Article 2/1).

Derogations – the usual derogations (for sex-specific jobs and maternity provisions) were inserted. The Commission, however, insisted that the former should be the subject of rigorous monitoring (Article 2/2). Protective legislation was in principle to be repealed but only after a lengthy period of review and consideration (Article 9/1). A special derogation was inserted (for the Netherlands) accepting the 'freedom' of private educational establishments in matters of vocational training.

Scope – the concern was clearly to keep this as limited as possible. A reference to 'general education' in the context of equal treatment in vocational training (intended to refer to option choices and careers advice in schools) was deleted on the grounds that the Community had no competence in the field of education.

The inclusion of social security provisions was also controversial. Barbara Castle, then the British Minister responsible, insisted that these should be removed from the scope of the Directive. The Commission here fought an effective rearguard action and said if they were removed, a firm commitment must be included to deal with them later in a separate Directive (Article 1/2).

Implementation – very little was added or deleted here. A suggestion from the European Parliament that an additional Article should be included, providing for independent bodies to monitor and support implementation in each country, was accepted by the Commission, but came too late to be seriously considered by the Council.

The Directive was finally adopted in February 1976 and came into force thirty months later in August 1978.[10] Once adopted a whole set of procedures came into effect, to review, monitor and interpret its application. This inevitably involved mechanisms and a network, some of the consequences of which are only now being felt – in the mid-1980s.

■ What conclusions should we draw from this process?

The history of these negotiations clearly illustrates the way in which institutionalized patriarchy operates the political process. One of the women involved in the earlier discussion of the Directive was so horrified by the sight of so many men discussing the draft in the working group, that she referred to the Directive ever afterwards as 'men's rules for women's rights'. The discussion in the ad hoc group, even though most of the women were government employees, seems to have been qualitatively different from that in the working group. The reason being that the women took the issue seriously (and had some knowledge of the situations being discussed), whereas by and large the men did not. This kind of difference is only likely to occur when a fairly large number of women are involved. A token woman – like Barbara Castle at the Council meeting – tends to act as a surrogate man.

The gradual down-playing of the importance of the issue of family responsibilities in the whole question of the position of women in the labour market was partly due to a genuine doubt about Community competence, but also to the gradual imposition of the patriarchal view. As discussion moved up the Commission/Council hierarchy, the number of people prepared to admit the centrality of this issue diminished. The treatment of the provision on positive discrimination is a further example of this. The already watered down reference in the draft Directive was dropped at the level of the social affairs attachés with virtually no discussion; clearly the Commission hierarchy had by this stage decided that this was not an issue to fight on. This may well be an illustration of the conceptual difficulty (referred to earlier) which the Community as a whole has over the adoption of *special* measures.

The weakest part of the Directive is the provision it makes for implementation and enforcement at the national level. As we have seen, this is a crucial area, essential if the terms of an equality law are to have any substantive effect. Surprisingly, neither the Commission nor the ad hoc group seems to have paid much attention to this, and the Parliament's suggestion (for independent monitoring bodies) came so late in the process that it was easy for the Governments to turn it down. The situation with regard to monitoring at the national level is in marked contrast to the strong Community procedures which exist to enforce the actual provisions of a Directive, that is to see that member states really do implement in their own systems the measures which have been agreed. So if the Directive had included more measures on implementation, the Commission would have had the right to take strong action to ensure that these were given effect within the member states.

One most noticeable aspect of the whole process is the lack of any popular involvement, or indeed any knowledge beyond a tiny group of what was going on. In Britain this was due partly to the general ambivalence about Community membership, and partly to a complete misunderstanding in certain quarters about the implications of Community legislation. But in other countries there seems to have been hardly more interest; the trade unions at national level were on the whole doubtful about such legislation and the women's movement indifferent. Neither group took it seriously.

The Equal Treatment Directive is therefore a law which on the whole reinforces formal rather than substantive equality. It attempts to deal with the employment problems of women as though these existed in a vacuum; it allows rather than encourages positive measures, and its provisions for implementation are weak. Despite these limitations, however, it has proved to have a certain force. This is partly because within the employment situation its scope is very broad, and partly because the strength of the Community's own monitoring system has obliged states either to introduce new legislation or look again at existing provisions. This puts the issue once more on the political agenda and opens the way for change. For example, the existence of the Directive means that sooner or later the British Government will have to amend the clause in the Sex Discrimination Act which excludes private households and businesses with less than six employees from its provisions, since such a derogation is not permitted by the terms of the Directive.

There are two other aspects of the Directive which could in the end have considerable effect. The first is the generally stringent attitude to derogations and exclusions – even ones at present permitted. All of these have to be rigorously monitored at Community level. As a start to this process, the Commission published in 1982 a report on protective legislation and other excluded activities in all members states (Halpern, 1982). This analyses the existing situation in a sensitive way, makes useful comparisons, and recommends policy for the future. It provides excellent material for any campaign on these questions.

The second aspect of the Directive which could be important, concerns the reference to indirect discrimination. In the Directive this is ambiguous, and so far there has been little attempt by the Commission to insist that member states include this concept in their legislation. However, in 1983 the Commission set up a network of independent experts (mostly labour lawyers and trade union officials concerned with women's employment problems) to review the application of the equal pay and equal treatment Directives in the member states. One of the tasks of this network is to devise a clearer definition of what indirect discrimination actually means, so that this part of the Directive can be better enforced.

All of these developments open the way for discussion and action on issues regarded as closed in many countries. Although the Equal Treatment Directive was adopted in 1976, its full potential is not yet known. To a large extent this will depend upon how far women in the different member states are willing and able to press for the full implementation and development of its provisions.

■ Trends in the women's movement

The impact of these developments, both in individual states and on the situation of women as a whole, needs much more study if any meaningful conclusions are to be drawn or trends identified. All that can be said at this stage, is that European initiatives are beginning to impose a common level of legislative provision on these issues throughout the Community.

Thus countries with existing legislation have been forced to make amendments (Britain); countries with inadequate legislation have been forced to introduce new provisions (Germany and Italy); and countries with no legislation at all have been encouraged to adopt national versions of Community Directives (Ireland and Greece). In France, the socialist Government, which has sought to introduce more effective legislation, has been able to draw on Community experience of what works and what does not. By doing this, France has now set a new level of provision which may in the end affect developments in other countries.

One important feature of the Community process in this respect is that it works very slowly. The situation requiring new measures developed in the 1960s; action was taken in the 1970s; and implementation is only really taking place in the 1980s, when circumstances have radically altered. Thus in the end the main effect of the legislation, which was intended to be 'progressive', may be that it makes more difficult the current attempts to weaken the position of women in the labour market.

The existence of this common framework makes links between women in the Community more meaningful. However, although in the women's movement there is now more interest in and knowledge of equality legislation, there is as yet no agreement about what strategy to pursue towards it. One recent trend in the women's movement (particularly noticeable in Germany but also evident elsewhere) is a new emphasis on the importance of women's ability to have children and capacity for human relations. This leads to a rejection of the man's world and of the demand for equality, and to a celebration of the qualities which spring out of women's central role in the family and the home. Where this leads (as with the Greenham women) to a direct challenge to patriarchal policies and assumptions, its effect is wholly positive, but where it leads to withdrawal and to a *de facto* acceptance of existing structures, then in political terms its effect can be reactionary. In Germany, for example, there is a disturbing convergence between some of the recent statements of the Kohl Government (idealizing the special qualities of women and attributing the lack of 'warmth' in German society to too many women working) and the analysis of certain sections of the German women's movement. This political ambivalence is also present in some of the arguments contained in Germaine's Greer's new book, *Sex and Destiny* (1984).

Some Italian feminists have adopted a different analysis. In Italy, the debate about 'equality and difference' has been going on a long time, and at the 1983 Turin conference on women's employment, two Italian women formerly active in feminist struggles in the trade union movement wrote a paper trying to draw the two strands together (Piva and Ingrao, 1983). Activist women in Italy, they stated, have tended to pursue either 'difference' or 'equality': 'The women who have stressed their "difference" as a value have refused to take up the task of transforming work, while those who have stressed the value of equality have taken up bargaining initiatives and have sought an alliance with the left.'

Now is the time, they argue, to make a synthesis. Equality brings women into the labour market, they must then try to use their 'difference' to transform the work-process and the context in which equality is defined. They use as an example the influx of women workers in the late 1970s into the major car factories of northern Italy – an influx made possible incidentally by the adoption in 1977 of Italian equality legislation to comply with the Equal Treatment Directive. Once there in large numbers, the women raised complaints about the organization of work and working conditions, which they hoped would be taken up more generally. As with the Commission's 'ad hoc group', once women entered in sufficient numbers into a particular work situation, the very fact of their different style and interest altered the form and nature of that activity. On this analysis, equality remains an important demand, but it has to be claimed in a way that preserves women's autonomy, and avoids co-option and tokenism. The objective of gaining equality is not to compete in a man's world but to transform the structures of patriarchal society.

Equality legislation, whether European or national, has its part to play in this and in the current situation can be a useful tool against attempts to reinforce traditional male/female stereotypes. Far more mobilization is needed, however, to get the right kind of legislation, and to ensure that it is implemented in a way that does not co-opt and isolate women but allows their 'difference' to take effect.

■ Notes

This article appeared in *Feminist Review* No. 20, 1985.

I should like to thank the members of ROW Europe – especially Nicky Coombes, Vanessa Hall Smith, Judy Keiner and Erika Szyszczak – who helped me to develop these ideas. Thanks also to Rebecca Frances Kides and Cynthia Cockburn for comments on the text and to the Nuffield Foundation for travel money.

1 The debate on 'equality and difference' is much further advanced in other European countries than it is in the UK. For a summary of the recent debate in Italy and France see the interesting discussion in 'Trade Unionism and the Radicalizing of Socialist Feminism' *Feminist Review* No. 16, Summer 1984.

2 Gabrielle Defrenne was a Belgian airhostess who complained about

discriminatory practices in the state airline, Sabena. Three cases about her situation were referred to the European Court of Justice. See ECJ cases: 80/1970, 43/1975, 149/1977.

3   *Clarke and Powell* v *Eley Kynock* (1982). In this case management and the union agreed that all part-timers should be made redundant before any full-timer. The judge ruled that since the majority of part-timers were women this constituted indirect discrimination under the Sex Discrimination Act.

4   The judgment in this case was given by the Industrial Tribunal in October 1984. The case was supported jointly by the Equal Opportunities Commission and the General Municipal Boilermakers and Allied Trades Union (GMBATU).

5   Law No. 93-635 of 13 July 1983. For a discussion of these issues see *La revue d'en face* Paris: *Editions Tierce* no. 11, Winter 1981 and no. 14, Autumn 1983.

6   The British Government, for example, while phasing out the controversial Housewives Non-Contributory Invalidity Pension (HNCIP) is in fact now making it more difficult for *anyone* to claim an invalidity pension.

7   A more overall account of policy development is given in Rights of Women Europe (1983) *Women's Rights and the EEC – A Guide for Women in the UK* (available from Rights of Women, 53/54 Featherstone Street, London EC1. Price £3.50 including postage and packing).

8   'Social Action Programme' *Bulletin of the European Communities* supplement 2/74. This contains both the Commission's proposal and the Council's Resolution of 21 January 1974.

9   The texts of both of these are given in Commission document COM (75) 36 final, 12 February 1975.

10 Council Directive of 9 February 1976, 76/207/EEC. The full text is published in the *Official Journal*, Series L, 14/2/76.

Going Private

Angela Coyle

This article is about the impact of 'privatization' on the conditions of employment of women who work as cleaners. It comes out of research in progress on the cleaning industry as a whole, but here the focus is on women's cleaning jobs in the National Health Service (NHS). It argues that as more and more cleaning services are sub-contracted out to private contractors, the already poor pay and conditions found in this work can be seen to be deteriorating even further. This is because it is very dificult to protect the pay and conditions of sub-contracted employment either through employment legislation or trade union organization. Women employed by cleaning contractors are very often placed entirely outside the scope of the Employment Protection Act, whilst it becomes even more difficult to apply other legislation such as the Equal Pay Act or the Health and Safety at Work Act. Trade union organization of this particularly dispersed and fragmented workforce has always been weak and uneven but the extension of sub-contracting is undermining the degree of organization that has been achieved amongst women cleaners.

Women who work as cleaners, one of the most hidden and neglected sections of the workforce, are now at the forefront of a Government strategy which seeks to 'free' or 'deregulate' the employer/employee relationship. Sub-contract work plus abolition of all legislation which controls and protects minimum pay and employment conditions have been key strategies in the Thatcher Government's policy of enabling 'market forces' to regulate wage levels and of enabling the lowest wage threshold to be found.

The extension of sub-contract work in the public sector, or

'privatization' as it is commonly labelled, has affected some men's jobs such as refuse collection and security work, but now it is a very serious issue for women, who make up such a significant number of public sector employees (one in three of all women's jobs are in the public sector). What is achieved through 'privatization' will set a baseline for women's pay in public *and* private sector work. However, it is also serious for all employees, for what is happening is that the most vulnerable sections of the workforce are at the *forefront* of a general dismantling of the regulation and control of employment. Women are being used to pave the way for a significant deterioration in terms and conditions of employment.

■ Cleaners: who are they?

Of more than 700,000 people currently working in cleaning jobs, most (75 per cent) are women, usually working on a part-time basis. Men tend to be employed in 'heavy cleaning', which can cover anything from the cleaning of factory production areas to the cleaning of streets, drains, the outside of buildings, and vehicles and machinery. Very often, men who work as cleaners are not called such, but rather are employed in 'general maintenance' or as 'general labourers'. Different titles differentiate men's cleaning work from women's and enable men to secure different gradings and better pay. Women tend to be employed in 'light cleaning' in, for example, offices, hotels, hospitals and schools. It is archetypal women's work, with very low status.

Cleaning has to be undertaken outside of the normal working day, so hours are invariably anti-social. Cleaning shifts can start as early as 5 a.m., some finish very late at night. Many cleaners work weekends, some work all night. Some cleaners work a split day shift. It is not uncommon to find women cleaners who combine two or three part-time cleaning jobs, and all for very low pay.

Rather like homeworking, women's reasons and needs for taking up this kind of work vary according to individual circumstances and employment opportunities in the local labour market. What is apparent is that, for *a range of reasons*, women who work as cleaners are a particularly 'trapped' section of the workforce: women from ethnic minorities who are likely to encounter particularly restricted job opportunities (Freeman, 1982; Phizacklea, 1982); women with children and/or dependent relatives, and older women with few marketable skills who, as the job market has become more restricted, are increasingly forced into such work.

In 1981 the Low Pay Unit conducted one of the largest surveys of women cleaners ever undertaken. The evidence of 475 respondents to this survey of women directly employed by the Civl Service confirmed the following 'profile' of the 'typical' cleaner. The researchers found that 'a young cleaner is a rare phenomenon' (Beardwell *et al*, 1981), and that the vast majority of cleaners in the Civil Service were between the ages of thirty-five and fifty-nine, married with family responsibilities, and with work histories that usually covered quite a range of low-paid, unskilled 'women's' work. Cleaning is undoubtedly 'returners'' work, if only because of the opportunity it offers for part-time work. It is now clear that part-time work is sought by women during that stage in their life when domestic commitments are at their most demanding. Three-quarters of all working women with children up to the age of ten years will be in part-time work (Ballard, 1984). So great is women's need for part-time work that the National Training Survey found that significant numbers of women with teaching, nursing and clerical qualifications were working as cleaners, solely because of the opportunities such work provided for part-time work (Elias and Main, 1982). However, it would be wrong to construe cleaning as convenient work for women. Cleaning hours cut right across the day and there is evidence that cleaning hours *disrupt* family relationships and activities rather than accommodate them (Beardwell *et al*, 1981).

As with most occupations in which women predominate, pay levels are very low indeed. There is no wages council for this industry and union organization is difficult (women cleaners work in small groups, dispersed around and between buildings). It is a labour-intensive industry in which labour is the main cost and consequently employers are always devising ways of keeping wages down. As in other labour-intensive work, women get these jobs *because* they can be paid lower wages than men.

Just how badly women cleaners are paid is hard to measure, since aggregate figures are available only on full-time rates and on *direct* employment, which in fact offers the best terms of employment for cleaning work. Recent figures taken from the New Earnings Survey (NES) show that average full-time earnings in cleaning are below the average manual wage. This is particularly so for men.[1] Male cleaners earn 79.6 per cent of the average male manual wage, whilst women cleaners earn 91.7 per cent of the average female manual wage.

The NES also indicated that public sector wage rates for cleaning are *significantly* lower than in the private sector. In a wage table of cleaners' full-time basic weekly rates made up of 102 different industry-wide wage agreements, cleaners' pay in the civil service (at £70.93 per week), local authorities (at £70.30 per week), the National Health Service (at £68.98 per week) and British Rail (at £60.40 per week) came close to the bottom (Labour Research, 1985a).

Not only are these very low pay rates – below the Trades Union Congress's (TUC) definition of low pay at £105 a week or £2.60 an hour – but the Labour Research findings also indicate that 'a significant proportion' of industry-wide, union negotiated wage agreements for cleaners have been set below the lowest unskilled manual rate (1985a: 38). This means that cleaners' pay rates are being set at a special rate (effectively a women's rate) and this is making the application of the Equal Pay Act even more difficult than it is already. Furthermore, these figures only indicate full-time pay in direct employment. The number of women working part-time and in sub-contract work is not recorded. It is possible only to guess. Whitley Council Rates, which are the hourly rates of pay agreed for cleaners employed by the Health Service, range from £1.72 to £2.10 per hour. Most contractors will pay a lot less than this. (My research in the West Midlands is revealing that contractors' rates average £1.30-£1.50 an hour for a fifteen-hour week.)

■ Cleaning in the Health Service

The National Health Service is one of the biggest employers in the United Kingdom. One and a quarter million people work for the NHS, and in 1984-5 it cost £16 billion to run. This NHS expenditure actually buys a bargain in national health care. In 1982 spending on health in the UK represented 5.3 per cent of the GNP and compared very favourably with 8.8 per cent and 8.1 per cent in West Germany and France respectively, and 9.9 per cent in the United States. Private does *not* necessarily mean value for money. Nevertheless, the NHS has become a target for cost-cutting, especially in hospital ancillary services – cleaning, laundry and catering services – which employ 160,000 people (mostly women) and cost the NHS £1 billion a year (*The Economist*, 3 November 1984). These ancillary services have now become a prime Government target for privatization.

■ What is privatization?

'Privatization' has become a 'buzz' word for Government policy and philosophy, which is seeking to transfer a great deal of public sector services provision into the private sector. The term quite usefully conveys the economic and ideological nature of its policy, but does not always convey the actual processes involved. What does the sale of British Telecom, for example, have in common with the demands of those women cleaners on strike at Barking Hospital?

The Thatcher Government has embarked on a radical programme of transferring public industries to private ownership and control and in doing so has rather successfully gained acceptance for an economic and ideological equation. Private equals competitiveness and efficiency: public equals protectionism and inefficiency. Whilst this represents the broad rationale for all privatization of the public sector, different parts of the public sector are being privatized in different ways, and for different reasons. British Telecom and British Gas (which looks as if it will be next to go) are profitable industries, whereas public expenditure in the NHS rises annually. Consequently, 'privatization' of the former is an economic strategy for raising money; in the latter, *it is one for saving money*. By contracting out, to contractors, work which has been undertaken by women ancillary workers as part of a direct NHS labour force, it is possible to achieve both considerable and immediate expenditure savings and reductions in the size of the labour force. Women cleaners are paying for those cost savings by a serious deterioration in their pay and conditions of employment and ultimately we are all paying by a serious deterioration in the standard and provision of health care in our hospitals.

■ The privatization countdown

In late September 1983, the then Secretary of State for Social Services, Norman Fowler, issued a circular requesting each of the 223 District Health Authorities (DHAs)[2] in the UK to put hospital cleaning, catering and laundry services out to private tender, *and* to provide a timetabled programme for privatization by April 1984, in order to meet an overall Government deadline for the programme by September 1986.

According to a National Union of Public Employees (NUPE) survey, ten DHAs decided not to comply with the directive to tender for the ancillary services but to ensure that wages and conditions were maintained at existing NHS levels, and another fifty-five, including half of those in Wales and all in Scotland, took no action at all (*Guardian*, 13 June 1984). Of the remaining 157 which have submitted timetables for tendering, few are on schedule for the

September 1986 target (*ibid.*).

When Authorities have put out services to private contractors, the experience has been very mixed. Of the three ancillary services, more cleaning services have 'successfully' gone out to private contractors than laundry or catering services. Undoubtedly the use of private contractors has secured big savings for the DHAs and in the tendering process very few cleaning contracts have stayed in-house. For example, it has been estimated that in contracting out cleaning, Maidstone District General Hospital saved £88,000 in the first year of operation, and Hitchingbrooke Hospital in Huntingdon saved £246,000 on its cleaning bill. It has been suggested that often these savings are 'loss leaders' and that contractors set ridiculously low costings in order to secure new contracts with the intention of upping the costs in subsequent contracts (*Guardian*, 3 July 1984).

This may not necessarily be the case, however, since even without 'loss leaders' private contract cleaners provide a service more cheaply than direct labour by reducing the standard of cleaning service and by significantly reducing cleaning hours. This means, as will be seen, that women work fewer hours but undertake proportionately more work, receive less weekly pay, are entitled to less sickness and holiday pay, and have fewer (if any) rights under the Employment Protection Act.

Sub-contract work alters the very nature of the employer/employee contract. Contract work often means that labour can be hired and fired at will without entitlement to redundancy or severance pay. Agreed rates of pay, hours of work and the place of work may be changed at the employers' will. And employers' legal responsibilities for providing a safe working environment can be more easily evaded.

Despite the very apparent savings that can be made, District Health Authorities have become even more wary of sub-contracting because of the widespread series of industrial disputes associated with private contractors and reports of appallingly dirty hospital facilities. Two hospitals in particular, Barking and Addenbrookes, have achieved nationwide notoriety.

The dispute at Barking Hospital has not, strictly speaking, been caused by privatization: the domestic cleaning services have been sub-contracted out for the past twelve years. However, when the contract came up for renewal at the end of 1983, the company holding the contract, Crothalls, introduced cuts in cleaners' hours and pay in order to deal with intensified competition from other cleaning contractors. Crothalls successfully regained the contract, with a new contract starting 1 April 1984 which set a 41 per cent price reduction over its own previous costings. These cuts in costs were inevitably achieved at the expense of the women cleaners. Crothalls cut cleaning hours by 41 per cent too, with the effect that some women had their take-home wages cut from £57 to £17 per week (Labour Research, 1985b). In addition to these cuts in working hours, cleaners had to accept new work rotas (which changed every three weeks), no entitlement to sick pay, reduced holiday entitlement and a fortnightly instead of weekly pay system.

In response to the conditions of the new contract offered to them, cleaners at Barking Hospital went on strike. Crothalls deemed these women 'sacked' and took on a new workforce. An Industrial Tribunal found Crothalls' sackings illegal and in March 1985 Crothalls offered the striking cleaners £22,000 to buy off the dispute. They refused and the dispute continues.[3] The effects of reduced hours, pay cuts and a greatly increased workload have, not unsurprisingly, led to a rapid deterioration of the cleaning service. Nurses have been reported as supervising cleaning instead of contractors, and as sometimes doing it themselves. An independent health inspector's report stated that there was no evidence of an overall system of regular organized cleaning such as is essential in a hospital (TUC, 1984).

Addenbrookes Hospital in Cambridge is another which has achieved widespread media publicity. There women cleaners have been on strike since October 1984, when the cleaning services went out to contract to OCS Hospital Cleaning Services Ltd. Although the contractors retained the £1.72 per hours rates that were paid under NHS employment, cleaners' hours were almost halved, they lost their sick pay entitlements, pension rights and bonus payments, and suffered a reduction of holiday entitlement. There have been reports that schoolchildren were being employed to do the work. Furthermore, as in Barking, a monitoring of the new cleaning service has revealed very poor cleaning standards.

Very unusually for an industrial dispute concerning ancillary workers, and women too, the cleaners at Addenbrookes gained the support of medical and professional staff. At Addenbrookes a consultant paediatrician resigned in protest over the sub-contracting of cleaning in the hospital:

> I believe that to save money by further separating the status of the professional from that of ancillary staff would not serve the end if it means employing the latter as casual labour. On my ward we value very highly the responsible and loyal work of our cleaners. (*Guardian*, 25 October 1984).

These kinds of experiences have made District Health Authorities wary of privatization, and the apparently *laissez-faire* philosophy of the Government has become increasingly directive and interventionist. For those DHAs which thought they could get around the problem by maintaining NHS rates as agreed by Whitley Council (£1.72 to £2.10 per hour), the following guidelines were issued in late 1984 by Kenneth Clarke, the then Minister of Health:

> Some Districts are seeking to require contractors who tender for the provision of NHS support services to employ staff on Whitley terms and conditions of service. This is contrary to the advice given by the Department last year in DA (83) 40; and it is, as John Patten made clear again in his letter this summer, unacceptable to Ministers ... We consider that it is quite wrong for authorities ... [to] specify the terms and conditions of service which private contractors should provide for staff working on NHS contracts. There is no sensible basis upon which a Health Authority can interfere in this way in the relationship between the contractor and its employees (Clarke, 1984).

Trade union lawyers had questioned the legality and the powers of the 1983 Department of Health circular and so the letter goes on:

> Some Authorities may also have been influenced by the argument that the circular itself is not a binding direction in law. This is quite irrelevant and is not any sudden or unexpected discovery. Circulars have always been worded in this way and we do not draft them to ensure that each circular is a legally binding document. We do not ordinarily expect to have to use the Secretary of State's legal powers of direction as we look upon our Health Authorities as partners in our aim of improving the National Health Service. However we have always expected Authorities to follow Government policies and we are entitled to continue to do so (*ibid.*).

Thus came a clear indication of the Government's intention.

Early in 1985 Norwich Health Authority – having learned from the Addenbrookes experience – accepted an 'in-house' tender costing £100,000 more than two competing contractors' bids. The in-house contract maintained cleaners' pay and conditions *and* cleaning standards. John Patten, the junior Minister for Health, ordered Norwich Authority to reconsider the contracts (*Guardian*, 19 January 1985). Cuts in cleaning hours have subsequently been made.

The year 1985 has been one for new offensives in the contracting out of Health Service cleaning services. Something like 30 per cent savings have been achieved on those services contracted out so far, and the Government aims to save £100 million a year from cleaning (*Sunday Times,* 20 January 1985). It has been estimated that sick pay and holiday pay equals 14 per cent of the NHS wage bill, pensions another 21 per cent. The Government has now opened the way for contractors not to provide these benefits and therefore the possibility of significantly reducing the £1 billion a year that it costs to provide cleaning, laundry and catering services.

■ Contractors: who are they?

Contract cleaning is not a new phenomenon. Some of the largest cleaning companies date back to the 1930s. It is, however, impossible to estimate the number of contract cleaners operating in the UK. Fierce competition means that contractors come and go, often taken over by large firms or operating on the grey margins of the economy. The market is dominated by a few very large companies and they or their subsidiaries are now in the forefront of the 'privatization' market. There is an association for contract cleaners, the Contract Cleaning and Maintenance Association (CCMA), which provides guidelines to contractors on price fixing, insurance cover and cleaning methods, but which has no power to influence pay and conditions. The CCMA is anxious to improve the image of contract cleaning and of the industry in general; away from its mop and bucket image to one of modern 'scientific' cleaning methods.

The contract cleaning business has been growing steadily since the war and had really taken off by the mid-1960s with the rapid expansion in office building (and hence office cleaning). By the mid-sixties, two of the largest UK-based firms, Pritchards and Initial Services, had multi-million-pound turnovers (Wandor, 1972: 225). Contract cleaning has continued to expand, and by 1980-1 the average return on capital in its business was 27.5 per cent – compared with an average 10 per cent for British industry as a whole (ICC Business Ratios, 1983). There are big profits to be made in this business, and the ICC projected considerable expansion throughout the 1980s provided 'privatization' contracts continued to grow and contractors were prepared to exploit new markets (*ibid.*).

Contract cleaning firms have done just this, pursuing new markets with enthusiasm. They themselves have been under economic pressure as recession and factory closures in the manufacturing sector have reduced the opportunities for industrial cleaning contacts in the UK. Large contractors have been diversifying their operations and, as well as office cleaning, have interests in laundry services, catering service and private health care. They have also been moving geographically by gaining cleaning contracts in the Middle East, South Africa and Latin America (GLC Economic Policy Group, 1983: 20).

However, public sector contracts within the UK provide contractors with attractively *stable* businesses, and along with seeking new contracts there, they have enthusiastically taken up the task of disseminating a public relations campaign for privatization. At a public meeting in the West Midlands (November 1984), a director of ISS Service Systems stated:

> I have no wish to be political. My sole concern is that of contract cleaning which represents an opportunity to reduce costs to ratepayers and taxpayers.

Contract cleaners certainly reduce cleaning costs. They can often cut the cleaning bill by up to 30 per cent, but not so much through their scientifically efficient cleaning methods as through the vice of the contract system. Competitive tendering forces contractors into a downward spiral of cost cutting in which the wage bill has to be their prime target. Both the National Prices and Incomes Board Report (1971) and the ACAS inquiry (1979) into contract cleaning found that the larger contractors favoured a wages council for industry with a fixed minimum wage. This would help regulate the tendering process. The fear of every contractor is that if they set wage rates higher than their competitors they will lose the contract. The logic of the competitive tendering process therefore is to 'play safe' and chip away at wage costs. And it is this that leads to the abuse of female cleaners: reduced hours, no benefits, increased workloads for fewer employees – and deteriorating cleaning standards.

■ The Fair Wages Resolution

There is nothing new about the sub-contracting of cleaning, nor about these related problems. Nor, for that matter, is there anything new about privatization. In 1967 the Government transferred out a third of the cleaning of government offices to contractors. The purpose was to cut cleaning costs and reduce the number of Civil Service employees. They certainly did. Three thousand five hundred cleaners were made redundant; cleaning costs were cut by 30 per cent, as were average wages, which dropped from £19.00 to £14.00 a week, and there were no guarantees of re-employment for those women made redundant nor was there consultation over disruptive new schedules (Sullivan, 1977).

In this instance the Civil Service Union (CSU) sought to fight the cleaners' wage reductions under the Fair Wages Resolution (FWR). This Resolution, passed by the Labour Government in 1946, sought to ensure that contractors to the government and local authorities should recognize employees' right to join a union and pay wages 'not less than those paid by the best employer in the trade'. For this requirement to be properly met, contractors cleaning government buildings would have had to pay the same rates as those found in *direct* cleaning employment. The CSU, however failed to get the FWR properly interpreted in this case. This was not surprising, since then, as now, the primary purpose of contracting out cleaning was to cut costs. There has never been effective enforcement of the FWR but nevertheless it has provided an important wage 'benchline'.

In 1970 the Government transferred two-thirds of its cleaning to contractors and thereby became the biggest single user of contract cleaners and hence in a powerful position to seek to regulate pay and conditions for employees of contract cleaners. It didn't. Again the Civil Service Union attempted to pursue parity for contract cleaners under the FWR and this time went for less, by claiming parity not with the best *direct* employment pay rates but with the public sector. The CSU asserted that:

> the pay of sub-contracted cleaners employed on public sector sites should not be less favourable than the pay and conditions of cleaners directly employed in that part of the public sector with which the contract is held (NBPI, 1971).

However, it was not until 1975 that it was agreed between Government, the CCMA and those trade unions involved, under the FWR, that:

> It is the Government's intention to introduce into contracts for the cleaning of Government offices, clauses requiring successful contractors to pay wages and to grant holidays with pay to their employees engaged in such contracts at rates no less favourable than those from time to time agreed for local authority staff engaged on similar work (Sullivan, 1977: 25).

This statement was important for cleaners and contractors alike. Importantly it allowed for *increasing* costs over the duration of a contract. For the commonest way for contractors to deal with rising costs within the time span of a contract is to employ fewer women to do the work: undermanning (*sic*) is endemic to contract cleaning.

The CSU was satisfied with this reinforcement of the FWR. However, it was limited in that it was to apply only to Government contracts, with no similar requirements placed on public corporations. There was evidence at the time that contract cleaners contracted by the Gas Board and Area Electricity Boards were paying very low rates of pay to their women cleaners.

■ Privatization 1980s style: a new offensive

The discussions that were taking place within the cleaning business in the 1970s about whether there should be a minimum wage rate, a wage council for the industry, or how to enforce the Fair Wages Resolution, now look rather quaint as the Thatcher Government has set about dismantling *all* forms of protection for minimum wages.

In 1980, the Government removed Schedule 11 from the Employment Protection Act which provided for 'the going rates for the job'. It importantly set informal guidelines for local wage rates. In 1983, the Government abolished the Fair Wages Resolution which stipulated that contractors had to pay at least the agreed wages and conditions on offer in the public sector. Although both were hard to establish in law – for example, during its entire existence only twenty or so cases were brought under the FWR – the Resolution still provided a crucial *basis* for wage negotiation. At least cleaners had an indication of what they *should* be earning. Now in 1985 the Government plans to abolish wages councils. Although there is not a wages council for cleaning, these bodies do set minimum rates of pay for nearly three million workers, and have provided some basis for comparability on pay levels in all sectors. Soon the only legislation that will exist to protect women's pay will be the Equal Pay Act.

There *is* a difference between the contracting out of cleaning in Civil Service buildings in 1967 and in hospitals in the 1980s. In the former, sub-contracting was an expedient strategy for cost cutting; in the latter, sub-contracting is a much larger offensive to lower wages, reduce employee benefits and to *deregulate* the employer/employee contract. The privatization offensive is seeking such a degree of cutbacks that it threatens to destabilize the contract cleaning business.

Contract cleaners find themselves in opposition to Government policy and advise District Health Authorities to maintain minimum wage rates and protection clauses in Health Service contracts. Eric Green, Chairman of Health Services Section, CCMA, stated the point clearly:

> What we have been doing has been opposed by the Government, which is why we are briefing Health Service administrators, telling them they need to meet these minimum rates to get suitable staff. Some of these savings recommended by the Department (Kenneth Clarke) are piddling – such as say £10,000 by not having a performance bond, which is a safety net if anything went wrong (*Guardian*, 26 November 1984).

■ Trade union organization

The effectiveness of legislation in protecting pay and employment conditions is crucially linked to the effectiveness of trade union organization in seeing that legislation is enforced. The unionization of cleaning work has always been very difficult indeed; recruitment is costly and time consuming because of the scattered nature of cleaning work. Only the very largest of organizations will have a cleaning force of any size. Many cleaners work in small groups; in twos and threes, or even on their own. Despite this, there was a sizeable growth of unionization amongst women cleaners in the late 1960s and early 1970s. The campaign to recruit women cleaners working for contract cleaners – the Night Cleaners Campaign – drew many women into unions for the first time, and in subsequent action to improve pay and conditions women cleaners undoubtedly benefitted from the larger backing of their union, the Transport and General Workers Union (Wandor, 1972). Public sector unionization amongst women also grew rapidly in this period. One union in particular, NUPE, made a big effort to recruit part-time women workers employed within both the Health Service and local authorities.

However, the sub-contracting of cleaning employment that is taking place is a crisis situation which institutionalized forms of trade union practice just cannot deal with. Whilst NUPE was successful at *recruitment* of women cleaners, it was no more successful than other unions in extending *representation* to this group of workers.

Fryer *et al* (1978) point out that NUPE has always suffered from problems of professional divisions, task fragmentation and union rivalry. This has made unified action and unity of interest hard to establish, especially at a local level. Consequently, there has been a continued and heavy reliance on establishing strong national agreements but this in turn has served to maintain a strong reliance on full-time officials, and NUPE has not seen the development of active shop stewards and rank-and-file participation.

That NUPE has enlarged its membership but not built an organization is painfully illustrated by the privatization experience. Although privatization is a Central Government directive, the sub-contracting process is being conducted not on a national level but at a local, District Health Authority level, with each union branch having to fight off contractors' tenders with an 'in-house' tender. This brings with it the dilemma of trying to protect existing pay and conditions whilst competing with private contractors. Small wonder that few contracts have gone in-house.

In one Birmingham hospital in 1985, the cleaning contract did 'successfully' stay in-house, but only after women cleaners had accepted the seemingly inevitable pay cuts (for some this was up to £20 a week), reduced hours, new shift rotas, new work practices and the ending of meal breaks. The NUPE official who presided over this new contract had to see trade union principles crumble. Members' pay and conditions could not be protected. This most hardworking and committed of trade union officials was in an impossible situation: if NUPE had not accepted these 'competitive' terms the cleaning services would have gone out to private contract. Thus, the very threat of contractors can be used to force lower pay and worse conditions of employment. It is certainly better that cleaning services remain in-house rather than going out to contract, for that maintains direct NHS employment, Whitley Council hourly rates of pay and union membership. For some women already on the margins of poverty, however, it can seem a rather academic distinction, and NUPE is losing membership as women clearly perceive that the union is not 'looking after them' as promised. As with other unions, deep-rooted paternalism is reflected in union structure: women are approximately 70 per cent of the membership but are only 10 per cent of the union's full-time officials. NUPE does not have a participative organization in which women *are* the union. The task of building that kind of structure is overdue.

■ Futures

The contracting out of hospital ancillary services will not be the beginning and end of the privatization experience. It has been argued that the Thatcher Government has decided upon a piecemeal and gradual programme for the privatization of the NHS in the recognition that total privatization at this point in time would be politically unacceptable (Labour Research, 1985b). After the sub-contracting of ancillary services, other services will follow: for example, portering, ambulancing and ground and building maintenance (jobs in which men predominate). The Health Minister is currently airing the idea of privatized hospital management.

Nor is privatization restricted to the Health Service. The Government is also frustrated by the slowness with which local authorities have responded to directives to tender their public services. By mid-1985 only forty-one out of 456 councils in England and Wales had begun to tender out to contract jobs that were currently undertaken by direct labour. Women make up 75 per cent of the manual labour force in local authority employment, so primarily where it has occurred it has been women's jobs that have been affected; school cleaning and the provision of school dinners being prime targets. Now the Secretary of State for the Environment is proposing a Bill which will *compel* local authorities to tender for the sub-contracting of school meals, school cleaning *and* refuse collection, the maintenance of council vehicles, street cleaning and the upkeep of parks and grounds. (Note, these are 'men's' jobs again.)

This issue of the private sub-contracting of work is marked for the way in which it has so far predominantly affected women's employment. Although there has been some support for privatization disputes, especially at a local level, it is also marked by its failure to gain *significant* support from the wider (male) labour movement. It will not be the first time that men, blinkered by sectional interests perhaps, have allowed 'women's' disputes to happen, unaware of the longer-term implications for themselves. It will not be the first time in the history of industrialized capital that the least organized and most vulnerable sector of the workforce has been used to pave the way for 'new' and more exploitative work practices. This extension of the sub-contracting of work is a serious extention of the casualization of work, and if uncontested, could be the most serious threat to pay, employment protection and rights since the war.

■ Notes

This article appeared in *Feminist Review* No. 21, 1985.

1

	Gross Hours	Basic Pay	Total (*including premia pay*)
Female cleaners	39.1	74.50	85.70
All-female manuals	39.4	78.10	93.50
Male cleaners	44.0	93.80	121.50
All-male manuals	44.3	113.90	152.70

Source: New Earnings Survey, 1984.

2 The NHS is run as a hierarchy. Fourteen Regional Health Authorities are responsible for strategic planning, and 241 District Health Authorities are responsible for administration at a local level. Although there is trade union and all-party representation, the structure of the RHA and DHA is Conservative dominated.

3 At the time of writing, the Barking women's dispute enters into its sixteenth month. Despite all the evidence of poor cleaning standards, poor management and very poor industrial relations, the DHA seems to have little control over the situation; it is caught between privatization policy and a real dependency on contract cleaners to provide the service.

Homeworking and the Control of Women's Work

Sheila Allen and Carol Wolkowitz

It's difficult to make money working at home when you've kiddies. I much preferred the evening shift, when my husband would have the kiddies and I could go to work and get on with the job without being interrupted.

You do not leave homework behind you when you come home from work.

What kinds of work obligations do homeworkers experience, and what social relations determine their character? Homeworking is dominated by contrasting, conflicting assumptions and interpretations. It was for long ignored or portrayed as an anachronism, peripheral to the economies of advanced industrial societies and of marginal importance as a source of livelihood (Bythell, 1978). In the mid-seventies research undertaken by the Low Pay Unit and others began to replace an image of housewives working for 'pin money' with a picture of homeworkers as women forced by dire economic need to accept appalling wages for work at home (Bolton, 1975; Brown, 1974; Crine, 1979; Field, 1976; Hope *et al*, 1976; Jordan, 1978). By the 1980s homeworking has been taken up for discussion by those who applaud, wholly or in part, paid work in the home as a form of employment (Atkinson, 1984; Burns, 1977; Gershuny, 1979; Gershuny and Pahl, 1979-80; Handy, 1984; IMS, 1984; Pahl, 1980; Postgate, 1984; Rose, 1983; Toffler, 1980). Some of them have argued that British firms can make their products more competitive, or utilize new technology to best advantage, by putting work out to workers at home, thereby enabling firms to adapt flexibly to changes in demand by treating labour as a completely variable factor. Others portray remunerated work at home as a way in which the unemployed can supplement household income and combat demoralization, permitting enterprising individuals to take up rewarding work as part of new, home-centred 'life styles'. Some even manage to reconcile both points of view. Only recently have these projections and assumptions begun to be critically examined (Allen, 1985; Allen *et al*, 1986; Pahl, 1984; Purcell *et al*, 1986; Redclift and Mingione, 1985; Wallace and Pahl, 1986).

Clearly there is a vital need for better-informed discussion on homeworking, the conditions homeworkers experience in their work, and its implications for women, who comprise the vast majority of homeworkers. Most importantly, undermining romanticized notions of homeworking, in which it is akin to cottage industries, is crucial to achieving improvements in homeworkers' employment status. At a theoretical level, the extent and conditions of paid work carried out in the home need to be incorporated into models of industrialization and de-industrialization. Attention to homeworking would contribute to the development of more adequate theories of the processes of production as they articulate with gender relations, both inside and outside the home. These developments are not possible within a sociology of work developed almost entirely in relation to male employment patterns, or within sociology of the family which characterizes the home in terms of consumption not production.

Yet getting behind existing images of homeworking is no easy matter. Local or small-scale independent research studies have highlighted the wide range of goods and services in which homeworking is involved, and the different types of enterprises which supply work, directly or through subcontracting arrangements (Allen, 1981A, 1983; Beale, 1978; Bolton, 1975; Brown, 1975; Dundee, 1984; Jordan, 1978; Newton-Moss, 1977). Clothing, food, toys, leisure goods, household furnishings, cleaning materials, paper garments for incontinents, greeting cards, boxes for chocolates and perfume, swimming pool cleansers, brushes, industrial transmission belts, fireworks and shoes are but a few of the products produced by homeworkers. They include goods and services of every level of quality, incorporated by firms into their final product or marketed by retail outlets through exclusive shops, high street chain stores, mail order houses, and market traders. Homeworkers are also involved in production for restaurants, preserving and pickling factories, local government services and regional health authorities, as well as firms of accountants, building societies, and central government departments. Other research studies have investigated the situation of homeworkers using new technology, some as comparatively well-paid systems analysts (Huws, 1984A, 1984B) and others as clerical workers (Posthuma, n.d.; Cragg and Dawson, 1981). However, attempts to estimate the extent of homeworking nationally are hampered by the general failure of official statistics to incorporate those involved in homeworking, whether as suppliers or workers. For a number of reasons even those figures which are available underestimate the scale of homeworking, and do not make it possible to identify sectors in which homeworking is increasing or decreasing.[1] The lack of adequate quantitative data on homeworking enables conflicting images of homeworking to co-exist.

Moreover, the persistence of different notions of homeworking relies on the lack of attention given to the analysis of the labour process (Allen 1981B). This article takes up for critical scrutiny the widely held view that because the work is done in the home it is free from the disciplines of industrial production, especially those of time constraints and measured effort, and therefore offers autonomous conditions of work easily accommodated within the domestic routine of women with family responsibilities. This article incorporates data from the ninety completed interviews with homeworkers in four areas of West Yorkshire, conducted mainly in 1980, following a survey of over 4,000 households. Interviews using detailed questionnaires were conducted in all but one case by women with local backgrounds and accents. We believe these data provide a more accurate picture than when outsiders and/or officials to whom homeworkers may fear revealing their homework are involved as interviewers or sponsors.[2]

■ The myth of autonomy

The autonomy homeworkers are thought to enjoy in deciding when and for how long they will work, and at what pace, is central to current thinking about homeworking and of particular significance so far as women are concerned. The time and effort control exercised over the assembly-line workers and all those who clock in and out of work is contrasted with a person working in her own home, with no supervisor or timekeeper. In the abstract, such a contrast appears to give the homeworkers a freedom and flexibility denied the factory or office worker. It is a critical component of positive evaluations of remunerated work at home, and a major reason why homeworking is assumed to be a boon for women who need to adjust their paid work around family responsibilities. But this view is quite misleading.

Many people work *at* or *from* home for payment of some kind, but they do so under a wide variety of contractual arrangements, and the confusion about homeworkers' conditions of work arises partly out of the tendency to conflate them. The Homeworkers (Protection) Bill 1979 provided a definition of homeworkers as in reality waged workers, distinguishing them from others who work *at* or *from* home under different sets of relationships.[3] The definition used in the Bill arose out of discussions among researchers and others concerned to improve homeworkers' conditions, and has since been adopted by many of those researching homework (Allen, 1981A, 1983; Crine, 1979; Dundee, 1984; Greater London Council, 1984; Leeds Tucric, 1984; Pugh, 1984). In contrast, most of the studies carried out or sponsored by the Department of Employment have focused on either Wages Council industries or the much broader category designated as home-based work (Hakim and Dennis, 1982; Hakim, 1984A, 1984B, 1985; Leighton, 1982, 1983). To understand homeworking, the first was too restrictive and the second is too broad. While interesting in itself for those concerned with patterns of work and the possible range of contractual relations, 'home-based work' rejects an analysis in terms of relations of production and makes it impossible to analyse the conditions of the different groups involved. Lumping together the plastic-bag packer with the redundant executive, or the consultant with the addresser of envelopes, inevitably leads to the conclusion that home-based work is characterized by diverse contractual relations and conditions of work and a wide range of remuneration. It then becomes impossible to identify the particular problems homeworkers as waged workers encounter or to frame legislation to ameliorate them.

Presumptions regarding conditions of work in homeworking have been highlighted by the few cases brought before industrial tribunals by homeworkers seeking to establish their rights to benefits conferred on employees by the Employment Protection (Consolidation) Act 1978. In such cases tribunals and the courts are asked to determine whether homeworkers' conditions of employment, including the control and supervision of their work, are in reality those of employees. Suppliers giving evidence in these cases, supported by bodies like the Inland Revenue, have drawn on assumptions about homeworkers' autonomy in work, arguing that homeworkers 'are not bound by conditions of normal employment', as they 'do the work when they like and for such hours as they want' (*D'Ambrogio* v

Hyman Jacobs (1978) quoted in Townshend-Smith, 1979: 1022). Where tribunals have examined actual conditions of work they judged in one case that insofar as the supplier of work determines 'the thing to be done, the manner of performance, and in reality the time and place of performance', the homeworkers should be considered as employees, with the same rights and benefits as other employees (*Airfix Footwear* v *Cope* (1978) quoted in Townshend-Smith, 1979: 1022). Like all industrial tribunal decisions, this ruling applies only to those individuals bringing the case. We consider the mechanisms of control operated by the suppliers of work in some detail based on our investigations.

However, apart from the homeworkers' relation to the supplier, including questions of employment status, and the need to distinguish between various contractual relationships governing paid work at home, it is important not to confine the discussion to these aspects alone. For the restrictions and obligations under which people work are not confined simply by those imposed as part of the wage labour contract. The notion of homeworkers' autonomy holds sway, in part, because of powerful associations made between ideas of home, privacy and the freedom of work constraints imposed by 'the rude, commercial, aggressive world' (Barker and Allen, 1976: 1). In order to appreciate homeworkers' actual position within the labour process we need to understand what the domestic sphere means for women and, in particular, the work obligations which women experience within it. It is only through confronting the diverse obligations which women experience that we can comprehend their conditions as homeworkers and relate these to women's working lives more generally.

■ Systems of control in homeworking

To turn labour into labour for profit requires a system of control (Thompson, 1983). To discipline and reward the workforce, and to supervise and evaluate its performance, entails authority over the workforce. The attempt to exercise this authority may be more or less hidden, more or less subtle, more or less successful. Control of the pace and intensity of work and the quality of output is in many cases exercised directly, through close supervision, or technically, through the design of machinery and work processes which demand a certain way of working and which leave the actual producers with little discretion over how they perform their jobs. This applies to both in-workers and homeworkers.

The attempt to exercise control over labour appears to reach its extreme in assembly-line production, in which the pace of work is set by the tempo of the line and the worker is to a greater or lesser extent subordinated to the machine. It is this kind of control to which most investigation has been directed, and which has come to symbolize the subordination of the workforce and its lack of autonomy at work (Braverman, 1974). Mechanisms through which labour is controlled directly or technically are often thought to account for the growth of factory production over 'putting out' in the rise of industrial capitalism. In addition, the development of 'scientific management' techniques in the twentieth century and the increasing utilization of computer technology in the past decade are portrayed in the same mould. All other modes through which labour is set to work have come to appear as inefficient survivals, in which workers are assumed to be free to set their own hours of work, to choose the pace and intensity of work, and to exercise control antithetical to high profits.

An example of control through the use of computers is the way in which the productivity of many office workers is tracked by computers in keystrokes per hour. As the General Manager of an American-owned offshore data-processing firm describes their system:

> When a worker turns on a machine, she must sign on with her identification number ... If she goes for a break, she must turn off the machine.

Nor can operators leave their machines running when they go to the toilet, the manager says:

> Yes, some think they are being smart and fooling us by leaving the machine on when they go to the bathroom, but we can tell when they do this, because their recorded productivity level drops since they've been gone from their terminal. (Posthuma, n.d.)

But control is not limited to direct supervision or to subordinating the workers to the machine. In homework, as in the factory or office, it is not the worker who organizes and exercises control but the supplier. Employers have available, depending on the context, a range of mechanisms through which to control output. Although production in the factory has come to appear as the dominant form by which labour is controlled, a substantial proportion of the labour force is subject to controls of other kinds. The mechanisms which determine the homeworkers' pace and quality of work are comparatively indirect.

Consequently homework can take on the appearance of autonomy which is more apparent than real.

The work task

Homeworkers are not independent contractors trading on their own account. The supplier purchases the materials and sells the product. The homeworker does not design or choose her work tasks. Much homeworking is in fact characterized by a division of labour in which production is subdivided into discrete, standardized tasks using standardized components, leaving the homeworker with discretion over only the most trivial aspects of the work process. In the production of greeting card decorations, for instance, we found that one set of homeworkers makes the decorations, another group of homeworkers attaches them to the cards, and yet another is employed to box the finished cards. The last homeworker acts as the quality controller who can refuse payment to the others. The homeworker who stitches together the ends of fan belts has no control over her work tasks. Any possibility of originality or skill has been organized out of the work of the majority of homeworkers. However, some homeworkers do complete the whole product and rely on craft skills. Hand-knitters are one of the best examples. They are skilled workers who knit whole garments. Before they are accepted as homeworkers they must prove their skill. Once they become homeworkers, they work with materials supplied by the employer, to a design and size specified by him or her. Those hand-knitters whose task does not include stitching together the pieces complained that they miss the satisfaction of seeing the finished product. Machinists who complete whole products, making through dresses, blouses, trousers, leisure wear and so on, do so from cut-out pieces supplied by the supplier and according to his or her instructions. For this reason, contrary to the view expressed by Campbell, machinists are unable to make extra money for themselves by making and selling extra garments out of the materials supplied (Campbell, 1978).

Output

Like the design and performance of work tasks, output is also effectively under the supplier's control. The homeworker only rarely has a meaningful choice in how much work she takes on. Although many homeworkers pointed to some degree of flexibility in their work, it is clear from our data that this operated within severely constrained limits.

The chief mechanism through which the supplier controls output is the payment system typical of homeworking. Homework is almost invariably piecework, and is usually so not only in manufacturing but also among clerical workers (Brown, 1974; Cragg and Dawson, 1981; Crine, 1979; Hakim, 1980, 1984A; Jordan 1978). Computer programmers are sometimes paid hourly wages (Huws, 1984A, 1984B), but their employers have both the financial resources and the technology to monitor the pace of their work with extreme accuracy. In the West Yorkshire survey all the homeworkers were paid at piecework rates and their hours and intensity of work were determined by it (Allen 1981A, 1981B, 1983).

Because payment by results establishes an immediate connexion between payment and pieces produced, it is one of the main mechanisms through which suppliers attempt to maintain or increase the intensity of work. In some kinds of employment, these attempts are not always successful. Factory employees evolve methods of work which enable them to establish norms of piece rates (Marriot, 1957; Ray, 1952). In most cases for in-workers, piece rates operate on top of basic hourly, daily or weekly wage rates. In the case of Wages Council industries, the flat rates are based on an hourly wage rate. In times of full employment, rate setting has led to frequent annual disputes, so that its cost to employers in time 'lost' over changes in piece rates has outweighed its other benefits to the employers (Baldamus, 1961; Bowey *et al*, 1982).

In homeworking, however, piecework operates much more successfully from the employer's point of view. In the situation known as 'sweating', piece rates can be pushed down almost indefinitely, making it necessary for homeworkers to require the help of family labour to make up their earnings or to meet deadlines. Not only is there no basic rate in the homeworker's wages, but the absence of a standard working day or week means that employers do not need to establish a notional hourly or daily or weekly wage from which to calculate piece rates. Moreover, employers have no need to consider collective action from their workers when the labour force is employed under casualized conditions and is largely unorganized.

Under such conditions the worker can come to see piecework earnings as the result of individual effort becoming 'a willing accomplice to his or her exploitation' (Braverman, 1974: 62). The homeworker is discouraged from seeing herself as a regular worker, earning a regular wage, and her earnings come to appear as deriving from the additional tasks she takes on by choice. It is because homeworkers are characterized as housewives and irregular earners, supported by a male wage, that the obvious constraints posed by piecework can be ignored so consistently in depictions of the homeworker's autonomy or flexible workload.

The ideological force of piecework, as a system of payment, is reflected in conflicting assessments by homeworkers themselves. For example, one homeworker with two children under five packed greetings cards for three hours a night, seven days a week. Her earnings were so low that even though her husband helped her most nights, they earned only £15 to £20 a week between them for forty-two hours work. Not surprisingly, she said that she was 'permanently tired', but went on to say that 'this is my own fault, I needn't take all the work I do'. In fact when the greetings cards work 'finished', she had to take another homeworking job packing rubbish bags for even less pay.

But homeworkers also recognize that the low piece rates make long hours essential. 'To earn anything worthwhile', one homeworker comments, 'you'd have to chain yourself to the envelopes.' Many recognize the peculiar meaning of choice in this context. As one homeworker put it:

> It was up to the worker to say how many boxes she wanted delivered to her in any week so I suppose there was an average order – but often I'd order ten boxes and only complete seven. Nobody complained – it was up to me just what amount of work I'd do. But then the less I did the less I got paid, so the incentive was there to do more.

They also recognize the severe limits on the extent to which piecework enables them to control their own earnings by taking on more work, for they rarely have any choice between differently rated products. Piecework earnings depend on the worker's being able to build up speed and accuracy with a consistent product. But homeworkers are asked to do anything within a broadly agreed range of products and level of skill. They may experience changes in the product from week to week, but the rates are not adjusted to reflect the difficulties and time necessary to complete different products. The supplier's control over earnings through the allocation of work is shown by the commonly recognized practice of rewarding more experienced homeworkers with work carrying higher piece rates. Homeworkers' earnings depend on the type of work they are given as well as the hours they are prepared to put in.

The homeworker's dependence on the employer for the type of work, regardless of the effect on earnings, is evident in the following comments from homeworkers in West Yorkshire:

> Earned £5 a week on average – occasionally I had thicker wool and earned about £6 a week. (Hand-knitter. Average hours 30 per week)

> Pay varied between £5 and £5.50 depending on the difficulty of the pattern, i.e. whether it is part or all Fair Isle. (Hand-knitter. Average hours 28 per week)

> The extra money was for a better-paid job that could be done more easily – splitting packs that hadn't sold well and repacking them in different combinations. (Card packer. Average hours $17\frac{1}{2}$ per week)

> Earned £9.25 last week, usually £7-£8 week. If I get all the higher paid overalls I can earn £10 a week. (Machinist. Average hours $16\frac{1}{2}$ per week)

> Earned £11.80 last week. Varies between £8-£11 depending on the amount of work done. Some cards take longer to do than others, e.g. larger, stiffer cardboard. (Card packer. Average hours 13 per week)

While suppliers are free to allocate work of different kinds as and when it suits them, the homeworker is obliged to accept the work provided and to complete it on time. Despite weekly or seasonal variations in the amount supplied, the homeworker expects to complete the work, filling rush and seasonal orders as necessary and going without her income when no work is supplied. Fifty-eight per cent of the sample stated that there had been times when they had been wanting to work but no work was available, and half said that there had been times when there had been more work than they could comfortably manage.

Apart from the piecework system and the control over the amount and type of work, the provision of machinery by the supplier is one of the more obvious modes through which the supplier ensures that homeworkers meet production targets. This is recognized by those industrial tribunals which have accepted suppliers' provision of machinery as evidence that the homeworker's work obligations are those of an employee. The clearest example we found of a supplier explicitly controlling output was the homeworker who stated:

He will provide £20 of work (weekly). If you drop below this he will take the machine away.

In this case the obligation was one-sided. This homeworker had been without work for three to four weeks on a number of occasions. Clearly the expectation was that she would take a set amount of work when the employer made it available or risk losing her job. The non-provision of work by her employer did not offset or reduce this obligation.

Equally important is that the supplier sets the times for the delivery of materials and the collection of finished work. Homeworkers therefore work to tight deadlines, leaving little scope for adjusting their hours to suit themselves. For 90 per cent of the West Yorkshire homeworkers, work was delivered and collected by the supplier, in some cases with such frequency that the management of the work flow was reminiscent of factory employment. Weekly collection and payment was most common, but in at least fourteen cases work was delivered/collected more than once a week and in two cases more than once a day. One supplier even made two deliveries on Fridays, so that the homeworker would have 'enough' work over the weekend. It is clear that these homeworkers had to adjust to the flow of work when it suited the supplier.

Quality of work

Employers' control over labour also includes the control of the quality of work. In much factory employment this is exercised through direct supervision. Where direct supervision is impractical, as in homeworking, or in highly skilled occupations where some degree of work autonomy is expected, other mechanisms are brought into play. The recruitment and training of workers can provide familiarity with the standard of work required and instil company loyalty and discipline as alternatives to direct supervision.

A significant minority of homeworkers in our sample (and 14 per cent in the Department of Employment sample; Hakim 1980) were working for firms at which they had previously been employed as in-workers. In several cases the approach had been made by the employer, and some employers were said to take on as homeworkers only those who had been previously in-working employees. In addition, twenty-five referred to some test or trial period, either in the factory or at home, during which they had to demonstrate their ability to complete a sample of work according to the employer's instructions, and five more referred to employers' demonstrating how the work was to be done. When asked specifically, forty of the ninety homeworkers said they had done some training at the firm.

Those employers who do not exercise this kind of control, which they are less likely to do if the work is unskilled, operate control on the quality of work through the piecework system. If work is found to be faulty, either payment is refused or work has to be made good before payment is made. In fact, very few homeworkers referred to not being able to complete their work satisfactorily, for if they find that they cannot do the work at a rapid pace to the standard required they earn almost nothing and look for other homework.

The organization of consent

Many methods for controlling output and retaining a loyal workforce rely upon apparently consensual co-operation between homeworker and supplier. The self-discipline required of the homeworker by the supplier of work indicates the extent to which suppliers prefer to engineer what appears to be voluntary compliance rather than exercise direct control. Because meeting production targets is made the responsibility of homeworkers as individuals it provides considerable scope for the supplier to present himself or herself as an 'understanding employer' (Freeman, 1982) willing to make allowances on occasions for the homeworkers' other commitments. This kind of interaction between supplier and homeworker ensures that production requirements are met, while at the same time fosters the illusion that homeworking permits an unusual degree of autonomy.

Existing research on homeworking reveals some differences among suppliers in their expectations regarding acceptable variations in the individual homeworker's output from time to time (Jordan, 1979; Saifullah Khan, 1979). Of the homeworkers interviewed in West Yorkshire, one half mentioned times when they had refused work or had been unable to complete work on time. Some had been told they would lose their job if it happened again. Other suppliers were reported to be more sympathetic to workers whose other commitments make it difficult for them to manage an identical allocation of work each week. They let it be known that they will allow some latitude in meeting obligations ('If you can't manage the work in a particular week,' says one West Yorkshire homeworker, 'you just tell the driver not to put you down for work.') Although in the abstract this appears a wholly reasonable approach, it legitimizes the homeworker's low pay and lack of employment security by confirming the primacy of her family responsibilities and the supposedly secondary importance of her paid employment.

Variations in output are of course not unique to homeworking. All employers allow for workers' holidays and illness in scheduling work, and few expect to meet their production targets all the time. But homeworkers are led to perceive commonly provided employee benefits as privileges. For homeworkers, holidays or sick leave, for which in-workers are usually paid, are unpaid and granted as a special favour. Although many homeworkers see the supplier's willingness to accept occasional refusals of work as an indication of the flexibility of the work, it is quite clear that homeworkers refuse work very rarely, and only on those occasions when in-workers expect paid leave. When asked if they had ever refused work, homeworkers replied with comments like the following:

> Once when going on holiday.

> Twice when ill, nothing happened.

> Another time I cut my finger and had to go to hospital. The firm didn't mind that the orders were not completed in time.

> Twice a year when I needed a break.

They were so grateful for the work and fearful of losing it that some felt the supplier to be sympathetic even when very little extra time was given to complete the work:

> Nothing much happened when I told them that I hadn't done the work. They said we will come next morning, have it ready as it has to be sent off for delivery.

> Oh, they don't care you know. I just tell them that this (or that) has happened. Like last week this girl next door died, so we had to go there ... so I had to leave it and then I finished it after. I'd 400 left, so I did 200 last night and have 200 (still) to do.

Women employers and subcontractors, or women employed as agents by the suppliers of homework, may be particularly likely to adopt the role of the 'understanding employer'. The relation between the female supplier of work and the homeworker is mainly that of employer-employee, but it is coloured by the supplier's own experience and expectations. One woman subcontractor we interviewed, an ex-homeworker who managed her business from home, sympathized with the stresses of the job, like sore fingers and frustration with detailed work, and said she was understanding if family problems interrupted work or her employees needed a break – without pay. She distributed bottles of sherry as a Christmas bonus. Her identification with the problems facing women working at home was no doubt sincere, but was clearly functional to keeping a loyal, hard-working labour force at no cost to herself in real employee benefits.

Another business which has sought a favourable reputation for its understanding of the difficulties of women workers is F International, a computer software contractor. It is headed by a woman and employs women programme analysts as homeworkers. One *Guardian* report readily accepted the claim that F International workers are well paid and able to combine looking after their children with work at home 'in hours to suit the individual' (Toynbee, 1985). But others have pointed out that, in practice, F International employees are required to spend part of the week in a firm's premises. They are paid much less than in-firm employees with the same training, and less than the employees of other software subcontractors (*Guardian* Women, Letters, 1985).

Suppliers also encourage homeworkers to identify with their employer's interests. Homeworkers recognize that the supply of work is contingent on their employers' obtaining contracts for further work, and this can be strategically emphasized by the supplier. We found that instructions to homeworkers could be accompanied by direct hints that further contracts depended upon the homeworkers' quality and speed of work. One firm which supplied fancy packaging to chocolate and perfume manufacturers mentioned this specifically in its written instructions to homeworkers.

In fact the mechanisms of control used to obtain the compliance of a homeworking labour force vary enormously. It has been suggested, for instance, that in homeworking quality of work depends upon forms of 'non-economic coercion', especially the mobilization of kinship ties between supplier and worker (Young, 1981). Kinship ties between supplier and worker have been found in the production of lace in South India (Mies, 1982), of carpets in Morocco (Maher, 1981) and of clothing by Cypriot and Bangladeshi homeworkers in London and the West Midlands (Anthias, 1983; Mitter, 1986). Although in these cases the husband or male relative controls production partly through the same mechanisms as other suppliers – through, for instance, the timing of the delivery and collection of work – his authority is patriarchal in character.

In contrast the West Yorkshire survey found no homeworkers employed by their husbands or other kin, and very few cases in which the husband mediated between the homeworker and the supplier. This suggests that kinship links are not essential to control of the quality of work, and where they exist they stem from somewhat different aspects of the organization of homeworking production. Or they may be important only when homeworkers are new entrants to the waged labour force, and consequently unfamiliar with factory discipline. This was not the case for the West Yorkshire sample, as nearly all the workers had previous experience of paid employment outside the home. In Britain most suppliers can rely upon a labour force which is already fully habituated to the demands of waged employment. The West Yorkshire homeworkers took pride in being seen as 'responsible' or 'reliable' workers turning out good work. Although their presentation of this image no doubt emerges partly as a strategic response to the limited and uncertain supply of homework, it reflects also widespread, cultural values regarding the 'fair day's work' owed an employer.

■ Non-wage obligations

So far we have been concerned to challenge those aspects of the myth of homeworkers' autonomy which derive from a confusion between the position of homeworkers and the self-employed. In view of the immediate benefits homeworkers would gain from legal recognition of their status as employees, this emphasis is not misplaced. But it must be stressed that this represents a very partial, and for that reason, misleading picture. Constraints associated with the wage labour contract are only one form through which control over labour is organized. When women's work is examined, we also have to consider other limitations on women's autonomy in setting their hours and pace of work.

These are limitations imposed by the sexual division of labour. The ability to realize those advantages which men often seek in self-employment, like the capacity to set one's own hours and pace of work, or to exchange time spent on leisure or family life for a higher income or more rewarding work (Scase and Goffee, 1982), rest in part on men's position as men. Homeworkers share with other women controls on their use of their own labour which men experience much more rarely.

The working day

Even when homeworkers are acknowledged to be employees, the freedom to set one's hours 'to suit oneself', to fit the work around housework and childcare, is believed to distinguish homework from other kinds of paid employment. In the course of discussing homework with academics, trade unionists, neighbours and friends, we have come across the extreme tenacity of this image. People retain an image of the homeworker popping out to do the shopping in a 'convenient moment' or stopping work to run a load of washing, to get the children's tea, or to comfort a crying baby, and then picking up work where she left off. Or the homemaker is thought to get down to work when the family is busy with other things.

Close attention to the real conditions of women's work, paid and unpaid, suggest that this image must represent a very partial picture of the homeworker's working day. This whole scenario, with its assumption of convenient moments and orderly routine, is misleading and smacks more of some imagined domestic idyll than the harassed coping strategies with which most women are familiar. Since homeworkers work the same number of hours, paid and unpaid, as women going out to work, they face most of the same problems. Added difficulties, distinctive to doing paid work at home, compound the problems.

Some studies of homeworking have repeated the conventional wisdom, arguing that it allows 'a more flexible, even easy-going day' than going out to work (Cragg and Dawson, 1981). Some homeworkers do perceive their work in this way. In the West Yorkshire survey, nine homeworkers cited working at their own pace or without supervision as a reason for enjoying homework, and twenty-one specifically mentioned that working to one's own pace or to fit in with one's own routine was an advantage homeworking offered or a reason for recommending it to others. However, the rest of the ninety homeworkers either saw no advantages in homeworking or mentioned other aspects. Some had begun homeworking with the idea that it would give them control over their hours of work, but as experienced homeworkers they had come to see the situation differently. As one homeworker commented: 'It starts off okay but then you get a lot of pressure put on you.' Another tried to hold on to the view that homeworking offered advantages but recognized that in her own case they had become illusory. She saw the advantages of homeworking as being able to 'work when you feel like it' and to 'fit it in' with household and children, but in practice found that she frequently worked 'until two in the morning' and had come to 'resent the pressure my boss is putting on me'. Since the actual workload is set by the supplier it does not offer much scope for the worker to fit it in at her convenience. When homeworkers in the West Yorkshire study were asked to explain the reasons why their hours of work varied, more cited the supply of work than all other reasons combined.

Homeworkers' own accounts provide striking evidence that the working day is tightly structured by the constant demands of paid work and unpaid domestic labour. This is true not simply exceptionally, as when children are ill (Cragg and Dawson, 1981), but as the normal condition of work. As the following reports demonstrate, the combination of homeworking, housekeeping, childcare and, in some cases, other paid work means that every moment is accounted for:

> I get the kids off to school, then do the washing and clean round for ten o'clock when the work is delivered. I work through until lunchtime, stop for a sandwich, and continue until four in the afternoon. About six, after tea and clearing it up, I work for another hour, get the youngest off to bed, start again about eight and work until eleven at night. Sometimes I stop work at about nine and get up early the following morning so it will be ready at ten in the morning, when the delivery comes. My day varies according to what crops up – some days the youngest goes to the speech therapist – and how fast I can do a certain job. I am faster at each job as I go along. But it always has to be done by 10 a.m. the next day.

> I get up and give the family breakfast and tidy the house. I try to start work about 9.30 a.m. and work until 3.30 in the afternoon with a break for lunch. Sometimes I work in the evenings if I have not been able to get enough done during the day due to the children needing attention.

> At 5.30 in the morning I clean an office at the bottom of the road. Then I get home, get breakfast and see the kids to school. I sew until lunchtime, and then get back to sewing … I am also childminding for two other children.'

Accounts like these show that despite the claims of some suppliers (Rubery and Wilkinson, 1981) homework is not done casually, in front of the TV, nor picked up and put down in odd moments. While there may be a few opportunities for day-to-day adjustment in the particular hours homework is done, this is limited by the employer's control of the amount of work and has to be seen within the context of an extremely long working week. Homeworkers work the same number of hours as women with jobs outside the home. In the West Yorkshire study, the majority did homework for eleven to thirty hours a week, and twelve worked over forty hours a week. Over a third worked in the evenings, as well as during the day, and nearly as many worked at the weekend. This is added to the time put into unpaid domestic labour. The real situation is that homeworking permits the worker to go on working until she drops. It allows her to extend the working day into unsocial hours, evening and night work, and the working week into a full seven days.

Indeed in many respects homeworking is more onerous than going out to work. This is partly because there is no spatial separation between paid and unpaid work. Homeworking is 'always on your mind, always there'. As homeworkers recognize, 'You do not come home from work and leave it behind you.' Moreover, while those going out to work are at least allocated tea breaks, the homeworker's day is so dominated by simultaneous demands on her labour that a break in one kind of work is used to get on with another. The use of domestic space means that this way of organizing work is not even convenient. Few homeworkers have a separate place to work, and they are therefore unable to leave their work set up. Three quarters of the West Yorkshire sample worked in the kitchen or living room, and had to clear work away to prepare meals or to make room for children to play, and then set up again, all in their 'own' time.

Further difficulties arise from the character of domestic responsibilities. Unlike work governed by commercial transactions, the time required by housework and childcare is not calculable or easily rationalized. Standards of work are established quite differently. Studies demonstrate that the domestic labour of women going out to work is rarely reduced or shared with other household members (Hunt, 1980; Hartman, 1981; Meissner et al, 1975), but household routine may be adjusted to some extent. Meals may be served earlier or later, or consist of different foods, or the house may be left untidy and cleaned in long hours put in at the weekend. In contrast, the homeworker's family still expect the services of a full-time housewife, including for instance the preparation of a cooked dinner in the middle of the day:

I get up at 7.30, give the kids breakfast and take them to school. Then I do the washing and clean the house and put my youngest to sleep. I set to work for about two hours from nine to eleven. I stop to prepare a cooked lunch, my husband comes home for this. When he leaves about one, I wash up, and then work until three when the kids come from school. I cook dinner for seven. After I've put the kids to bed I work from eight to ten, and then to bed.

Nor is homework as readily combined with the care of young children as is sometimes supposed. It is true that homeworking enables mothers to be at home with children young enough to require the presence of an adult, but this is simply a caretaker role. Homeworkers recognize that despite being at home they are still unable to give their children their full attention, and have the same worries as women working outside the home:

> It took my attention away from the three-year-old if I did only 250 boxes a week. Five hundred, and I neglected home, children, husband.

> I have to work very hard to earn a worthwhile wage, and can't look after my children properly.

> The house is neglected and the children play out long hours.

> Can't pay attention to the children, care for their clothes, cleaning.

Considerations like these make it evident that there is little about homeworking which is convenient for the worker. The homeworker adapts herself to the amount of work, and makes time for it through a lengthening of her working day. Her position is a particularly vivid example of the situation of women with dependants more generally. Part-time work outside the home is also portrayed as fitting into the other responsibilities of women workers. In practice, however, employers hire part-time workers to cover periods of high customer demand or to keep machinery running during breaks in the work of full-time employees (Robertson and Wallace, 1984). For part-time workers also, other responsibilities must be fitted around the hours set by the employer, however inconvenient they may be (Coyle, 1984).

Family expectations: the husband's control

> My husband says *I should* be here for the kids if they're ill etc., and *I have* to take them to and from school in case of accidents. Also he doesn't want me to meet other men or women who'd put ideas in my head. (italics added)

Who defines and enforces the sexual division of labour within conjugal households? In addition to the more general ideological and practical constraints on the homeworker's working day, homeworkers may be subject to more personalized controls over the terms under which they sell their labour. Husbands exercise considerable control over homemakers' conditions of work.

In the West Yorkshire sample, the husbands did not directly exploit or appropriate women's labour as homeworkers. As we have already mentioned, none were employed by their husbands and only a few gave their wages to the husband. Two homeworkers had a husband and one a father-in-law who were employed or who had previously been employed by the firm which supplied the homework. These men brought the work home and returned it to the factory, but their role did not extend beyond this. For our sample, homeworking was clearly waged employment, not unpaid family labour controlled or supervised by male family members.

However, the decision to do homework rather than go out to work is frequently made by the husband. Fifty homeworkers (55 per cent of the sample) said that their families expected them to stay at home rather than go out to work. In a large number of these cases the husband's opinion was seen to be crucial. Homeworkers were aware that their husbands had definite preferences either in favour of or against their wives' working outside the home.

Husbands' views were justified in terms of a number of rationales. In some cases the husband's view was that it was 'a woman's place' to be in the home and his to be the breadwinner:

> My husband feels he should support the family financially.

> He likes me to stay at home. My husband is willing to work longer hours to discourage me going out to work.

More usually, however, the husband's preference for a wife at home was expressed in terms of the wife's obligations to their children:

> My husband objects to me not looking after our child.

> He would not like the idea of a childminder.

Husbands also made references to their own needs. The nature of these varied, but each showed a high expectation that the wife should fit in with the husband's routine:

> My husband is away a lot so he wants me to be at home on the days he has off.

> My husband prefers it – because sometimes he finishes work at 3.00 p.m. and expects me to be in when he comes home.

> He likes me at home although he wouldn't force me to. He likes me to be at home when he gets in from work. He doesn't like coming in to an empty house.

> My youngest child has asthma and I'm expected to be here in case he's ill. My husband likes meals ready when he gets home also.

The overriding impression is that many husbands expected their wives to fit in with their definition of satisfactory family life or acceptable standards of housekeeping. With some exceptions, both husband and wife accepted the husband's right to determine the use of the wife's labour. Even those husbands who were said to have no preference were given this right:

> My husband does not prevent me going out to work. I have to think of the children – so I decided.

> My husband lets me please myself.

Several homeworkers whose opinion differed from the husband's still gave way to his views, feeling this to be part of their marital bargain:

> He thinks that women should be in the home. He is a male chauvinist pig, but I let him get away with a lot because he treats me well.

Husbands who preferred a wife to go out to work did not express concern for the children's situation but left it to the wife to sort out. Consideration of the children's welfare was treated as the wife's responsibility.

> My husband would like me to go out and earn – I cannot because of the children.

Particularly significant is that where husbands preferred their wives to be at home, the couple sometimes saw housekeeping and childcare as a full-time job which left no room for paid employment:

> I have a full-time job at home. I don't want to go out to work, as there is enough to do at home. My husband likes us to relax at night, he doesn't like to see me ironing.

In this situation, in which the wife is perceived as *already* doing a full-time job, then the homework becomes invisible as work and as a source of income. When homeworkers collude in this definition, homework becomes the wife's 'choice' in the use of her free time rather than an extension of the working day. The importance of her earnings to family living standards is only half-acknowledged, at least by the husband:

> My husband still insists that we don't need my homework money, but he's glad of the extra really.

The strength of the conventional view of women as wives and mothers is obvious in these cases. Some husbands object only to their wives' work outside the home, and to compensate for the loss of these earnings are willing to help with homework ('He helped to get more done, he wanted a little extra money and hated my outside cleaning job'). But in other cases even homeworking was resented. It is in this context that some of the family tensions mentioned by homeworkers should be situated. Twelve referred to problems between themselves and their husbands arising out of their homework. Our general impression was that these often reflected the husband's irritation at his wife being occupied in this way while he was there:

> There are no serious problems, but all the knitting got on my husband's nerves.

> Some tension but slight. It gets on my husband's nerves sometimes.

Sometimes the dissatisfaction was expressed in terms of mess or inconvenience, but even then it could reflect other underlying tensions. An example is the homeworker whose husband complained about her 'neglect of the children' and 'the mess in the house from all the fluff'. However, she also mentioned that 'my husband has all the say if his wage is the only income'. It is not unlikely that her wish 'for a bit of economic independence' contributed to their arguments. She concluded that homework was 'too badly paid to be worth the upset to the family'.

Of course note needs to be taken of those husbands who condemned the fact that suppliers were getting away with paying wages so far below average (see also Sharpe, 1984). But in a few cases their comments about this aspect of homework were somewhat ambiguous. One homeworker reported that:

> Sometimes my husband gets annoyed because I regularly work at knitting until two in the morning. He complains about the poor pay and thinks I'm a fool 'cos I'm frightened to ask for more.

Another said that she and her married daughter had not told their husbands how little they earned, for fear the men would have 'thrown the sewing machines out of the window'.

Of course we have no reason to believe that homeworkers were working at home primarily because of their husbands' overt demands. Many husbands expect a wife at home as an integral part of married life; others do not care so long as their own needs are met. But in general husbands do not *need* to express their opinion directly. Forty-one of the ninety homeworkers said without comment that their families did not expect them to stay at home. But none of the husbands appeared to have contemplated the kind of shift in the household division of labour which would have made wives' work outside the home more practicable. Taken-for-granted ideological expectations of the division of labour are so effective that overt control need never emerge. It is these that are the most successful in controlling women.

■ Hidden labour

The interplay of controls on the homeworker's labour is most starkly apparent in the extent of the hidden labour of other members of the household, friends and neighbours. Low piecework rates, and the need to have work ready for collection despite the other demands on homeworkers' time, mean that homeworkers require the help of others. The labour of other family members was mentioned by thirty-nine of the homeworkers in West Yorkshire. The husband's contribution was most often mentioned (twenty-four cases), followed by the homeworker's young children (nine cases) and adult relations (sons, daughters, mothers, mothers-in-law, and sisters being the most common).

Husbands and other adult relatives usually did the same work as the homeworker, although husbands sometimes did only part of the process. They worked in the evenings, or, if they were unemployed or off sick, for part of the day. Children worked after school or in the evening. Much of the child labour was packaging. For example, one homeworker paid each of her four children, aged between five and eleven, $\frac{1}{2}$p for every teddy bear they turned to the right side after she had machined the parts together. The children also helped package them. The woman received 9p per teddy bear and earned 90p an hour. The stuffing of the bears was done by other homeworkers. In another family, an eight-year-old, the eldest of four children, stacked greeting cards for three hours every night. His mother earned 38p an hour and gave him 50p for several nights' work.

The unrecorded labour of family members means that hourly wage rates in homeworking are even lower than total earnings suggest at first sight. For instance, one homeworker appeared to be earning £2.19 an hour, one of the highest wages we recorded. This was her eighth job in five or six years of homeworking. She lived with her husband, a mechanic, and their four children and looked after two other children after school and during the holidays. She was able to begin work only in the evenings, four hours a night, twenty hours a week. She assembled Easter egg boxes, pleating the silk linings and attaching them to the boxes. Her husband worked with her every evening, sticking double-sided tape to the inside of the boxes. When his labour is included, their hourly wage rate works out at only £1.09 an hour.

In organizing the help of other members of the family, these homeworkers are forced to discipline their children's work and monitor their husband's, saving the supplier the costs of this supervision but adding still greater tension and fatigue to their working day. Over half of these homeworkers paid other family members for their help. Although mothers and sisters were said to be willing to 'help out', female adult relatives were normally paid for their work, and usually worked on a regular basis. These women were apparently sharing among themselves the few available jobs and their meagre rewards (see also Wallace and Pahl, 1986). Many of the children were paid, usually in the form of pocket money but sometimes as in the cases cited above, on something like a piece or time rate.

The terms under which husbands contribute to homework offer insight into a wife's perceived right to call upon a husband's labour as compared to his rights to her unpaid domestic services. A husband's labour had to be bought or carefully negotiated. Four husbands were paid for their time, and another four worked the same hours as their wives and shared the pay equally. Fifteen husbands were not actually paid, but the homeworkers indicated that the husband helped his wife 'to get more done' because all the earnings were being used for household expenses. Even so, homeworkers avoided direct requests for help:

> The homework sometimes created tension at home between my husband and me, if I wanted to get down to the work and he didn't feel like it.

> He didn't mind helping as long as he felt he didn't have to.

In discussing husbands' perceptions of homework, it was apparent that many interpret it as a leisure-time activity, and prefer to ignore the reasons why women are forced to accept such low-paid work. However, the contribution made by some husbands suggests that others are well aware of the competing demands of their wives' labour and the importance of meeting these demands to the functioning of the household. But while these husbands benefit materially from and contribute to homeworker earnings, they are still able to enjoy the status traditionally associated with being able to keep a wife at home.

■ Conclusions

Working 'in one's own home' conjures up a picture of work autonomy which is quite misleading. Homeworkers are thought to set their own hours of work and to combine homeworking with all their other obligations within the home and outside it. It is true that they do not have to clock in and do not have a supervisor leaning over their shoulder. In practice, however, their obligations to the supplier are those of an employee, and they are, if anything, more constrained than those who go out to work. The supplier establishes the hours of work through the times set for the delivery and collection of work and payment by the piece, and their earnings are limited not by their willingness to work but by the availability of work and the allocation of work with different piece rates. Homeworkers are not paid for work until it meets the supplier's specifications. Hours, pace and quality of work are so effectively controlled by the supplier that direct physical supervision is not required.

The disadvantages of paid work at home also reflect the many other demands on women's labour. Many of the assumptions regarding working at home are couched within a male perspective. These imply that waged work outside the home and bureaucratically imposed controls are the main constraints on personal autonomy. People are assumed to be free of the demands of the workplace once they return home. But for women, of course, this is far from the case. The domestic sphere incorporates other work obligations enforced by the explicit demands and implicit expectations of other family members. The woman who goes out to work returns to another set of demands on her labour. Calls on the labour of the homeworker are even more extensive, for with no spatial separation between her paid and unpaid labour family members do not lower or adjust their expectations. Husbands, children and elderly relatives are free to interrupt her paid work, and this may account for the preference by families that the woman work at home. Popular images of working at home – flexible working hours, more time to spend with one's children, a reduction of work pressure, a less stressful day – have nothing to do with the experience of homeworking. The women experience the two sets of constraints simultaneously on a day-to-day basis. Homeworking is very far from being a boon to women, for instead of liberating them from or reducing the burden of the 'double day' it intensifies the pressures of both waged work and unpaid domestic labour.

Those who argue that homework represents the future 'lifestyle' and will replace going out to work in 'proper jobs' are either unaware of, or ignore, the evidence on present patterns of homeworking. As much evidence shows, the unemployed lack the resources to participate either in the formal or informal sections of the economy as self-employed (McKee and Bell, 1986; Miles, 1983), but homeworking in the manufacturing sector may be an available form of paid work for them (Wallace and Pahl, 1986). This cannot be interpreted as a viable 'lifestyle' or a freely chosen option, given the data analysed here.

If the future lies with home-based work, then serious attention needs to be paid to the conditions of those presently carrying out waged labour at home, to ensure they are guaranteed basic rights and minimum levels of pay and, in a broader context, to questions of class and gender subordination within the economy and the household. Without these, autonomy will remain a highly functional myth.

■ Notes

This article is based in part on one chapter of *Homework: Myths and Realities* by the same authors, to be published by Macmillan, and appears with their permission. We wish to acknowledge the financial support for the research received from the University of Bradford (September 1978–May

1979 and October 1983–September 1986) and from the ESRC, formerly the SSRC (September 1979–April 1981). Our thanks are due to Julia Graham, Research Assistant (March 1980–April 1981), and to the interviewers, but above all to the homeworkers and others who spared the time to answer our questions and discuss the issues of homework with us.

1   For a full discussion of the collection and analysis of quantitative data on homeworking, see Allen and Wolkowitz, forthcoming.

    The West Yorkshire survey gives some idea of the density of homeworking in one region. The number of homeworkers in the door-to-door survey in the Metropolitan District of Bradford, which included both private and council housing estates, was 1.2 per cent of the total number of households, and 2.6 per cent of the number at home at the time of the survey. If these figures are taken as proportionate, then the number of homeworkers in the city can be estimated as between 1.06 and 2.6 per cent of those officially recorded as economically active. These figures can be compared with the 2.8 per cent cited by an official survey which used a much broader definition of home-based workers (Hakim, 1984A). We also tried to obtain at least a partial picture of the range of suppliers in the area. Using several different methods, eighty-eight firms were found to be supplying homework, over seventy within the region and twelve outside it.

2   See Allen (1981C) for details of the research design and interviewing programme.

3   The Homeworkers (Protection) Bill 1979 defined a homeworker as:

> an individual who contracts with a person not being a professional client of his for the purpose of that person's business, for the execution of any work (other than the production or creation of any literary, dramatic, artistic or musical work) to be done in domestic premises and not under the control or management of the person with whom he contracts, and who does not normally make use of the services of more than two individuals in the carrying out of that work. (HMSO, 1979)

It was placed before Parliament by Frank White, MP, in November 1979, and again in January 1981, but defeated both times (Crine, 1981).

Notes on Contributors

Sheila Allen is Professor of Sociology at the University of Bradford where she teaches courses on gender divisions, race relations and the sociology of economic life. She has written books and articles in all these fields. Since 1978 she has been involved in research on homeworking and is a member of the National Homeworking Group.

Veronica Beechey is a sociologist who has written extensively about women's employment. She is currently writing a book on part-time work, *A Matter of Hours* (with Tessa Perkins) to be published by Polity Press, and chairs the Open University Women's Studies course, 'The Changing Experience of Women'.

Irene Breugel has taught Economics at North East London Polytechnic and is an active feminist and trade unionist. She now works for the Greater London Council.

Nicola Charles teaches in the Department of Sociology and Anthropology at the University College of Swansea. Prior to this she worked on a research project exploring food and the sexual division of labour within the family. The research on which her article is based was carried out at Sheffield City Polytechnic in collaboration with David Brown and was funded by the European Foundation for the Improvement of Living and Working Conditions.

Cynthia Cockburn has worked in print, studied at the London College of Printing and is a member of the National Union of Journalists. She is a researcher in the Department of Social Science and Humanities at the City University, London, where she has worked on 'gender and technology' with support from the Equal Opportunities Commission and the Economic and Social Research Council. Her article has been published previously in Donald McKenzie and Judy Wajcman (eds.) *The Social Shaping of Technology*, The Open University Press, 1985.

Angela Coyle is the Director of the Women and Work Programme at the University of Aston in Birmingham. This article came out of research on the cleaning industry funded by the Equal Opportunities Commission. She is author of a study of female unemployment, *Redundant Women* (Women's Press), and is currently writing a book on equal opportunities in employment to be published by Macmillan.

Diane Elson teaches Economics at the University of Manchester. She is active in developing links between working women in Britain and the Third World through the Manchester International Women's Group, *Working Women Worldwide* and *International Labour Reports*.

Catherine Hoskyns teaches International Relations at Coventry (Lanchester) Polytechnic. She has been active in the women's movement and now works with Rights of Women in London. She is part author of *Women's Rights and the EEC – ROW a Guide for Women in the UK* (Europe, 1983). An earlier version of her article was delivered as a paper to the Political Science Association annual conference in April 1984.

Mary McIntosh is a member of the *Feminist Review* Collective and teaches Sociology at the University of Essex. She has written articles on state policy and women's oppression and a book with Michèle Barrett, *The Anti-social Family*.

Amina Mama is a psychologist and researcher. She lives in London and is doing postgraduate research on Black women's subjectivity. She has worked with various Black organisations and was one of the editors of *Feminist Review* No.17, August 1984: *Many Voices One Chant: Black Feminist Perspectives*.

Janine Morgall worked as a clerical worker/secretary for fifteen years. She was a shop steward for a group of secretaries in Copenhagen and an active member of the clerical workers' union. She is trained as a sociologist and has been a consultant for the World Health Organization on issues of women and health, and has been a teaching assistant at Roskilde University in Denmark. She is at present doing doctoral research at the University of Lund in Sweden.

Ruth Pearson is a Research Fellow at the School of Social Sciences, the Open University. She is an economist who has worked in Argentina and Mexico on technology transfer and industrialization and dependency. She now lives in Norwich, where she teaches Third World Studies and is engaged in research on the service sector and women's employment. She is active in local women's campaigns around health and is a member of the editorial board of *Capital and Class*.

Anne Phillips lectures in Politics at the City of London Polytechnic. She is the author of *Hidden Hands: Women and Economic Policies*.

Mandy Snell was for three and a half years a research officer at the London School of Economics, on the Equal Pay and Opportunity Project. She has worked in the Industrial Sociology Unit at Imperial College and now works for the Women's Committee Support Unit at the Greater London Council. She is a member of the *Feminist Review* Collective.

Barbara Taylor is a feminist historian and author of *Eve and the New Jerusalem*, Virago, 1983. She is currently writing a book on Mary Wollstonecraft and early feminist theory.

Carol Wolkowitz has been involved in the University of Bradford research project on homeworking since 1983, and has also done research on women's political activities in India. She is one of the editors of *Of Marriage and the Market: Women's Subordination in International Perspective*, CSE Books, 1982, and is a past member of the editorial committee of *Capital and Class*.

References

ACAS (1981) Report No.20, February.

ADAMSON. O., BROWN, C., HARRISON, J. and PRICE, J. (1976) 'Women's Oppression Under Capitalism' *Revolutionary Communist* No.5.

ALLEN, Sheila (1981A) 'Invisible Threads' *Institute of Development Studies Bulletin* Vol.12, No.3 Sussex: Institute of Development Studies.

ALLEN, Sheila (1981B) 'The Labour Process and Working at Home', Sociologists in Polytechnics Annual Conference, Reading (mimeo); *Social Scientist* (forthcoming) Delhi.

ALLEN, Sheila (1981C) 'Homeworking in the West Yorkshire Conurbation' *S.S.R.C. Final Report*, September.

ALLEN, Sheila (1983) 'Production and Reproduction: The Lives of Women Homeworkers' *Sociological Review* Vol.31, No.4.

ALLEN, Sheila (1985) 'Protective Legislation for Home Based Production'. Paper presented to the Conference on Women and the Household, New Delhi, January.

ALLEN, Sheila, PURCELL, Kate, WATON, Alan and WOOD, Stephen (eds.) (1986) *The Experience of Unemployment* London: Macmillan.

ALTHUSSER, Louis (1971) *Lenin and Philosophy and Other Essays* London: New Left Books.

AMOS, Valerie and PARMAR, Pratibha (1984) 'Challenging Imperial Feminism' *Feminist Review* No.17.

AMSDEN, Alice H. (ed.) (1980) *The Economics of Women and Work* Harmondsworth: Penguin.

ANTHIAS, F. (1983) 'Sexual Divisions and Ethnic Adaption: The Case of Greek-Cypriot Women' in Phizacklea (1983).

ANTHIAS, F. and YUVAL-DAVIES, N. (1983) 'Contextualizing Feminism: Gender, Ethnic and Class Divisions' *Feminist Review* No.15.

APEX (1979) *Office Technology: The Trade Union Response*, First report of the APEX word processing working party London: Apex.

APTHEKER, B. (1982) *Woman's Legacy: Essays on Race, Sex and Class in American History* Massachusetts: University of Massachusetts Press.

ARMSTRONG, Peter (1982) 'If It's Only Women It Doesn't Matter So Much' in WEST, J. (1982).

ATKINSON, John (1984) *Flexibility, Uncertainty and Manpower Management* Sussex: Institute of Manpower Studies Report No.89.

AZIKWE, N. (1962) 'The Future of Pan-Africanism' in LANGLEY, A. (1979).

BAIN, G.S. and PRICE, R. (1972) 'Union Growth and Employment Trends in the United Kingdom 1964-1970' *British Journal of Industrial Relations* Vol.10, November.

BALDAMUS, W. (1961) *Efficiency and Effort: An Analysis of Industrial Administration* London: Tavistock.

BALLARD, B. (1984) 'Women Part-time Workers: Evidence from the 1980 Women and Employment Survey' *Employment Gazette*, September.

BARKER, Diana Leonard and ALLEN, Sheila (eds.) (1976) *Dependence and Exploitation in Work and Marriage* London: Longman.

BARKER, Jane and DOWNING, Hazel (1980) 'Word Processing and the Transformation of Patriarchal Relations of Control in the Office' *Capital and Class* No.10.

BARRETT, Michèle (1980) *Women's Oppression Today* London: Verso.

BARRETT, Michèle and McINTOSH, Mary (1980) 'The Family Wage: Some Problems for Socialists and Feminists' *Capital and Class* No.11.

BARRETT BROWN, M. and HUGHES, J. (eds.) (1978) *Full Employment – Priority* Nottingham: Spokesman Books.

BARRON, Iann and CURNOW, Ray (1979) *The Future with Microelectronics: Forecasting the Effects of Information Technology* London: Frances Pinter Ltd.

BARRON, R.D. and NORRIS, E.R. (1976) 'Sexual Divisions and the Dual Labour Market' in BARKER, D.L. and ALLEN, S. (1976).

BAUDOUIN, T., COLLIN, M. and GUILLERM, D. (1978) 'Women and Immigrants: Marginal Workers' in CROUCH, C. and PIZZORNO, A. (1978).

BEALE, Sally (1978) *A Study of Homeworking in a Limited Geographic Area* University of Bath: School of Management MSc unpublished dissertation.

BEARDWELL, I., MILES, D. and WORMAN, E. (1981) 'The Twilight Army' Low Pay Unit Pamphlet No.19.

BEECHEY, Veronica (1977) 'Some Notes on Female Wage Labour in Capitalist Production' *Capital and Class* No.3.

BEECHEY, Veronica (1978) 'Women and Production: A Critical Analysis of Some Sociological Trends of Women's Work' in KUHN, A. and WOLPE, A. (1978).

BEECHEY, Veronica (1982) 'The Sexual Division of Labour and the Labour Process: A Critical Assessment of Braverman' in WOOD, S. (1982).

BELOTTI, Elena (1975) *Little Girls* London: Virago Press.

BENET, Mary Kathleen (1973) *The Secretarial Ghetto* New York: McGraw-Hill.

BERG, Maxine (ed.) (1979) *Technology and Toil in Nineteenth Century Britain* London: CSE Books.

BIRD, E. (1980) *Information Technology in the Office: The Impact on Woemn's Jobs* London: Equal Opportunities Commission.

BIRNBAUM, Ben (unpublished paper) 'Women, Skill and Automation: A Study of Women's Employment in the Clothing Industry 1946-1972'.

BLACK PATIENTS AND HEALTH WORKERS GROUP (1983) 'Psychiatry and the Corporate State' *Race and Class* Vol.25, No.5.

BLAKE, Myrna (1979) 'Asian Women in Formal and Non-formal Sectors – Review and Proposals for Research-Education-Mobilisation' *Occasional Paper 2* United Nations Asian and Pacific Centre for Women and Development.

BLAND, L., BRUNSDON, C., HOBSON, D. and WINSHIP, J. (1978) 'Women "Inside and Outside" the Relations of Production' in WOMEN'S STUDIES GROUP (1978).

BLAXALL, Martha and REAGAN, Barbara (eds.) (1976) *Women and the Workplace* Chicago and London: University of Chicago Press.

BLIVEN, Bruce Jnr (1954) *The Wonderful Writing Machine* New York: Random House.

BOLTON, Brian (1975) *An End to Homeworking* London: Fabian Society Tract No.436.

BOSERUP, Ester (1970) *Women's Role in Economic Development* London: Allen & Unwin.

BOWEY, A.M. *et al* (1982) *Effects of Incentive Payment Systems, United Kingdom 1977-1980* London: Department of Employment Research Paper No.36.

BRAVERMAN, Harry (1974) *Labor and Monopoly Capital: The Degradation of Work in the Twentieth Century* London and New York: Monthly Review Press.

BRIGHTON LABOUR PROCESS GROUP (1977) 'The Capitalist Labour Process' *Capital and Class* No.1.

BROVERMAN, G. *et al* (1970) 'Sex Role Stereotypes and Clinical Judgements of Mental Health' *Journal of Consulting and Clinical Psychology* 34.

BROWN, G. and HARRIS, T. (1981) *The Social Origins of Depression* London: Tavistock.

BROWN, Marie (1974) *Sweated Labour: A Study of Homework* London: Low Pay Unit Pamphlet No.1.

BRUEGEL, Irene (1985) 'Will Women Lose Out Again?' *New Socialist* July.

BURNS, S. (1977) *The Household Economy* Boston: Beacon Press.

BYTHELL, Duncan (1978) *The Sweated Trades: Outwork in the Nineteenth Century* New York: St Martin's Press.

CAMPBELL, Beatrix (1978) 'Lining Their Pockets' *Time Out* 13-19 July.

CAMPBELL, Beatrix and CHARLTON, Valerie (1978) 'Work to Rule: Wages and Family' *Red Rag*.

CARDOSA-KHOO, Jane and KHOO, Kay Jin (1978) 'Work and Consciousness: The Case of Electronics "Runaways" in Malaysia'. Paper presented to Conference on the Continuing Subordination of Women in the Development Process, Institute of Development Studies, University of Sussex.

CAVENDISH, Ruth (1982) *On The Line* London: Routledge & Kegan Paul.

CENTRE FOR CONTEMPORARY CULTURAL STUDIES, RACE AND POLITICS GROUP (1982) *The Empire Strikes Back* London: Hutchinson.

CHARLES, Nicola (1979) 'An Analysis of the Ideology of Women's Domestic Role and its Social Effects in Modern Britain' University of Keele: unpublished PhD thesis.

CHARLES, Nicola and BROWN, David (1981) 'Women's Shiftwork and the Sexual Division of Labour' *Sociological Review* Vol.29, No.4.

CHESLER, P. (1972) *Women and Madness* New York: Doubleday.

CHILD, John (1967) *Industrial Relations in the British Printing Industry* London: Allen & Unwin.

CHRISTIAN, L. (1983) *Policing by Coercion* London: Greater London Council.

CLARKE, K. (1984) Letter from the Minister of Health to All Regional Health Chairmen, 9 October.

COCKBURN, Cynthia (1983) *Brothers: Male Dominance and Technological Change* London: Pluto Press.

COOLEY, M. (1979) 'Computers, Politics and Unemployment' *European Computing Review*.

CONFERENCE OF SOCIALIST ECONOMISTS (1976) *The Labour Process and Class Strategies* London: Stage 1.

COUNTER INFORMATION SERVICES (1976) *Women Under Attack* London: CIS.

COUNTER INFORMATION SERVICES (1979) *The New Technology* London: CIS.

COYLE, Angela (1982) 'Sex and Skill in the Organisation of the Clothing Industry' in WEST, J. (1982).

COYLE, Angela (1984) *Redundant Women* London: The Women's Press.

COWARD, Rosalind (1978) 'Rethinking Marxism' m/f No.2.

CRAGG, Arnold and DAWSON, Tim (1981) *Qualitative Research Among Homeworkers* London: Department of Employment Research Paper No.21.

CRAIG, Christine, RUBERY, Jill, TARLING, Roger and WILKINSON, Frank 'Abolition and After: The Paper Box Wages Council', Research paper by the Labour Studies Group, London: Department of Employment.

CRINE, Simon (1979) *The Hidden Army* London: Low Pay Unit.

CRINE, Simon (1981) *The Pay and Conditions of Homeworkers: Submission to the House of Commons Select Committee on Employment* London: Low Pay Unit.

CROUCH, C. and PIZZORNO, A. (1978) *A Resurgence of Class Conflict* Vol.2 London: Macmillan.

CUTRUFELLI, M. (1983) *Women of Africa* London: Zed Press.

DANIEL, W. and STILGOE, E. (1978) *The Effects of the Employment Protection Act* London: Policy Studies Institute.

DAUBLER-GMELIN, H. (1977) *Frauenarbeitslosigkeit* Hamburg: Rowolt.

DAVIES, Margery (1979) 'Woman's Place is at the Typewriter' in EISENSTEIN, Z. (1979).

DAVIES, M. (ed.) (1983) *Third World, Second Sex* London: Zed Press.

DAVIS, A. (1981) *Women, Race and Class* London: The Women's Press.

DeCASTRO, J. (1956, revised 1973) *The Geopolitics of Hunger* New York: Monthly Review Press.

DELGADO, Alan (1979) *The Enormous File: A Social History of the Office* London: John Murray Publishers.

DELPHY, Christine (1977) *The Main Enemy* London: Women's Research and Resources Centre.

DEPARTMENT OF EMPLOYMENT (1978) 'Age and Redundancy' *Employment Gazette* September.

DEX, S. (1978) 'Measuring Women's Unemployment' *Social and Economic Administration* Summer.

DONZELOT, Jacques (1980) *The Policing of Families* London: Hutchinson.

DOYAL, L. *et al* (1981) 'Your Life in Their Hands: Migrant Workers in the National Health Service' *Critical Social Policy* Vol.1, No.2.

DUNDEE INNER CITY NEIGHBOURHOOD ACTION CENTRE (1984) *Working at Home: A Feasibility Study on the Extent, the Problems and the Future Requirements of Homeworkers in Dundee* Dundee: Inner City Neighbourhood Action Centre.

EISENSTEIN, Zillah (ed.) (1979) *Capitalist Patriarchy and the Case for Socialist Feminism* London and New York: Monthly Review Press.

ELIAS, P. and MAIN, B. (1982) *Working Women's Lives: Evidence from the National Training Survey* Warwick: University of Warwick Institute for Employment Research.

ELLIS, J. (ed.) (1978) *West African Families in Britain* London: Routledge & Kegan Paul.

EL SADAWI, N. (1980) *The Hidden Face of Eve* London: Zed Press.

ENGELS, Frederick (1972) *The Origin of the Family, Private Property and the State* London: Pathfinder Press.

ENGELS, Frederick (1976) *The Condition of the Working Class in England* St Albans: Panther.

EVANS, Mary and UNGERSON, Clare (eds.) (1983) *Sexual Divisions: Patterns and Processes* London: Tavistock.

FARLEY, Lin (1980) *Sexual Shakedown* New York: Warner Paperback.

FEMINIST REVIEW (1984) 'The Women's Movement and the Labour Party: An Interview with Labour Party Feminists' *Feminist Review* No.16.

FERBER, M. and LOWRY, H. (1976) 'Women, the New Reserve Army' in BLAXALL, M. and REAGAN, B. (1976).

FERRIS, Elizabeth (1978) 'Sportswomen and Medicine, The Myths Surrounding Women's Participation in Sport and Exercise' in Report of the 1st International Conference on Women and Sport, Central Council of Physical Recreation, London.

FIELD, Frank (1976) *Seventy Years On: A New Report on Homeworking* London: Low Pay Bulletin No.10-11, August-October.

FINCH, Janet (1983) *Married to the Job: Wives' Incorporation in Men's Work* London: George Allen & Unwin.

FIRESTONE, Shulamith (1971) *The Dialectic of Sex* London: Jonathan Cape.

FONER, N. (1976) 'Women, Work and Migration: Jamaicans in London' *New Community*, Vol.5.

FOUCAULT, M. (1965) *Madness and Civilization* New York: Random House.

FREEMAN, Caroline (1982) 'The "Understanding" Employer' in WEST, J. (1982).

FROBEL, Folker, HEINRICHS, Jurgen and KREYE, Otto (1979) *The New International Division of Labour* Cambridge: Cambridge University Press.

FRYER, B., MANSON, T. and FAIRCLOUGH, A. (1978) 'Notes: Employment and Trade Unionism in the Public Services' *Capital and Class* No.4.

GAME, Ann and PRINGLE, Rosemary (1984) *Gender at Work* London: Pluto Press.

GARDINER, J. (1976) 'Women and Unemployment' *Red Rag* No.10.

GEORGE, D. (1925) *London Life in the XVII Century* London: Kegan Paul.

GERSHUNY, J.I. (1979) 'The Informal Economy: Its Role in Industrial Society', *Futures* Vol.2, No.1, February.

GERSHUNY, J.I. and PAHL, R.E. (1979-80) 'Work Outside Employment: Some Preliminary Speculations', *New Universities Quarterly* Vol.34, No.1, Winter.

GOODY, E. (1978) 'Delegation of Parental Roles in West Africa and the West Indies' in SHIMKIN, D.B. *et al* (1978).

GORZ, André (ed.) (1978) *The Division of Labour* Brighton: Harvester Press.

GRAMSCI, Antonio (1971) *Selections from the Prison Notebooks* New York: New International Publishers.

GREATER LONDON COUNCIL (1983) 'A Strategy for Homeworking in London: Report by the Director of Industry and Employment', 13

December, unpublished paper.

GREATER LONDON COUNCIL ECONOMIC POLICY GROUP (1983) 'The Contract Clean-Up' *Strategy Document* No.9.

GREER, Germaine (1984) *Sex and Destiny: The Politics of Human Fertility* London: Secker & Warburg.

GREGORY, Jeanne (1981) 'Formal or Substantive Legality: The Future of Protective Legislation' *Occasional Paper 3* Middlesex: Middlesex Polytechnic.

GRIFFITHS, Dorothy and SARAGA, Esther (1979) 'Sex Differences and Cognitive Abilities: A Sterile Field of Enquiry' in HARTNETT, O. *et al* (1979).

GROSSMAN, Rachel (1979) 'Women's Place in the Integrated Circuit' *Southeast Asia Chronicle* No.66 (joint issue with *Pacific Research* Vol.9, No.5-6).

GUARDIAN WOMEN (1985) Letters, *Guardian*.

GUTZMORE, C. (1975) 'Imperialism and Racism: The Crisis of the British Capitalist Economy and the Black Masses in Britain' *The Black Liberator* Vol.2, No.2.

GUTZMORE, C. (1983) 'Capital, "Black Youth" and Crime' *Race and Class* Vol.25, No.2.

HAGERTY, Eileen M. and TIGHE, Joan E. (1978) 'Office Automation and the Clerical Worker'. Speech presented at MIT Lecture Series: 'Technology and Work: The Worker's Perspective'.

HAKIM, Catherine (1978) 'Sexual Divisions in the Labour Force' *Employment Gazette*, November.

HAKIM, Catherine (1979) *Occupational Segregation: A Comparitive Study of the Degree and Patterns of the Differentiation Between Men's and Women's Work in Britain, the United States and Other Countries* Research Paper No.9 London: Department of Employment.

HAKIM, Catherine (1980) 'Homeworking: Some New Evidence' *Employment Gazette*, October.

HAKIM, Catherine (1981) 'Job Segregation Trends in the 1970s' *Employment Gazette*, December.

HAKIM, Catherine (1984A) 'Employers' Use of Homework, Outwork and Freelances' *Employment Gazette*, April.

HAKIM, Catherine (1984B) 'Homework and Outwork: National Estimates from Two Surveys' *Employment Gazette*, January.

HAKIM, Catherine (1985) Employers' Use of Outwork: A Study Using the 1980 Workplace Industrial Relations Survey and the 1981 National Survey of Homeworking, Department of Employment Research Paper No.44.

HAKIM, Catherine and DENNIS, Roger (1982) *Homeworking in Wages Councils Industries: A Study Based on Wages Inspectorate Records of Pay and Earnings* Research Paper No.37 London: Department of Employment.

HALL, S. *et al* (1978) *Policing the Crisis* London: Macmillan.

HALPERN, Monique (n.d.) 'Protective Measures and Activities not Falling

Within the Field of Application of the Directive on Equal Treatment – Analysis and Proposals' EEC Commission Document V/707/3/82.

HANDY, Charles (1984) *The Future of Work: A Guide to Changing Society* Oxford: Basil Blackwell.

HARMAN, Chris (1979) *Is a Machine After Your Job?* London: SWP.

HARRIS, D.F. and TAYLOR, F.J. (1978) *The Service Sector*, Research Series No.25 London: Centre for Environmental Studies.

HARTMANN, Heidi (1979A) 'The Unhappy Marriage of Marxism and Feminism: Towards a More Progressive Union' *Capital and Class* No.8.

HARTMANN, Heidi (1979B) 'Capitalism, Patriarchy and Job Segregation by Sex' in EISENSTEIN, Z. (1979).

HARTMANN, Heidi (1981) 'The Family as the Locus of Gender, Class and Political Struggle: The Example of Housework' *Signs* Vol. 6, No.3, Spring.

HARTNETT, O. *et al* (1979) *Sex Role Stereotyping* London: Tavistock.

HER MAJESTY'S STATIONERY OFFICE (1979) *Homeworkers (Protection): A Bill to Amend the Law to Provide for the Future Protection of Homeworkers*, etc., 29 November.

HEYZER, Noeleen (1978) 'Young Women and Migrant Workers in Singapore's Labour Intensive Industries'. Paper presented to the Conference on the Continuing Subordination of Women in the Development Process, Institute of Development Studies, University of Sussex.

HOBSBAWM, E.J. (1964) *Labouring Men* London: Weidenfeld & Nicholson.

HOOKS, B. (1981) *Ain't I A Woman: Black Women and Feminism* London: Pluto Press.

HOPE, Emily, KENNEDY, Mary and DE WINTER, Anne (1976) 'Homeworkers in North London' in BARKER, D.L. and ALLEN, S. (1976).

HUGHES, J. (1978) 'A Rake's Progress' in BARRETT BROWN, M. and HUGHES J. (1978).

HULL, G. *et al* (1982) *But Some of Us Are Brave* New York: The Feminist Press.

HULT, Marit (1980) *Technological Change and Women Workers: The Development of Microelectronics*. Submitted to the World Conference of the United Nations Decade for Women, Copenhagen, Denmark 14-30 July. A/CONF 94/26.

HUMPHRIES, J. (1976) 'Women as Scapegoats and Safety Valves' *Review of Radical Political Economy*.

HUMPHRIES, J. (1981) 'Protective Legislation, the Capitalist State and Working Class Men: The Case of the 1842 Mines Regulations Act' *Feminist Review* No.7.

HUNT, Pauline (1980) *Gender and Class Consciousness* London: Macmillan.

HURSTFIELD, J. (1978) *The Part Time Trap* London: Low Pay Unit.

HUWS, Ursula (1982) *New Technology and Women's Employment* Leeds: TUCRC.

HUWS, Ursula (1984A) *The New Homeworkers: New Technology and the*

Changing Location of White Collar Work London: Low Pay Unit Pamphlet No.28.

HUWS, Ursula (1984B) 'New Technology Homeworkers' *Employment Gazette*, January.

ICC BUSINESS RATIOS (1983) *Contract Cleaners* (2nd edn. 1982-3).

INSTITUTE OF MANPOWER STUDIES AND MANPOWER LIMITED (1984) *Flexible Manning – The Way Ahead: Report of a Joint Conference* Sussex: IMS Report No.88.

JAMES, Edward (1982) 'The Role of the European Community in Social Policy' *Yearbook of Social Policy*.

JAYAWARDENA, K. (1982) *Feminism and Nationalism in the Third World in the Nineteenth and Early Twentieth Centuries* The Hague: Institute of Social Studies.

JENNESS, L., HILL, H., REID, N.M., LOVELL, F. and DAVENPORT, S.E. (1975) *Last Hired, First Fired* New York: Pathfinder Press.

JOSEPH, G. and LEWIS, J. (1981) *Common Differences: Conflict in Black and White Feminist Perspectives* New York: Anchor Press.

JORDAN, David (1978) *The Wages of Fear: A 1978 Report on Homeworking* London: Low Pay Unit Bulletin No.20.

KOLKO, G. (1979) 'Working Wives, Their Effect on the Structure of the Working Class' *Science and Society*, Fall.

KENDRICK, Jane (1981) 'Politics and the Construction of Women as Second-Class Workers' in WILKINSON, F. (1981).

KUHN, Annette (1978) 'Structures of Patriarchy and Capital in the Family' in KUHN, A. and WOLPE, A. (1978).

KUHN, Annette and WOLPE, AnnMarie (eds) (1978) *Feminism and Materialism* London: Routledge & Kegan Paul.

LABOUR RESEARCH (1985A) *Bargaining Report* No.38 London: Labour Research Department.

LABOUR RESEARCH (1985B) Vol.74, No.4 London: Labour Research Department.

LAND, Hilary (1980) 'The Family Wage' *Feminist Review* No.6.

LANGLEY, A. (1979) *Ideologies of Liberation in Black Africa 1856-1970* London: Rex Collings.

LAWRENCE, E. (1982) 'Just Plain Commonsense: The "Roots" of Racism' in CENTRE FOR CONTEMPORARY CULTURAL STUDIES, RACE AND POLITICS GROUP (1982).

LEEDS TRADE UNION AND COMMUNITY RESOURCE AND INFORMATION CENTRE (1984) 'Background Report on Homeworking for Leeds City Council', unpublished paper.

LEIGHTON, Patricia (1982) 'Employment Contracts: A Choice of

Relationships' *Employment Gazette*, October.

LEIGHTON, Patricia (1983) *Contractual Arrangements in Selected Industries: A Study of Employment Relationships in Industries with Outwork* Research paper No.39 London: Department of Employment.

LEWENHAK, S. (1977) *Women and Trade Unions* London: Earnest Benn Ltd.

LIM, Linda (1978) 'Women Workers in Multinational Corporations in Developing Countries – The Case of the Electronics Industry in Malaysia and Singapore' *Women's Studies Program Occasional Paper* No.9, University of Michigan.

LITTLEWOOD, R. and LIPSEDGE, M. (1982) *The Aliens and the Alienists: Ethnic Minorities and Psychiatry* Harmondsworth: Penguin.

LLOYD, C.B. (ed.) (1976) *Sex Discrimination and The Division of Labour* New York: Columbia University Press.

LOW PAY UNIT (1984) *Women and Work in the West Midlands* Birmingham: Low Pay Unit.

MACKAY, D.I., BODDY, D., BRACK, J., DIACK, J.A. and JONES, N. (1971) *The Labour Market Under Different Employment Conditions* London: George Allen & Unwin.

MACKINTOSH, Maureen (1982) 'Gender and Economics: The Sexual Division of Labour and the Subordination of Women' in YOUNG, K., WOLKOWITZ, C. and McCULLAGH, R. (1982).

MAHER, Vanessa (1982) 'Work, Consumption and Authority Within the Household: A Moroccan Case' in YOUNG, K., WOLKOWITZ, C. and McCULLAGH, R. (1982).

MARKOFF, John and STEWART, Jon (1979) 'The Microprocessor Revolution, an Office on the Head of a Pin' *In These Times* 7-13 March.

MARKS, S. (1970) 'The Zulu Disturbances in Natal' in ROTBERG, I. and MAZRUI, A. (1970).

MARKS, S. and ATOMORE, A. (1971) 'Firearms in Southern Africa' *Journal of African History* Vol.12, No.2.

MARRIOT, R. (1957) *Incentive Payment Systems: A Review of Research and Opinions* London: Staples Press.

MARTIN, Jean and ROBERTS, Ceridwen (1984) *Women and Employment: A Lifetime Perspective* London: Her Majesty's Stationery Office.

MARX, Karl (1973) *Grundrisse* Harmondsworth: Penguin.

MARX, Karl (1976) *Capital Vol.1* Harmondsworth: Penguin.

MASSEY, Doreen (1983) 'The Shape of Things to Come' *Marxism Today* Vol.27, No.4.

MAYO, Marjorie (1983) 'Rejoinder to Teresa Perkins' in EVANS, M. and UNGERSON, C. (1983).

McKEE, Lorna and BELL, Colin (1986) 'His Unemployment; Her Problem: The Domestic Consequences of Male Unemployment' in ALLEN, S. *et al* (1986).

MEISSNER, M. *et al* (1975) 'No Exit for Wives: Sexual Division of Labour and the Cumulation of Household Demands' *Canadian Review of Sociology and Anthropology* XII,4.

MENTAL HEALTH ACT (1959) *Review* London: Her Majesty's Stationery Office.

MIDDLETON, C. (1979) 'The Sexual Division of Labour in Feudal England' *New Left Review* No.113-114, January-April.

MIES, Maria (1982) *The Lace Makers of Narsapur: Indian Housewives Produce for the World Market* London: Zed Press.

MILES, I. (1983) *Adaption to Unemployment?* Sussex: Science Policy Research Unit Occasional Paper Series No.20.

MILKMAN, R. (1976) 'Women's Work and Economic Crisis' *Review of Radical Political Economy*.

MILLETT, Kate (1971) *Sexual Politics* London: Rupert Hart-Davis.

MITCHELL, Juliet (1975) *Psychoanalysis and Feminism* Harmondsworth: Penguin.

MITTER, Swasti (1986) 'Industrial Restructuring and Manufacturing Homework: Immigrant Women in the UK Clothing Industry', *Capital and Class*, No.27.

MOORE, B., RHODES, J., TARLING, F. and WILKINSON, F. (1978). *Economic Policy Review* Cambridge: Cambridge University Press, Department of Applied Economics.

NATIONAL BOARD OF PRICES AND INCOMES (1972) *Report* London: Her Majesty's Stationery Office.

NATIONAL CAMPAIGN AGAINST THE POLICE AND CRIMINAL EVIDENCE BILL (1983) *Bulletin*.

NEWTON-MOSS, Janie (1977) *Homeworkers: A Study of Women Working at Home* University of York Diploma in Social Administration, unpublished dissertation.

NIELSON, Ruth (1983) *Equality Legislation in a Comparative Perspective – Towards State Feminism* Copenhagen.

NIEMI, B. (1976) 'Geographical Immobility and Labour Force Mobility: A Study of Female Unemployment' in LLOYD, C.B. (1976).

NOBLE, David F. (1979) 'Social Choice in Machine Design: The Case of Automatically Controlled Machine Tools' in ZIMBALIST, A. (1979).

NORMAN, Colin (1980) *Microelectronics at Work: Productivity and Jobs in the World Economy* Washington D.C. Worldwatch Paper 39.

OAKLEY, Ann (1972) *Sex, Gender and Society* London: Temple Smith.

OBBO, C. (1980) *African Women: Their Struggle for Independence* London: Zed Press.

OECD (1976) *The 1974-5 Recession and the Employment of Women* Paris: Organization for Economic Co-operation and Development.

OFFICE OF POPULATION CENSUS AND SURVEYS, (1974, 1976)

General Household Survey London: Her Majesty's Stationery Office.

OFFICE OF POPULATION CENSUS AND SURVEYS (1979) 'The Changing Circumstances of Women' *Population Trends* London: Her Majesty's Stationery Office.

OFFICE OF POPULATION CENSUS AND SURVEYS (1982) *Labour Force Survey 1981* London: Her Majesty's Stationery Office.

OFFICE OF POPULATION CENSUS AND SURVEYS (1982) *Population Trends* No.28 London: Her Majesty's Stationery Office.

PAHL, R.E. (1980) 'Employment, Work and the Domestic Division of Labour' *International Journal of Urban and Regional Research* Vol.4, 1 March.

PAHL, R.E. (1984) *Divisions of Labour* Oxford: Basil Blackwell.

PAHL, R.E. and WALLACE, Claire (1985) 'Household Work Strategies in Economic Recession' in REDCLIFT, N. and MINGIONE, E. (1985).

PEACH, C. (1968) *West Indian Migration to Britain* London: Oxford University Press.

PERKINS, Teresa (1983) 'A New Form of Employment: A Case Study of Women's Part-time Work in Coventry' in EVANS, M. and UNGERSON, C. (1983).

PEARSON, R. (1986) 'The Grooming of Women's Labour: Multinational Companies and their Female Work Force in the Third and First World' in PURCELL, KATE *et al* (1986).

PHILLIPS, R. (1975) 'The Black Masses and the Political Economy of Manchester' *Journal of Black Liberation* Vol.2, No.4.

PHIZACKLEA, A. (1982) 'Migrant Women and Wage Labour: The Case of West Indian Women in Britain' in WEST, J. (1982).

PHIZACKLEA, A. (ed.) (1983) *One Way Ticket: Migration and Female Labour* London: Routledge & Kegan Paul.

PIVA, Paola and INGRAO, Chiara (1983) 'Equality and Difference'. Paper presented to the Conference on Women's Employment, Turin. A considerably altered and revised version of the paper is published in *Feminist Review* No.16, 1984.

POLLERT, Anne (1981) *Girls, Wives, Factory Lives* London: Macmillan.

POPKIN, Maggi (1975) 'Raises Not Roses' *The Second Wave* Vol.4, No.1.

POSTGATE, Richmond (1984) *Home: A Place for Work? Possibilities and Snags Explored* London: Calouste Gulbenkian Foundation.

POSTHUMA, Anne (n.d.) 'High Tech Job Wars', unpublished paper.

PORTER, Marilyn (1982) 'Standing on the Edge: Working Class Housewives and the World of Work' in WEST, J. (1982).

PRANDY, K. (1979) 'Alienation and Interests in the Analysis of Social Cognitions' *British Journal of Sociology* Vol.XXX, No.4.

PUGH, H.S. (1984) *Estimating the Extent of Homeworking* London: City University Social Statistics Research Unit Working Paper No.15.

PURCELL, Kate, WOOD, Stephen, WATON, Alan and ALLEN, Sheila

(eds.) (1986) *The Changing Experience of Employment: Restructuring and Recession* London: Macmillan.

RAMSAY MACDONALD, J. (ed.) (1904) *Women in the Printing Trades: A Sociological Study* London: P.S. King & Son.

REDCLIFT, Nanneka and MINGIONE, Enzo (eds.) (1985) *Beyond Employment: Household Gender and Subsistence* Oxford: Basil Blackwell.

REITA, Rayna (ed.) (1975) *Toward an Anthropology of Women* New York: Monthly Review Press.

ROBERTSON, O. and WALLACE, J. (1984) 'Growth and Utilization of Part-time Labour in Great Britain' *Employment Gazette*, September.

RODGERS-ROSE, L. (ed.) (1980) *The Black Woman* Beverley Hills: Sage.

ROGERS, J. (1967) *Sex and Race* New York: H.M. Rogers.

ROSE, Richard (1983) *Getting By in Three Economies* Strathclyde: University of Strathclyde Centre for the Study of Public Policy.

ROTBERG, I. and MAZRUI, A. (1970) *Protest and Power in Black Africa* Oxford: Institute of Race Relations.

ROWBOTHAM, S. (1973) *Hidden From History* London: Pluto Press.

ROY, Donald (1952) 'Quota Restrictions and Gold Bricking in a Machine Shop' *American Journal of Sociology* No.57.

ROYAL COMMISSION ON THE DISTRIBUTION OF INCOME AND WEALTH (1978) *Lower Incomes* Report No.6 London: Her Majesty's Stationery Office.

RUBERY, Jill (1980) 'Structured Labour Markets, Worker Organisation and Low Pay' in AMSDEN, A.H. (1980).

RUBERY, Jill and WILKINSON, Frank (1979) 'Notes on the Nature of the Labour Process in the Secondary Sector' *Low Pay and Labour Markets Segmentation Conference Papers* Cambridge.

RUBERY, Jill and WILKINSON, Frank (1981) 'Outwork and Segmented Labour Markets' in WILKINSON, F. (1981).

RUBIN, Gayle (1975) 'The Traffic in Women: Notes on the Political Economy of the Sexes' in REITER, R. (1975).

RUNNYMEDE TRUST STATISTICS AND RACE GROUP (1982) *Britain's Black Population* London: Heinemann.

SAFIOTTI, H.I.B. (1978) *Women in Class Society* London and New York: Monthly Review Press.

SAIFFULLAH KHAN, Verity (1979) 'Work and Network: South Asian Women in South London' in WALLMAN, S. (1979).

SCASE, Richard and GOFFEE, Robert (1982) *The Entrepreneurial Middle Class* London: Croom Helm.

SHARPE, Sue (1984) *Double Identity: The Lives of Working Mothers* Harmondsworth: Penguin.

SHARPSTON, Michael (1975) 'International Subcontracting' *Oxford Economic Papers*, March.

SHARPSTON, Michael (1976) 'International Subcontracting' *World Development* Vol.4, No.4.

SHIMKIN, D.B. *et al* (eds.) (1978) *The Extended Family in Black Societies* New York: Morton.

SHYLLON, F. (1974) *Black Slaves in Britain* Oxford: Institute of Race Relations.

SIVANANDAN, A. (1976) 'Race, Class and the State: The Black Experience in Britain' *Race and Class* Vol.17, No.4.

SLEIGH, J., BOATWRIGHT, B., IRWIN, P. and STANVON, R. (1979) *The Manpower Implications of Micro-electronic Technology* London: Department of Employment.

SMITH, D. (1981) *Unemployment and Racial Minorities* London: Policy Studies Institute No.594.

SOLOMOS, J. *et al* (1982) 'The Organic Crisis of British Capitalism and Race: The Experience of the 70s' in CENTRE FOR CONTEMPORARY CULTURAL STUDIES, RACE AND POLITICS GROUP (1982).

STEADY, F. (ed.) (1981) *The Black Woman Cross-Culturally* Massachusetts: Schenkman.

SULLEROT, Evelyn (1970) *L'emploi des femmes et ses problèmes dans les etats membres de la Communauté Européenne* Brussels: European Commission.

SULLIVAN, J. (1977) 'The Brush Off' London: Low Pay Unit Pamphlet No.5.

SZASZ, T. (1970) *Ideology and Insanity* Harmondsworth: Penguin.

THOMAS, A. and SILLEN, S. (1972) *Racism and Psychiatry* New York: Brunner Mzel.

THOMPSON, Edward P. (1963) *The Making of the English Working Class* London: Victor Gollancz.

THOMPSON, Paul (1983) *The Nature of Work: An Introduction to Debates on the Labour Process* London: Macmillan.

TINKER, H. (1974) *A New System of Slavery: The Export of Indian Labour Overseas 1830-1920* Oxford: Oxford University Press.

TOFFLER, A. (1980) *The Third Wave* London: Collins/Pan Books.

TOWNSEND-SMITH, Richard (1979) 'Law of Employment: Recognising a Contract of Employment – II' *New Law Journal* Vol.CXXIX, 5926, 18 October.

TOYNBEE, Polly (1985) 'Guardian Women', *Guardian*, 15 April 1985.

TRANSPORT AND GENERAL WORKERS UNION (1980) 'Women's Handbook, Policies and Action for the Transport and General Workers Union' London: TGWU.

TRADES UNION CONGRESS (1984) *The Privatization Experience* London: TUC.

TRIVEDI, Parita (1984) 'To Deny Our Fullness: Asian Women in the Making of History' *Feminist Review* No.17.

TYPOGRAPHICAL ASSOCIATION (1893) Report of the Delegate Meeting in Sheffield, December 1893.

UNIT FOR MANPOWER STUDIES (1976) *The Role of Immigrants in the Labour Market* London: Unit for Manpower Studies.

UNEMPLOYMENT STATISTICS (1972) *Report on an Interdepartmental Working Party* London: Her Majesty's Stationery Office.

WAJCMAN, Judy (1983) *Women in Control* Milton Keynes: Open University Press.

WALLACE, Claire and PAHL, Ray (1986) 'Polarisation, Unemployment and All Forms of Work' in ALLEN *et al* (1986).

WALMAN, Sandra (ed.) (1979) *Ethnicity at Work* London: Macmillan.

WALVIN, J. (1973) *Black and White: The Negro in English Society 1555-1945* Harmondsworth: Penguin.

WANDOR, M. (ed.) (1972) *The Body Politic* London: Stage One.

WERNEKE, D. (1978) 'The Economic Slowdown and Women's Employment' *International Labour Review* January-February.

WEST, J. (ed.) (1982) *Work, Women and the Labour Market* London: Routledge & Kegan Paul.

WHITEHEAD, Ann (1978) 'The Intervention of Capital in Rural Production Systems: Some Aspects of the Household'. Paper presented to the Conference on the Continuing Subordination of Women in the Development Process, Institute of Development Studies, University of Sussex.

WHITEHEAD, Ann (1979) 'Some Preliminary Notes on the Subordination of Women' *IDS Bulletin* Vol.10, No.3.

WILKINSON, Frank (ed.) (1981) *The Dynamics of Labour Market Segregation* London: Academic Press.

WILLIAMS, E. (1964) *Capitalism and Slavery* London: Andre Deutsch.

WILLIS, Paul (1977) *Learning to Labour* Westmead: Saxon House.

WILSON, Amrit (1978) *Finding a Voice: Asian Women in Britain* London: Virago Press.

WOLPE, AnnMarie (1978) 'Education and the Sexual Division of Labour' in KUHN, A. and WOLPE, A. (1978).

WOMEN'S STUDIES GROUP, CENTRE FOR CONTEMPORARY CULTURAL STUDIES (1978) *Women Take Issue* London: Hutchinson.

WOOD, Stephen (ed.) (1982) *The Degradation of Work?* London: Hutchinson.

YOUNG, Kate (1981) 'Domestic Out-work and the Decentralisation of Production: A New Stage in Capitalist Development'. Paper for the ILO Regional Meeting on Women and Rural Development, Mexico, 24-28 August.

YOUNG, Kate and HARRIS, Olivia (1976) 'The Subordination of Women in Cross-cultural Perspective' in *Papers on Patriarchy* London: PDC and Women's Publishing Collective.

YOUNG, Kate, WOLKOWITZ, Carol and McCULLAGH, Roslyn (eds.) (1982) *Of Marriage and the Market: Women's Subordination in International Perspective* London: CSE Books.

ZEITLIN, Jonathan (1981) 'Craft Regulation and the Division of Labour: Engineers and Compositors in Britain 1890-1914' PhD Thesis, Warwick University.

ZIMBALIST, A. (ed.) (1979) *Case Studies in the Labor Process* London and New York: Monthly Review Press.

Index

Published February 1987

IS THE FUTURE FEMALE?
Troubled Thoughts on Contemporary Feminism
Lynne Segal

In one of the most provocative books for many years, Lynne
Segal challenges many of the current feminist orthodoxies – on
female sexuality, pornography, war and peace, psychoanalysis
and sociobiology. She argues against the exponents – Mary
Daly, Andrea Dworkin and Dale Spender among them – of the
new apocalyptic feminism, which says that men wield power
over women through terror, greed and violence and that only
women, because of their essentially greater humanity, can save
the world from social, ecological and nuclear disaster. She
urges that to base the politics of feminism on innate and
essential differences between men and women is mistaken,
dangerous, and basically a counsel of despair, since its logical
conclusion is that nothing can change. Things emphatically
have changed for women, she asserts, and we must build on
these changes, combining autonomy with alliances to alter
power relations and forge a new future for women *and* men.

Published January 1987

DIVIDED LOYALTIES
Anne Phillips

Feminists – and critics of feminism – have been polarised around an insistent dilemma: are the divisions in our society primarily based on sex or class? It is these divided loyalties which are the concern of Anne Phillips' book and she believes it is essential for feminists to take into account both polarities if feminism is not just to be seen as a middle-class matter. The choices that face feminism are complex ones, and often additionally complicated by questions of class. How do we battle for wider opportunities at work while refusing working conditions that are unacceptable? How do we combine our demands as workers with our needs as mothers? Drawing on historical and contemporary material, the author describes earlier struggles to illuminate our own: the tensions of class solidarity versus sisterhood were felt in such turn of the century debates as the vote ('A good husband is much better worth having than a vote'), and over protective legislation at work – sex discrimination or sisterly benevolence? Today we continue to do battle around such issues with the state, local councils and trade unions, facing difficult choices between what seem equally pressing needs. With boldness and clarity, Anne Phillips focuses on these questions and their changing and challenging consequences.

MARRIED WOMEN'S WORK
Clementina Black

Married Women's Work provides, in the words of Clementina Black, its editor, an account of the 'true condition of thousands of married women's lives in Great Britain in the earliest quarter of this century'. The survey, made between 1909 and 1910 by the Women's Industrial Council, looked at the 'crying evil' of low wages and at women's burden of 'combined household and industrial toil far too heavy for any creature'. Fired by the conviction that substantial knowledge was needed to get public support for legislative reform, the investigators looked at the vast range of work done by married women and widows in all the major cities and many rural areas of Britain. In fascinating detail, we learn about the work conditions and home life of mantle makers, rag pickers, charwomen, weavers, fruit pickers, shopkeepers, hawkers – and many, many more. The overwhelming evidence from the information gathered here is that 'the mental effect upon the women themselves of being wage-earners is good'. What was wrong was not that married women worked, but their scandalous underpayment and the lack of training and childcare facilities.

Out of print since 1915, this is a formidable source book for historians, and contributes, with all-too-much relevance, to the unresolved debates around women, work and the family. But it is more than this: like its famous companion volume, *Round About a Pound a Week*, it is a marvellously rich portrait of the daily lives of working people, and their endurance in the face of overwork, ill health and poverty.

WOMEN IN TRADE UNIONS
Barbara Drake

"Men trade unionists are accused of sex privilege and prejudice
... A belief in the divine right of every man to his job is not
peculiar to kings and capitalists, and men in organized trades
are not disposed to share these advantages with a host of
women competitors." Barbara Drake, 1920

In this remarkable and influential work, produced by the
Labour Research Department and the Fabian Women's Group
in 1920, its author Barbara Drake, niece of Beatrice Webb,
provides an impressively comprehensive study ranging from
eighteenth-century "combinations" to the First World War in
which women became cheap "substitute" labour. In a detailed
survey of different industries and unions – amongst them,
textile, printing, food and tobacco, and clerical work – she
analyses the particular problems of women organizing in trade
unions. Obstacles such as the lack of recognition by male trade
unions, the disruption of women's working lives by family
demands, little or no job training, and centrally, the refusal of
equal pay for equal work – all are cited as part of the "old
suspicions and prejudices which set men and women in
antagonism and retard the growth of labour solidarity".
Women in Trade Unions is much more than an impressive
historical document for it presents to us issues which are still as
relevant, still as crucial to the future of women in the eighties as
they were in the 1920s.

Women's studies from Virago

HALF THE SKY
Bristol Women's Studies Group

Half the Sky introduces over two hundred extracts spanning
more than three centuries of feminist thought and action. The
selections include material from history, sociology, fiction and
poetry, literary criticism, anthropology, psychology and art
history, as well as articles from newspapers, journals and
government reports. Here are writings from Simone de
Beauvoir, Mrs Beeton, Christine Delphy, Shulamith Firestone,
Margaret Mead, Sheila Rowbotham, Marie Stopes, Jill
Tweedie and many more. Each chapter develops a theme
central to women's lives – childhood, health, sexuality,
marriage and motherhood, work – with linking passages and
lists of further reading. This interdisciplinary anthology also
provides a discussion of and suggestions for starting and
running courses. With a comprehensive bibliography and
resources section *Half the Sky* is a vital source book for use in
schools, further and adult education classes, polytechnics and
universities.

'An impressive collection ... stimulating and enjoyable ... an
excellent introduction to Women's Studies'—*Dale Spender,
WRRC Newsletter.*

Women's Studies from Virago

WOMEN IN SOCIETY
Cambridge Women's Studies Group

Women in Society is one of the most important books on
feminist theory and practice to emerge in recent years. Based on
the course of the same name at Cambridge University, it
comprises four integrated sections, each developing a theme
central to the understanding of women's place in society. To
each essay the authors have brought the expertise of their
respective disciplines – history, economics, psychology,
sociology, anthropology, physiology, semiotics. Combining
original research with critical examination of existing
arguments, this authoritative book offers new and sometimes
provocative perspectives on the family, work, the state, the
economy, sexuality, motherhood, violence, sex differences,
mental health, the nature/culture debate, patriarchy – and
much else. With a comprehensive bibliography, this is essential
reading for all those concerned with the many and complex
issues raised by feminism.

'An innovative interdisciplinary reader ... excellent, extremely
accessible and highly recommended'—*Marxism Today*
'This book should prove both inspiring and invaluable for the
future study of women'—*British Book News*